Lecture Notes in Computer Science 6660

Commenced Publication in 1973
Founding and Former Series Editors:
Gerhard Goos, Juris Hartmanis, and Jan van Leeuwen

Ngoc Thanh Nguyen (Ed.)

Transactions on Computational Collective Intelligence IV

 Springer

Volume Editor

Ngoc Thanh Nguyen
Wroclaw University of Technology, 50-370 Wroclaw, Poland
E-mail: ngoc-thanh.nguyen@pwr.wroc.pl

ISSN 0302-9743 (LNCS)   e-ISSN 1611-3349 (LNCS)
ISSN 2190-9288 (TCCI)
ISBN 978-3-642-21883-5   e-ISBN 978-3-642-21884-2
DOI 10.1007/978-3-642-21884-2

Springer Heidelberg Dordrecht London New York

Library of Congress Control Number: 2011929659

CR Subject Classification (1998): I.2, C.2.4, I.2.11, H.3-5, D.2, I.5

Typesetting: Camera-ready by author, data conversion by Scientific Publishing Services, Chennai, India

Printed on acid-free paper

Springer is part of Springer Science+Business Media (www.springer.com)

Preface

Welcome to the fourth volume of *Transactions on Computational Collective Intelligence* (TCCI). It is the second issue in 2011 of this Springer journal which is devoted to research in computer-based methods of computational collective intelligence (CCI) and their applications in a wide range of fields such as group decision making, Semantic Web, social networks and multi-agent systems. TCCI strives to cover new methodological, theoretical and practical aspects of CCI understood as the form of intelligence that emerges from the collaboration and competition of many individuals (artificial and/or natural).

This issue includes six papers divided into two parts. The first part contains Ireneusz Czarnowski's paper entitled "Distributed Learning with Data Reduction," which consists of 120 pages and has a monograph character. The second part consists of five regular papers selected from high-quality submissions addressing advances in the foundations and applications of CCI. The first entitled "Data Clustering Based on an Efficient Hybrid of Kharmonic Means, PSO and GA" by Malihe Danesh et al., deals with new PSO-based algorithms for clustering problem. The second paper, "A Study of Probability Collectives Multi-agent Systems on Optimization and Robustness" by Chien-Feng Huang and Bao Rong Chang, presents an interesting study on optimization and robustness of probability collectives multi-agent systems. In the third paper, titled "Inference Rules in Multi-agents' Temporal Logics," Vladimir Rybakov presents a framework for computation inference rules valid in agents' temporal logics. The next paper, "Selecting ISPs" by Andrzej Siemiński contains the description of the analysis of several properties of the network connection that is offered by Internet service providers. The last paper titled "AbSM—Agent-Based Session Mobility" authored by Günther Hölbling, Wolfgang Pfnür, and Harald Kosch presents a novel system for supporting session mobility that enables the user to create a relation between the session and himself.

TCCI is a double-blind refereed and authoritative reference dealing with the working potential of CCI methodologies and applications, as well as emerging issues of interest to academics and practitioners. The research area of CCI has been growing significantly in recent years and we are very thankful to everyone within the CCI research community who has supported the Transactions on Computational Collective Intelligence and its affiliated events including the International Conferences on Computational Collective Intelligence: Technologies and Applications (ICCCI). The first ICCCI event was held in Wroclaw, Poland, in October 2009. ICCCI 2010 was held in Taiwan in November 2010 and ICCCI 2011 will take place in Gdynia, Poland, in September 2011. We are very pleased that TCCI and the ICCCI conferences are strongly cemented as high-quality platforms for presenting and exchanging the most important and significant advances in CCI research and development.

It is our pleasure to announce the creation of the new Technical Committee on Computational Collective Intelligence within the Systems, Man and Cybernetics Society (SMC) of IEEE.

We would like to thank all the authors for their contributions to TCCI. This issue would not have been possible without the great efforts of the editorial board and many anonymously acting reviewers. We would like to express our sincere thanks to all of them. Finally, we would also like to express our gratitude to the LNCS editorial staff of Springer, in particular Alfred Hofmann, Ursula Barth, Peter Strasser and their team, who have supported the TCCI journal.

April 2011   Ngoc Thanh Nguyen

Transactions on Computational Collective Intelligence

This Springer journal focuses on research in applications of the computer-based methods of computational collective intelligence (CCI) and their applications in a wide range of fields such as the Semantic Web, social networks and multi-agent systems. It aims to provide a forum for the presentation of scientific research and technological achievements accomplished by the international community.

The topics addressed by this journal include all solutions of real-life problems for which it is necessary to use computational collective intelligence technologies to achieve effective results. The emphasis of the papers published is on novel and original research and technological advancements. Special features on specific topics are welcome.

Table of Contents

Distributed Learning with Data Reduction

Regular Papers

Distributed Learning with Data Reduction

Ireneusz Czarnowski

Distributed Learning with Data Reduction

Ireneusz Czarnowski

Department of Information Systems, Gdynia Maritime University
Morska 83, 81-225 Gdynia, Poland
irek@am.gdynia.pl

Abstract. The work deals with the distributed machine learning. Distributed learning from data is considered to be an important challenge faced by researchers and practice in the domain of the distributed data mining and distributed knowledge discovery from databases. Currently, learning from data is recognized as one of the most widely investigated paradigms of machine learning. At the same time it is perceived as a difficult and demanding computational problem. Even more complex and still to a large extent open is learning from the distributed data. One of the approaches suitable for learning from the geographically distributed data is to select from the local databases relevant local patterns, called also prototypes. Such prototypes are selected using some specialized data reduction methods. The dissertation contains an overview of the problem of learning classifiers from data, followed by a discussion of the distributed learning. The above includes the problem formulation and the state-of-the-art review. Next, data reduction, approaches, techniques and algorithms are discussed. The central part of the dissertation proposes an agent-based distributed learning framework. The idea is to carry-out data reduction in parallel in separate locations, employing specialized software agents. The process ends when locally selected prototypes are moved to a central site and merged into the global knowledge model. The following part of the work contains the results of an extensive computational experiment aiming at validation of the proposed approach. Finally, conclusions and suggestions for further research are formulated.

Keywords: learning from data, distributed learning, machine learning, distributed data mining, data reduction, A-Team, multi-agent system.

1 Introduction

In the contemporary world the quantity of data produced every year can be, by some estimates, measured in zetabytes. Huge databases are developed and maintained in meteorological, financial, medical, industrial or science domains. Since traditional techniques of the analytical processing are not fit to effectively deal with such massive datasets, their owners more and more often require applying data mining or machine learning techniques enabling discovery and extraction of yet undiscovered knowledge and useful patterns. Such a need has motivated, in the recent years, an exceptional global research effort devoted to finding new

N.T. Nguyen (Ed.): Transactions on CCI IV, LNCS 6660, pp. 3–121, 2011.

techniques, methods and approaches bringing machine learning and data mining closer to the successful real-life applications.

Machine learning is the study of computer algorithms that improve automatically through experience. Applications range from data mining programs that discover general rules in large data sets, to information filtering systems that automatically learn users' interests [151]. Machine learning is also seen as a scientific discipline that is concerned with the design and development of algorithms that allow computers to evolve behaviors based on empirical data. In this work the focus is on supervised learning where the task is to induce a function from pairs of data consisting of an input object (typically a vector) and a desired output value (typically a class label). A supervised learning algorithm through analyzing the training data produces a classifier. The classifier should predict the correct class label any valid input vector. This requires the learning algorithm to generalize from the training data to unknown situations with the satisfactory accuracy. It is well known that the size of the training dataset might be a critical factor when inducing a classifier.

Unfortunately, the sheer size of the databases is not the only problem facing machine learning. The databases may also be geographically, physically or logically distributed. In such cases it is often unrealistic or unfeasible to pool together the distributed data for centralized processing. Hence, applying traditional approaches to knowledge discovery from the distributed data sources may not be possible [116]. The need to extract potentially useful patterns out of the separated, distributed data sources created a new, important and challenging research area, known as the distributed data mining (DDM) or knowledge discovery from multi-databases [231] or, simply, distributed learning. Needless to say, the distributed learning is more challenging than the "classic" machine learning. It is also less mature and contains more space for searching for new methods and solutions. The above facts have played a decisive role in motivating the author to undertake the presented research work.

This work focuses on the distributed learning problem. Learning from multi-databases is considered to be a more complex and difficult task than learning from a single database, and one of the main challenges is to create systems that learn automatically from distributed datasets [178], [235]. So far several approaches to the distributed learning have been proposed. Among them there are: integration of independently derived hypotheses by combining different classifiers to make global classification decisions [39], models aggregating classifiers [66], or global level combination of learning results obtained through using the so called meta-learning technique [161]. The most obvious approach to the distributed learning it to move all data into a centralized location, merge the data and build, using a typical machine learning algorithm, a single global knowledge model. However, in practice pooling together data for further processing can be impossible due to a restricted communication bandwidth among sites or some other reasons [125], [178]. Instead, in the distributed learning some partial analysis of the data at each of the separate (local) sites can be carried-out individually and in parallel, with a view to obtain samples of data. Such an approach can be seen as a mean of addressing the scalability issue of mining large datasets. However, one disadvantage of a simple sampling approach is that the sampled set may not sufficiently represent the local data.

The idea of this dissertation is to deal with the distributed learning problem through replacing sampling by a data reduction process which can be carried-out at separated sites. The overall objective of data reduction is to process training data with a view to finding patterns, also called prototypes, references vectors, or regularities within certain attributes, which can replace the original training set during further steps of the supervised learning. Data reduction can be achieved through selection of instances, selection of attributes or simultaneous reduction in both dimensions (see, for example, [142]).

In this work a novel approach to the distributed learning is proposed. It includes a family of instance reduction algorithms using an original similarity measure. The author proposes to reduce the original training set through calculating for each attribute vector from the training dataset the value of its similarity coefficient and then grouping instances into clusters consisting of vectors with identical values of this coefficient. From such clusters a representation is selected and the reduced dataset is formed. Selection in this case covers both - instance and attribute reduction. It is expected that selecting the relevant data from the distributed databases can eliminate or reduce some of the problems facing traditional distributed learning approaches. Data reduction should also speed up the global knowledge extraction process. A distributed learning approach based on data reduction can be also much more efficient computationally than moving all distributed datasets into the centralized site for learning the global model.

The author proposes also to integrate the selection procedure required for the data reduction with the classifier learning. Taking into account the fact that data reduction and learning classifier from the distributed data are both computationally difficult optimization problems, the idea is to construct an effective population-based family of algorithms solving the above outlined selection task. Such algorithms are proposed and constructed using the state-of-the-art agent technology and an A-Team architecture, which allows for a parallel computation at the separated sites carried-out by teams of agents. The proposed approach to the distributed learning uses a set of agents which process the local data and communicate results to other agents controlling and managing the learning process at the global level. The approach involves two stages, both supported by agent collaboration - local, in which the selection of prototypes from the distributed data takes place and global, producing the global model.

In view of the above the thesis of this dissertation is formulated as follows:

The proposed method of solving the distributed learning problem based on data clustering and data reduction schemes integrated with a classifier learning through the population-based family of algorithms, implemented within the A-Team architecture, is an effective and competitive approach to the distributed learning.

The detailed objectives of this work are as follows:

1. To propose a set of procedures for data reduction through simultaneous instance and attribute selection with the cluster-based prototype selection carried-out by program agents executing population learning algorithm. The above requires in particular:
   a. To review data reduction approaches.
   b. To identify properties of the data reduction methods based on similarity measures and other extended approaches including these based on integrating data reduction with learning classifiers or supporting multi-objective data reduction.
   c. To propose different variants of the cluster-based data reduction approaches with prototype selection carried-out by an agent-based population learning algorithm.
   d. To verify and evaluate the proposed algorithms experimentally using benchmark datasets.
   e. To compare the proposed method with other data reduction approaches known from the literature.
   f. To identify factors which have a direct influence on the effectiveness of the proposed data reduction method.
2. To design and implement an agent-based framework for learning classifiers from the reduced and distributed data. The above requires in particular:
   a. To review strategies and approaches to the distributed learning.
   b. To review technologies and architectures for the distributed learning.
   c. To propose an agent-based distributed learning algorithms.
   d. To verify and evaluate experimentally different variants of the agent-based distributed learning algorithms and different strategies for instance and attribute selection.
   e. To compare the proposed method with other approaches to distributed learning known from the literature.
   f. To identify factors which have a direct influence on the effectiveness of the proposed distributed learning algorithms.

The remainder of this dissertation is organized as follows. In Section 2 the problem of learning from data is formally defined. Possible taxonomies of the problem are reviewed and the learning process components including data preprocessing are explained. The following parts of the section discuss learning evaluation measures and offer a brief and general overview of the techniques and algorithms used for the classifier construction.

Section 3 provides basic notation and formulation of the distributed learning problem. It also contains a review of the strategies of the distributed learning followed by the state-of-the-art review of the current approaches to the problem. The section ends with a discussion of technologies, architectures and systems for distributed learning.

In Section 4 the data reduction problem is discussed. Some remarks on the scope and goals of data reduction are followed by the problem formulation, a review of techniques and algorithms for data reduction and taxonomy of data reduction algorithms. The next part of the section discusses approaches to data reduction including also the proposed by the author. The section also identifies basic properties of the approach based on integrating data reduction with learning classifiers and discusses several integration schemas. Finally, the multi-objective data reduction problem is briefly analyzed.

Section 5 presents the proposed agent-based framework for data reduction and distributed learning. The main feature of this framework is that it is based on the learning process executed by the team of agents. The section contains a description of the A-Team architecture including its main features, and a review of several applications of the population-based, multi-agent algorithms. The section provides details of the proposed agent-based framework for learning classifiers from reduced and distributed datasets and gives descriptions of the suggested agent-based algorithms for data reduction and for multi-objective data reduction.

Section 6 describes experimental evaluation of the proposed approach. It contains summarized results of computational experiments obtained for learning from the reduced and distributed datasets.

Finally, Section 7 groups conclusions and outlines further research directions.

2   Learning Classifiers from Data

2.1   Problem Formulation

The key objective of the machine learning is to design algorithms that are able to improve performance at some task through experience [151]. These algorithms are called *learners*. The learner uses the examples of a particular task to perform learning. The examples (instances, objects) belong to the set U, where U is a non-empty, finite set called the *universe* or, in short, *data*.

The example $x \in U$, based on the Mitchell's attribute-values representation [151], is described by a fixed set of attributes, $A = \{a_1, a_2, \ldots, a_n\}$, where n is the number of attributes. Each attribute, a_i, can be assigned a value, $a_i(x) \in V_{a_i}$, where V_{a_i} is the set of all possible values for attribute a_i and denotes *attribute domain*. Formally, each example can be identified by the vector of attributes and it is described by:

$$x \equiv [a_1(x), a_2(x), \ldots, a_n(x)] \equiv [x_1, x_2, \ldots, x_n]. \tag{1}$$

Learning from examples is one of the most popular paradigms of machine learning. It deals with the problem of identifying the regularities between a number of independent variables (attributes) and a target or dependent categorical variable (attribute) in a given dataset [201]. If such a dataset is categorical then the problem occurring as a result is called a *classification problem*.

It should be also noted that when a dataset is categorical learning from examples is considered with respect to some external information, which is sometimes referred to by a broad term of a *concept* [38],[151]. Such case is merged with *supervised learning*, as one basic machine learning technique, where each example is additionally labeled with a class [151],[175]. The class label of each example can take any value from a finite set of decision classes (categories) $C = \{c_l : l = 1, \ldots, k\}$, which has cardinality k. Hence, the data U for a classification task can be defined as:

$$U = \{[x_{ij}, d(x_j)] : i = 1, \ldots, n; j = 1, \ldots, N\}, \qquad (2)$$

where $[x_{ij}, d(x_j)]$ represents a single data vector (example), N denotes the number of examples, d is a function, such that $d(x)$ is the value of decision class for the example x, where $\forall_{x \in U} d(x) \in C$.

Learning from examples is understood as the process of finding a model (or function) that describes and distinguishes data classes or concepts. The model is called a *classifier* [96]. The process of finding a classification model that is considered here is also called a *learning process* or a *learning classifier* [96].

Formally, the learner outputs a classifier $h \in H$, called the *hypothesis*, that has been induced based on the set U, where H is the hypothesis space, i.e. a set of all possible hypotheses that a learner can draw on in order to construct the classifier. Thus, a learning algorithm outputs an element $h \in H$. The hypothesis may be viewed as a logical predicate that may be true or false with respect to the considered data, or a function that maps examples into, for example, category (data class) space [38]. In [212] it was mentioned that such a function expresses knowledge obtained by a learner from examples.

Based on the above, the problem of learning from data in a formal manner can be formulated as follows:

Definition 1. Given a dataset U, a set of hypotheses H, a performance criterion (or a set of performance measures in case of the multi criteria approach being considered) F, the learning algorithm L outputs a hypothesis $h^* \in H$ that optimizes F. The goal of learning from data is to find L producing $h^* \in H$ to optimize the performance criterion F.

The performance criterion may incorporate many different measures and an assumed performance measure is optimized. Without the loss of generality it can be also assumed that the performance criterion is maximized. Thus, assuming that the performance measure expressed as f_U (where $f_U \in F$) and defined with respect to U is scalar, the learning process may be formulated as a process of finding optimal hypothesis, h^*, such that:

$$h^* = \arg \max_{h \in H} f_U(h). \qquad (3)$$

It is a fact that in reality the learning process is caried-out using a limited set of examples, so-called *data source*, $D \subset U$, where $|D| < |U|$. In machine learning the available set of examples used in learning is also called a *training set*. Thus, the learning classifier is guided by f_U estimate f computed using examples from the training set [131]. In machine learning it is assumed that the results obtained from D generalize to U. In the machine learning such case has the *inductive* character [151].

In the inductive learning some additional assumption must be made to obtain a good generalization. Without a prior assumption about the training target, or inductive bias, a learner has no rational basis for predicting the class of a new, unseen instances [151]. The inductive bias denotes a rule or method that causes a learning process to choose one classifier over another, i.e. to select the classifier that fits perfectly the training set [152]. The inductive biases of learning algorithms can be defined with respect to a subset of H which should be considered by the learner and with respect to a way of searching for a classifier within the selected subset [86].

Considering the above, it should be also underlined that the learner may not be able to find the optimal classifier that is optimal with respect to the training set. Additionally, the set D can not be fixed when the problem size grows i.e. when the number of attributes and the number of examples grow, and that causes the cardinality of the hypothesis space to grow. As it has been pointed out in [131], in such case, for many inducers the growth of the cardinality of the search space is exponential with respect to the description length. In [131] the author also points out that, in general, it is difficult to search in the hypothesis space based on a measure of the performance of the induction algorithm. The above factors ensure that the task of finding the hypotheses to NP-hard optimization problem is considered [26],[152],[226].

Thus, the goal of learning from examples is merely to find a hypothesis $h = L(D)$ that is a good approximation of the target concept, where the hypothesis is optimal with respect to a selected performance criterion such that $f(h) < f(h^*)$. Ideally $f(h) = f(h^*)$. In the end, the learning task takes the following form:

$$h = \arg\max_{h \in H} f(h). \tag{4}$$

Finally, the role of a classification model (classifier) is to predict the class of objects whose class labels are unknown [96]. If for given $x \in D$, $h(x) = d(x)$ then h makes a correct decision with respect to x.

Thus, a learning algorithm for a classification consists of two components: a learning component, where the hypothesis is learned from training data and a classification component, where the learned hypothesis is used to classify new, previously unobserved, examples. These components create a *classification system* [212]. The last component of a classification system can be more precisely defined as follows:

Definition 2. A classifier h is a function that assigns instances from D to predefined sets of decision classes, that can be expressed as:

$$h : D \to \{\emptyset, C_1, C_2, \ldots, C_k\} \tag{5}$$

where $C_{l:l=1,\ldots,k}$ denotes subsets of data set D, such that examples are labeled by a class $c_{l:l=1,\ldots,k} \in C$, where the following two conditions are fulfilled:

1. $\bigcup_{l=1}^{k} C_l = D$.

2. $\forall C_j \subset D, C_l \subset D : C_j \cap C_l = \emptyset, j, l = [1, k], j \neq l$.

The case $h(x) = \emptyset$ denotes that a classifier is not able to assign an example to a predefined class.

Having formulated the learning problem and taking the classifier definition into account, the classification problem can be defined as follows:

Definition 3. Classification is the assignment of a class, $c \in C$, to an example $x \in D$.

2.2 Learning from Data – The Problem Taxonomies

Differences between practical approaches to learning from data can be derived from the following:

- Structure of data
- Number of categories
- Attribute domain
- Performance criterion or criteria incorporated with learning process
- Features of the data source.

With respect to the structure of the data source the learning from example has been referred to as:

- Supervised learning and
- Unsupervised learning.

It has been mentioned before that in supervised learning the objective is to generalize from the training examples defined by a set of inputs and the correct outputs (classes). In the case when no class values are provided, i.e. that data are given without specified knowledge of the number of classes and that the learner is given only unlabeled examples, the learning is unsupervised and the aim of learning is to describe the training data with a view on its statistical properties and to determine how the data are organized. In the unsupervised learning the classes are defined by the learner through data clustering. Unsupervised learning is also called unsupervised classification [76]. In the following chapter only the supervised learning is considered.

The machine learning techniques are more often based on the assumption that the training samples are uniformly distributed among different classes. It means that learners are trained on a balanced dataset and such process is called *learning from the balanced data* [213]. The effect of imbalanced class distribution is often ignored. However, many datasets in real applications involve imbalanced class distribution. The imbalanced class distribution problem occurs in the case when the number of examples in one class is significantly greater than the number of examples in the other class in dataset. Such case of a learning problem is called *learning from the imbalanced data* [98],[229].

Taking into account the cardinality of the set of decision classes, the learning classifier problem is called:

- *Binary*, it is a case with $|C| = 2$
- *Multi-class*, otherwise.

In machine learning, examples provide the input to learning algorithm. Each example is characterized by its values on fixed, predefined set of attributes which can be of various types. Most machine learning algorithms deal with the following [219]:

- Numeric attributes - real or integer values
- Nominal attributes - values from a predefined, finite set of possibilities and are sometimes called categorical
- Ordinal attributes - generally called numeric or nominal but without the implication of mathematical continuity.

The type of attributes can influence the way of solving a given learning problem and can enforce the implementation of specialized approaches. With respect to the discussed type of attributes in literature the different types of learning from data are considered, for example: *learning from numeric data* [134], *learning with symbolic attributes* [41], or *learning problem with categorical data* [158].

As it has been mentioned in the previous section, the performance criterion may incorporate many different measures, like, for example: the function of accuracy of classification, the complexity of the hypothesis, the classification cost or the classification error. In such case an optimized performance criterion F can be identified, with a vector of criteria which takes the following form $F = [f_1, f_2, \ldots, f_J]$, where J is a number of pre-decided criteria. It is the case referred to as multi-criteria classifier evaluation and also called *multi-objective learning classifiers from data*, which has been considered in [18].

In numerous cases the data volume is physically and geographically distributed. It is the case where the data are distributed among multiple separated sites, so-called *distributed data sources*. The data may be distributed because of various reasons. The distributed data can be collected by a particular organization especially if the organization has different databases. The distributed data can be collected by different communities or organizations. In this case the data can be shared, however they may have different structures (format differences, semantic differences, etc.) [231]. On the other hand, the data may be artificially partitioned among different sites for achieving better scalability. In the general case, the data site may be *homogenous*, i.e. each site stores the data for exactly the same set of attributes. More often sites store data for different sets of attributes, possibly with some common attributes among the sites. It is case of the *heterogeneous* data. The homogenous and heterogeneous cases are also called horizontal and vertical data fragmentation [116]. Thus, based on the above, learning classifiers from data is very often called *learning classifiers from the distributed data*, or in short *distributed learning*, and its variants, respectively, *learning classifiers from the homogenous* or *heterogeneous data*.

The basic approach to learning classifier from data is based on the assumption that the data are static and the learning process remains unchanged during the time of the learner operation. However, in many real-world learning classifier problems, the environment in which the learner works is dynamic, i.e. the target concept and its statistical properties change over time and the changes cannot be predicted in advance. It is referred to as the *data streams* where the class distribution of the streaming data is imbalanced. When the changes of data properties are observed they are also incorporated with data drift and a dynamic character of data source is observed [35],[176]. This problem is also known as the *concept drift* [217] and such learning is called as *learning drift concept* [123] or *learning classifiers from the streaming data* [237].

2.3   Learning from Data – Components of the Process

Having formulated the learning and the classification problems it is also necessary to point out other components of the learning process. The quality of the classification systems is notably dependent on the data quality that they operate on. When the quality of the data is poor then the learning process is also more difficult. Data pre-processing, which provides a set of techniques dedicated for improving the quality of data, can be considered as an important component of the machine learning process. Another relevant component of the learning process is its evaluation. This section discuses the data preprocessing and the problem of learning evaluation.

2.3.1   Data Pre-processing

Data pre-processing can often have a significant impact on generalization performance of a learning algorithm. For many real world applications, data pre-processing is a must to enhance the data quality before the actual learning process takes place. This fact is particularly emphasized in commercial applications of machine learning methods to large databases that take place, for example, in the knowledge discovery in databases (KDD). In KDD it is pointed out that if there is much irrelevant and redundant information present or the data are noisy and unreliable, then the knowledge discovery during the training phase is more difficult [231]. The importance of data pre-processing has been also shown in [52], where an artificial neural network was designed and implemented for solving a time-series prediction problem.

The aim of data pre-processing is to check and modify the original data by noise and outliers elimination, resolve data conflicts or replace missing data, or eliminate irrelevant and redundant information. Data pre-processing includes data cleaning, data transformation and data reduction. Data pre-processing algorithms are executed before the main learning step, thus the product of data pre-processing is the final training set [130].

Data cleaning deals with detecting and removing errors and inconsistencies from data in order to improve their quality. Data cleaning algorithms are also dealing with determining whether data contains duplicate representations of the same entity. Incomplete data is an unavoidable problem of the real world data sources. There are several methods which can possibly be used to deal with the problem of missing data, among them these based on: ignoring the instances with unknown attribute value and substituting the feature mean value computed from available cases to fill in the missing data values on the remaining cases. The overview of methods for handling missing data is provided in [138], [163].

Data transformation allows the mapping of the data from their given format into the format expected by the appropriate application. Data transformation methods are dedicated for value conversions or translation. For example, when normalization or z-score standardization is performed, the numeric values are conformed to minimum and maximum values, or with respect to mean values and standard deviations respectively [163]. Data transformation includes also methods for discretization dedicated for reducing the number of possible values of the continuous attributes. Discretization is a key when a large number of possible attribute values contributes to slow and ineffective learning process [130].

Data pre-processing viewed by data reduction includes reduction of the dimensionality of data. This part of data pre-processing is dedicated to attribute selection and instance selection. Attribute selection is a process of identifying and removing irrelevant and redundant attributes as possible. Instance selection is not only used to handle noise but also to identify and eliminate duplicate instances. In [29] instance selection is joined with improving the quality of the training data by identifying and eliminating mislabelled instances prior to applying the chosen learning algorithm. More details of the data reduction are included in Section 4.

2.3.2   The Learning Evaluation

As it has been defined, the goal of learning from data is to find a learner producing classifier to optimize the performance criterion. There are a lot of supervised learning algorithms for classification problems but no algorithm is superior to all classification problems. Thus, it is beneficial to select an appropriate algorithm for the considered problem [220]. Such selection is performed by evaluating the number of candidate learning algorithms or classifiers.

There are many different types of criteria that can be used for the classifier evaluation. The most common type is the classification error rate measured as the fraction of misclassified instances on a particular data set. Alternatively, the accuracy of classification, measured as the fraction of well classified instances within a particular data set, is used for classifier evaluation. Let $\eta(D, h)$ denote the accuracy of classification, then it can be expressed as a function:

$$\eta(D, h) = \frac{1}{|D|} |\{x \in D : h(x) = d(x)\}|. \tag{6}$$

However, the estimation of these two criteria is more trustworthy when it is performed on instances that were not used for training [219]. Thus, the available dataset is often used to define two subsets: the training set, $D \subset U$, and the test set, $D_t \subset U$, such that $D \cap D_t = \emptyset$, and a performance criterion is estimated on the test set.

The classifier can also be evaluated by the 0-1 function, where the cost associated with different misclassifications is possible to analyse. An alternative metric is the TP/false alarm rate, which refers to the rate of incorrect positive predictions. The last one is used for classifier evaluation by the confusion matrix [219].

The classifier can be also evaluated basing on minimizing the cost of misclassification which is the goal in a cost-sensitive classification. In such case costs can be ignored at the training time but taken into consideration at the prediction time. An alternative is to consider the cost of misclassification at both the predictions and the training time, which would be a reasonable approach in case of the cost-sensitive learning [219].

A graphical technique for the classifier evaluation is a Receiver Operating Characteristic curve (ROC curve). ROC curve is a plot of the true positive rate against the false positive rate. ROC curves depict the performance of classifier regardless class distribution or error costs. In general, ROC analysis is a common tool for assessing the performance of various classifications. An overview of other classifier evaluation criteria can be found in [139],[219].

The classifiers can be also evaluated with respect to their complexity. Complexity, as an evaluation criterion, can be measured in many different ways. For example, it can be calculated as the number of hidden units or layers of an artificial neural network or the number of leaves or nodes in a decision tree. In such case complexity allows to make comparisons between classifiers of different types. To the most common approximate measures of complexity belong the Minimum Description Length and the Vapniak-Chervonenkis dimension. These and other measures have been discussed in [139].

Learning algorithms are more often evaluated indirectly by evaluating a number of generated classifiers [139]. Taking this into account, the learning process can be viewed as a process of the learner configuration evaluation where the goal of learning is to find the best set of configuration parameters of a given learning algorithm. In [131] it has been observed that configuration parameters of a learning algorithm affect the learning process and influence the learning quality. The parameters depend on the type of learner used. For example, the parameters may concern the architecture of the neural network, the structure of a decision tree, rules for decision rule algorithm or the way the data should be transformed during the data pre-processing.

There is a number of methods for algorithm configuration evaluation, among them are the following: cross-validation, leave-one-out, hold-out, random subsampling and bootstrap [212]. Cross-validation (CV) is one of the popular methods for evaluating configurations and is often used together with classifier evaluation methods. A cross-validation test is performed by partitioning the available dataset into n subsets. The training and evaluation is repeated n times using a different dataset partition as the test set for each trial. 10-fold CV is the recommended method for classifier selection [126].

2.4   Techniques and Algorithms

The methods developed for classifier construction may be divided into the following groups [130]:

- Logic-based algorithms
- Statistical learning algorithms
- Perceptron-based techniques
- Support vector machines.

Decision tree algorithms are a well known and widely used family of machine learning algorithms for constructing classifiers from labeled examples. Decision tree algorithms belong to the logic-based class of algorithms. Decision tree structures consist of nodes representing attributes in the example to be classified, branches represent values that the node can assume and leaves correspond to class labels. Classifiers based on the tree structures are induced by splitting the source data into subsets based on the attribute value test. Such process is repeated recursively for each branch. Algorithms for decision trees induction differ from each other in terms of the criterion that is used to choose the attribute at each node of the tree. Different decision tree algorithms use also several different techniques to improve their comprehensibility, among them pruning, prepruning, logic operators or estimating error rates. Among well-known algorithms for inducing decision trees are, for example, the C 4.5 [166], the ID3 [165] or the CART [28]. The first algorithm, i.e. the C 4.5, employs two steps: the growing phase and the pruning phase. During the first phase the best split of data is found and the tree continues to grow recursively using the same process. During the second phase the tree is pruned [20]. The pseudo-code of the algorithm for growing a C 4.5 tree is shown as Algorithm 1.

Algorithm 1. *The C 4.5 growing algorithm - Grow(D, τ)* [20]

Input: D - the original training set; τ - a root node.
Output: T - a trained decision tree appended to the root.
1. If D is pure then assign class of pure examples to root τ and goto 5.
2. If no split can yield minimum number of examples split off then assign class of the node as the majority class of D and goto 5.
3. Find an optimal split that splits D into subset $D_{i:i=1,...,t}$.

4. For each subset $D_{i:i=1,...,t}$ create a node τ_i under root τ and run $Grow(D_i, \tau_i)$.
5. Return T.

Decision trees can be transformed into a set of rules. It is done by creating separate rules for each path in the tree [166]. However, machine learning offers methods for rule induction directly from the data. In general, the main aim of the rule induction algorithms is to obtain a small set of rules well describing the relationship between instances of individual classes. Most of them are an implementation of special covering procedures whose aim is to induce rules. Examples of classification rule algorithms are the AQ algorithm [148] and the CN2 algorithm [43]. Other approach to learning a set of rules has been proposed in [68], where for classification rules generation the multi-objective genetic algorithm has been proposed.

Statistical learning approaches have an explicit underlying probability model that specifies the probability of the examples belonging to particular classes. Bayesian methods are the most powerful statistical methods. Bayesian learning simply assumes calculating the probability of each hypothesis, based on the available data, and makes predictions on that basis. Predictions are made by using all the hypotheses weighted by their probabilities. A Bayesian Network is the graphical model for probability relationships among the set of attributes and its structure is a graph. The basic schema of learning for a Bayesian Network is to estimate the number of parameters from the data provided. Such parametric learning is often simple and effective, but can produce an oversimplified model. A classifier based on the network and on the given data returns the class label, which maximizes its posterior probability. An example of a very simple Bayesian Network is the Naïve Bayes Network, called also the Naïve Bayes classifier, where a deterministic prediction can be obtained by choosing the most likely class [108].

Instance-based learning algorithms belong to the nonparametric statistical learning class methods. These are referred to as lazy-learning algorithms [2], [151]. Lazy-learning algorithms construct hypotheses directly from the training data. Lazy-learning algorithms require less computation during the training process in comparison to other learning algorithms such as Bayes Networks or decision trees. However, the classification process can be very computation time consuming and very complex. The best example of the lazy-learning algorithm is the nearest neighbour algorithm [1]. A typical k-Nearest Neighbour (kNN) is based on the assumption that the examples within a dataset which are situated in a close proximity have similar properties. Thus, in the case of the classification problem the class label of an unclassified example is determined by the class of its neigbours. The key problem of kNN is the choice of k, that affects the performance of the kNN algorithm. The performance of the kNN algorithm also depends on the choice of the similarity function that is used to compare examples [89]. The pseudo-code of the nearest neighbor algorithm is shown as Algorithm 2.

Algorithm 2. *The kNN algorithm*

Input: D - the original training set containing examples with known class labels; k- the number of neighbors (a user-defined constant); x - unlabelled example to be classified.
Output: Class label of x.
1. Calculate distances between x and all the examples in D.
2. Sort all examples belonging to D according to the distance measure $d(x, x_i)$, where $x_i \in D$.
3. Select the first k examples from the sorted list which are the k closest training samples to x.
4. Assign a class to x based on majority vote.

Another class of well-known algorithms base on the perceptron processing [82]. In general, a perceptron is a type of a simple artificial neural network. It computes the sum of weighted inputs and produces the output value according to an adjustable threshold. The perceptron is a simple binary classifier which maps its input to the output value. It works most naturally with numeric attributes and it involves finding a set of weights of links between the input and processing units. Training process is considered as adjusting values of these weights using a set of training examples. The perceptron can only classify linearly separable sets of examples. A way to solve nonlinear problems is to use a multi-layer neural network, also called a multi-layer perceptron, which can be obtained by adding nonlinear layers between the input and the output. Other example of a multi-layer structure is a Radial Basic Function (RBF) network [103], [234].

Artificial neural networks are, nowadays, being used for solving a wide variety of real-life problems. The main advantages of the artificial neural networks include the ability to tolerate imprecision and uncertainty and still achieving tractability, robustness and low cost of practical application. Since training perceptron structures for practical applications is often very time consuming, an extensive research is being carried to accelerate this process. Another problem with artificial neural network training is the danger of being caught in a local minimum. Hence, researchers look not only for algorithms that train neural network quickly but rather for quick algorithms that are not likely, or less likely, to get trapped in a local optimum. An example of such development is a specialized A-Team applied to train the feed-forward artificial neural networks proposed in [55]. Other example is a specialized A-Team applied to train the cascade correlation learning architecture proposed in [53].

Support vector machines (SVM) in comparison to the previously mentioned methods, is a relatively new supervised machine learning technique. The idea is to use linear models to represent the nonlinear class boundaries. SVM transforms the examples space into a new space. A linear model constructed in the new space can represent a nonlinear decision boundary within the original data [30], [219]. Training the SVM is done by solving Nth dimensional quadratic programming problem, where N is the number of examples. It is well known that standard quadratic programming may be time-consuming from a computation point of view when the problem is large. Thus, several modifications of SVM have been proposed so far (see, for example, [79], [159]).

Although all the above algorithms can be directly used for the multi-class learning problem there are more specialized approaches to solving such problems. In [187] the n^2-classifier algorithm for solving multi-class learning problem has been proposed. The n^2-classifier belongs to the group of multiple classifiers. It consists of $(n2 - n)/2$ binary classifiers, where each one specialize in discriminating a respective pair of the decision classes only. All binary classifiers are used to provide the final classification decision, after their predictions are aggregated. The examples of other approaches to multi-class learning problem are one-per-class method and error-correcting output codes [70].

An increasing interest in integration of multiple learning models into one multiple classification system, also called the combined classification system or ensemble model, has been observed recently. Classification systems using the multiple learning models are practical and effective solutions to different classification problems, when the single algorithms are rather specialized to solve some learning problems and cannot perform best in all situations [187]. It was mentioned in [100] that the aim of the integration of multiple learning models is to achieve optimal accuracy. In [100] strategies for classifier integration are also referred to as the coverage optimization methods.

The integration of the multiple learning models can be achieved in many ways. The so-called weak classifiers can be constructed by the same - homogenous, or different - heterogeneous, learning algorithms. One multiple classification system can use different learning algorithms on the same dataset. Based on such an approach, for example, the stacking method [211] and meta-learning [44] have been proposed. Others combine multiple, homogenous learner, induced using the same dataset, but with different distributions, as it happens in the cases of bagging, boosting or random subspace methods [16], [99], [167]. In [149] the problem of integration of the multiple learning algorithms is discussed in the context of hybrid systems exhibiting the attributes of both heterogenous and homogenous ensemble models.

An interesting approach based on integrating gene expression programming with cellular genetic programming to induce expression trees, which, subsequently, serve as weak classifiers, is proposed in [113]. From the induced trees stronger ensemble classifiers are constructed using majority-voting and boosting techniques. In [109] it is also discussed that the ensemble members may also learn from different subset of attributes.

In the multiple classification system the base models can be linked in many ways depending on the adopted aggregation rule. It must be emphasised though, that in reality what is linked are the results of the predictions of these models. Having at one's disposal a fixed set of designed classifiers, the aim is to find an optimal combination of their decisions. More often strategies for optimal combination are referred to as decision optimization methods or decision combination methods [100]. In [223] decision combination methods are divided with regard to the method of generating the classification result into the following groups:

- Abstract-based methods - the final model generates the class the observation belongs to. Among them are the following: majority voting, weighted majority voting, plurality voting and Behaviour-Knowledge Space.
- Rank-based methods - the final model generates the set of classes arranged by their posterior probabilities. The example of this group of methods is the Borda count method.
- Measurement-based methods - the final model generates the vector of posterior probabilities. Typical aggregation rules of this group of methods are: generalized mean, weighted average, arithmetic average, probabilistic product, fuzzy integral and others.

The overview of all approaches to decision combination mentioned above may be found, for example, in [83], [100], [223].

3   Distributed Learning

3.1   Problem Formulation

In the distributed learning, a dataset D is distributed among data sources. Each data source contains a fragment of the data D. In general, the data may be fragmented into a set of relations which can lead to the fragmentation of a data set [36]. Two types of data fragmentation can be considered, i.e. *vertical and horizontal*. The first type of fragmentation is linked with the heterogeneous data, the second with the homogenous data.

Let D be distributed among the sites $1, \ldots, K$, respectively, $D_{i:i=1,\ldots,K}$ denote the distributed data sources and $N_{i:i=1,\ldots,K}$ denote examples, which are stored in separated sites. Let also the following property holds: $\sum_{i=1}^{K} N_i = N$. When the distributed data are homogenous all attributes are presented at each location, i.e. $\forall_{i,j:i,j=1,\ldots,K} A_i = A_j$, otherwise $\exists_{i,j:i,j=1,\ldots,K} A_i \neq A_j$.

The problem of learning from distributed data might also be subject to the set of constraints Z, imposed on a learner. Such constraints may for example prohibit transferring data from separated sites to the central location, or impose a physical limit on the amount of information that can be moved, or impose other restrictions to preserve data privacy.

Definition 4. Given the distributed datasets $D_1, \ldots, D_K$ described by the sets of attributes $A_1, \ldots, A_K$, a set of hypotheses H, a performance criterion (or a set of performance measures in case of the multi criteria approach being considered) F, the task of the distributed learner L_d is to output a hypothesis $h \in H$ optimizing F using operations allowed by Z.

From the above, one can observe that the problem of learning from a single (centralized) data set D is a special case of learning from the distributed data where $K = 1$ and Z is empty. Additionally, having the horizontal fragmentation of the data the following equation is true: $D = D_1 \cup D_2 \ldots \cup D_K$.

It was also established in [36] that L_d is relative to its centralized learner L. It is true if the hypothesis produced by L_d is identical to the one produced by L from data D obtained by appropriate merging of the datasets $D_1, \ldots, D_K$, where the value of the performance measure is the same. Further details with respect to the formulation of the general problem of learning from the distributed data can be found in [36].

3.2   Strategies of the Distributed Learning

Majority of learning algorithms used in case of the non-distributed learning is not effective or simply can not be applied in case of the distributed learning. Traditional approaches to learning from data base on the assumption that all training data are pooled together in a centralized data repository. It is a basic limitation of these approaches when the data are physically distributed. The above motivates the development of the new algorithms for solving the distributed learning problem.

From the literature, there are many reported algorithms proposed for distributed learning. Considering the current research effort on the distributed learning, it is possible to observe that the proposed algorithms are designed using the following strategies [10], [125]:

- Parallel computing strategy
- Centralized strategy
- In-place strategy
- Intermediate strategy
- Cooperation-based strategy
- Hybrid strategy.

The parallel computing strategy has been considered in the early work on the distributed learning. This strategy appeared in response to the need of scaling up learning algorithms to a large dataset [125]. In this strategy, the data are divided into subsets, and can be distributed, in order to increase the efficiency of the learning process, whereas typical distributed learning assumes that the data are inherently distributed and autonomous [230]. In other words, approaches based on the parallel computing strategy exploit parallel processing for scaling up machine learning algorithms to work with large datasets [116], [180]. Several approaches focused on parallelizing learning algorithms have been proposed so far (see, for example, [48], [53], [55], [60], [63], [114], [204]).

The following approaches for parallelizing learning algorithms have been proposed [180]:

- Approximate concepts
- Partial concepts
- Independent search.

The first approach assumes that the data are divided into subsets and the copies of the sequential learning algorithm are executed on each subset. The second assumes dividing the data into subsets on attributes, i.e. partitioning by the columns to which they refer, and executing a special variant of the learning algorithm on these subsets to derive a final learning model. Independent search bases on a decomposition of the learning problem into subproblems. Although the parallel computing strategy has been proposed to increase the efficiency of the learning process, as it is pointed above, it may be combined with other strategies described below to increase the quality of the distributed learning process.

A centralized strategy assumes moving all of the data to a central site, merging the data and building a single global model. Moving all data into a centralized location can be very time consuming, costly from the commercial point of view, and it may not be feasible due to restricted communication bandwidth among sites, high expenses involved, or some other reasons [125], [132], [178]. In other words, it can be unrealistic to collect distributed data for centralized processing and applying algorithms that require pooling together data from the distributed data sources [178].

Many current distributed learning approaches base on the in-place strategy. The strategy is to leave the data in place and to perform partial analysis of data at each of the separate sites, called the local sites, individually and at the same time, and build the local models. Then, the local models can be moved to a central site, where they are merged into the global knowledge model [10].

As it has been pointed out in [203], from the practical point of view, the in-place strategy is less expensive but also less accurate, while the centralized strategy is more expensive and also more accurate. A good compromise is the intermediate strategy which may take advantage of the strengths of both strategies described above i.e. in-place and centralized. In such an approach it is assumed that at the local level the local patterns can be identified for local decision and for local knowledge model representation. Finally, the local patterns and/or the local models are forwarded to the global level, where a set of global patterns or, in general, a global knowledge model is produced [231]. It is important to note that when the local patterns are forwarded these must inherit the features of the local dataset. It is especially important when only a limited set of the local patterns may be forwarded to the global level and they must be useful at the global level. However, it is difficult to identify which of the forwarded patterns are really useful for the global analysis [231]. In general, the intermediate strategy, including local and global analyses, is considered as a fundamental methodology for distributed learning and can be seen as a mean of addressing the scalability issue of learning from the large distributed datasets [231], [235].

The cooperation-based strategy seems to be a good alternative, where many distributed learning algorithms use the cooperation to obtain the final result. This strategy aims at improving the quality of the local models by exchanging qualitative information, simultaneously minimizing the amount of information which needs to be communicated [90]. An example of the implementation of the cooperation-based strategy can be found in [116], where cooperation is used to exchange data between learning models. Such approach to the collaboration is also discussed in [203]. A rule learning algorithm which bases on the cooperation to find acceptable local rules, that are satisfactory as global rules, is proposed in [162]. Using the cooperation-based strategy in [140] the distributed boosting algorithm has been proposed, where the main idea was also collaboration by exchanging learning models between learners. In [235] a multiple model exchange schema has been proposed, where the exchange of local models from time to time is assumed to help the model estimation task at the global level. In [235] such learning scheme is called *cross learning*.

The hybrid strategy seems to be the best alternative for designing distributed learning algorithms. The hybrid strategy is here understood as the approach integrating advantages of all the above strategies, where the distributed learning algorithms perform partial analysis of data at each of the separate sites and cooperate by data or/and local models exchange and building the global knowledge model at the central site. It should be also possible to exploit parallel processing for improving learning performance and scaling up algorithms to work with huge datasets. In [62] the approach to the distributed learning using the hybrid strategy idea has been proposed. Section 5 contains its extended version.

3.3   Distributed Learning – State-of-the-Art

Several algorithms for distributed learning have been proposed. The majority of them are extensions of "classic" machine learning algorithms invariably operating on the centralized data. The fuzzy algorithm extended to learning classifiers from large and distributed datasets was presented in [42]. A well-known tool in the distributed learning is a decision tree, which has been used in distributed learning in [9], [87]. In [230] the hybrid tree parallelism has been discussed. In [94] learning decision tree in parallel from disjoint data has been investigated. The approach assumes converting trees to rules and combining the rules into a single rule set.

Many of the algorithms for the distributed learning assume horizontal fragmentation. An approach to inducing decision tree from vertically fragmented data has been discussed in [116], [36]. In [37] the extensions of the following algorithms: Naïve Bayes, Support Vector Machine and k-Nearest Neighbors have been also proposed for learning from vertically fragmented data. The review of data mining algorithms and their classification with respect to homogenously and heterogeneously distributed data is also included in [178].

Among the methods used for the distributed learning several were based on the collaborative learning [39] and integration of independently derived hypotheses by combining different classifiers to make global classification decisions [160]. Most of the discussed methods have been also developed as an extension of the typical machine learning approaches. For example, Bayesian methods have been adopted for distributed learning and the model aggregating Bayesian classifiers was discussed in [65].

Combining classifiers is a fairly general method for distributed learning. In such case, different models of data from different sites are combined. The main aim of combining classifiers is to improve predictive performance and overcome some disadvantages of the base classification algorithm. The final prediction model can be constructed through combining thus obtained local classifiers. Among widely used approaches developed for aggregating multiple models are statistical methods, like bootstrap, bagging, boosting and stacking [16], [167], [40].

In general, the bootstrap and bagging approaches generate multiple models from different data sets and then average the output of the models. These approaches to aggregating multiple models have been initially introduced with a view of increasing the accuracy of data mining algorithms. Approaches focusing on improving the performance of the distributed learning using the boosting technique, have been proposed in [141], [150]. Bagging as the technique for improving distributed learning has been proposed in [39]. These approaches, belonging to ensemble learning class, have been extended by sending and sharing the local models.

The boosting strategy creates multiple learners that are induced from the weighted training set. The approach assumes that a weak classifier can be learned from each of the considered weighted training sets and then weak classifiers are combined into a final classifier. Subsequently, their applications have also been extended to combining models in the distributed learning.

The stacking approach combines the outputs of multiple models that are learned from independent data sets. Stacking with respect to the number of distributed nodes was investigated in [211].

Other methods for constructing combined classifiers include voting pools of classifiers [15], committees of classifiers and their combinations [198]. In particular, the committees can consist of the models of the same or different types. The committees may also differ in instance distribution and subsets of attributes used for learning [198].

An alternative approach to distributed learning is the concept of the genetic-based machine learning methods, also called Learning Classifier Systems (LCSs). The architecture of the distributed learning classifier system has been proposed in [67]. Several approaches to learning from the distributed datasets have been also discussed in [32].

The related notion of the so called meta-learning provides mechanisms for combining and integrating a number of classifiers learned at separated locations, finally producing a meta-classifier. In this sense, the main idea of meta-learning is to execute a number of learning process on a number of data subsets in parallel, and then combine the models through another phase of learning [161]. Meta-learning also improves predictive performance by combining different learning models. Meta-learning approaches differ in the strategy of induction of the final model. Distributed meta-learning techniques and several combiner strategies have been developed in [161]). Among them there are such strategies as voting and weighted voting implemented when only the labels of predicted classes from classifiers are available. When measures of the performance, confidence and others, with respect to classifier models, are available, also several other different rules for combining these measures have been suggested in [121]. It should be also noted that finding the optimal meta-learning model for a given problem is NP-hard [107] and, in general, meta-learning algorithms focus on finding approximation of the optimal knowledge model.

In [5] it has been pointed out that a majority of the meta-learning algorithms and ensemble learning algorithms are suitable for learning classifiers from homogenous distributed data. In [201] the authors conclude that meta-learning methodologies view data distribution as a technical issue and treat distributed data sources as a part of a single database. It is also pointed out that such an approach offers a rather narrow view of the distributed learning, since the data distributions in different locations are often not identical. For example, data relating to a disease from the hospitals around the world might have varying distributions due to different nutrition habits, climate or the quality of life [201]. Alternatively, in [201] an approach to clustering local classification models induced at physically distributed databases is proposed. Another approach, focusing on improving the performance of the distributed learning based on a boosting technique, has been proposed in [141].

When a partial analysis of data with the final merging of the partial analysis results into the global knowledge model is performed, the local level analysis can be carried-out by simple sampling of data [137], [153]. However, the sampled set of data may not sufficiently represent the local level data, that is one disadvantage of such an approach.

Selecting out of the distributed databases only the relevant data can eliminate or reduce the restrictions typical to sampling methods. As it was mentioned in [186], learning models based on the reduced datasets combined later into a meta-model seem to be one of the most successful approaches to the distributed learning and it is much more efficient computationally than moving all distributed datasets into the centralized site for learning the global model. Although sometimes an implementation of such an approach can be limited by such properties of data like sensitivity or privacy, it is worth being considered for the distributed learning [235].

Selection of the relevant data is the process often referred to as a *data reduction* [142], [178]. In the considered case, the main goal of the data reduction is to reduce the number of instances in each of the distributed data subsets, without the loss of the extractable information, to enable either pooling the data together and using some mono-database mining tools or effectively applying meta-learning techniques [238]. It means that the data reduction also plays an important role in the distributed learning. The development of techniques and strategies which will allow extracting the most important information from the distributed data remains still an open research area in the domain of the distributed learning [49], [221], [231], [232], [233], [235].

3.4   Technologies, Architectures and Systems for Distributed Learning

Agent technology seems to be a natural tool for the distributed systems and systems fundamentally designed for the collaborative problem solving in the distributed environment. The field of the autonomous agents and multi-agent systems is a rapidly expanding area of research and development. It uses many ideas originating from distributed computing, object-oriented programming and software engineering [8]. Combining approaches to distributed learning with agent technology has been pointed as the promising and at the same time challenging problem in the distributed learning research [125], [228].

The collective intelligence of multi-agent systems seem to fit quite well for analysis of the distributed data carried-out by different agents in parallel. In [125] the use of agent technology for distributed learning has been discussed with respect to:

- Access to the autonomous and distributed data sources
- Interactive and dynamic process of distributed learning
- Scalability of the learning system to large distributed data
- Multi-strategy of distributed learning
- Data manipulation under the umbrella of privacy and security.

In [231] an agent paradigm was proposed as a tool for integration of different techniques into an effective strategy of learning from data. The proposed hybrid learning system integrates basic components of the learning process. Hence, data pre-processing, data selection and transformation and induction of the learning and post-learning models are carried-out by a set of agents cooperating during the task execution.

Several agent-based architectures have already been proposed to solve the distributed learning problems. It is usually assumed that each site can have one or more associated agents, processing the local data and communicating the results to other agents that control and manage the knowledge discovery process. For example, in [77], [88], [161], [183], [186], [200] different distributed agent-based data-mining systems, including components dedicated to solving the learning problem, denoted respectively as PADMA, JAM, Kensington, Papyrus, MALE, ANIMALS and MALEF have been proposed. The example of the system developed for mining heterogeneous data set is BODHI [10]. In [5] the EMADS conceptual framework and its current implementation are shown. EDMAS is a hybrid peer-to-peer agent based system comprising a collection of the collaborating agents, including a collection of the classifier data mining agents that are placed in a set of containers. These containers can be distributed across a network.

Common to all of the above approaches is that they aim at integrating the knowledge discovered from different and distributed data sites with minimum amount of network communication and maximum of local computation [125]. However, the development of methods that would be appropriate to minimize the amount of data shipped between the sites and to reduce the communication overhead is still an important goal of the future research [228].

It can be concluded that agent-oriented software engineering seems to be an attractive tool for implementation of systems dedicated for the distributed learning (see, for example [125], [190]). Although several examples of agent-based distributed data mining systems have been recently described, complex architecture of systems for learning from massive and mostly heterogeneous datasets are also still an active field of research (see also, for example [36], [116], [119], [227], [231]). Systems based on interaction and integration of technologies from machine learning domain with techniques developed by the agent-oriented software engineering is an important and promising challenge. Trends and open issues in the field of the agent-based architecture applicable to the distributed learning are further discussed in [172].

4   Data Reduction

4.1   Scope of the Data Reduction

One of the current focuses of research in the field of machine learning are methods of selecting relevant information. Selection of the relevant information is the process often referred to as a *data reduction* [142], [178]. Data reduction techniques aim at decreasing the quantity of information required to learn a good quality classifiers. In practice it means that data reduction approaches are concerned with selecting informative instances and, finally, with producing a minimal set of instances or prototypes to represent a training set and presenting the reduced dataset to a machine learning algorithm [215]. It is obvious that removing some instances from the training set reduces time and memory complexity of the learning process [97]. The data reduction through removing attributes which are irrelevant for the classification results is equally important. In the real-world problems, relevant attributes are often unknown a priori and, therefore, many attributes are introduced with a view to represent the domain better [66]. Many of these attributes are not only irrelevant from the point of view of classification results but may also have a negative influence on the accuracy and on the time required for classifier learning. The presence of the redundant attributes introduces unnecessary noise to the data analysis and results in the increased computational complexity of the learning process. As it has been observed in [174], the number of instances needed to assure the required classification accuracy grows exponentially with the number or irrelevant attributes present. The concept of relevance with respect to instance and attribute selection problems has been investigated in [73], [127], [168], [224].

Data reduction carried-out without losing extractable information is considered as an important approach to increasing the effectiveness of the learning process. This holds especially true when the available datasets are large, such as those encountered in data mining, text categorization, financial forecasting, mining the multimedia databases and meteorological, financial, industrial and science repositories, analysing huge string data like genome sequences, Web documents and log data analysis, mining of photos and videos, or information filtering in E-commerce [118], [206], [225]. Finding a small set of representative instances for large datasets can result in a classification model "*superior to the one constructed from the whole massive data building and may help to avoid working on the whole original dataset all the time*" [236].

Data reduction is perceived as an important step in the knowledge discovery in databases. When KDD is defined as a nontrivial process of identifying valid, novel, potentially useful, and ultimately understandable patterns in data, then it assumes that the process of data selection by data reduction plays a pivotal role in successful data mining and should not be overlooked [80]. Much of the research effort from the KDD domain concentrates on scaling up data mining algorithms or scaling down the data. In the later case, the major issue is to select the relevant data and then to present it to a data mining algorithm [143]. When mining of extremely large datasets becomes a difficult task, one possible solution to this problem is to reduce the number of instances [118].

The selection of the relevant data is also one of the approaches to the distributed learning, in case data is stored in the separated and physically distributed repositories. Moving all of the data to a central site and building a single global learning model may not be feasible due to a variety of reasons including, for example, restricted communication bandwidth among sites or high expenses involved. The selection of relevant data in distributed locations and then moving only the local patterns can eliminate or reduce the above restrictions and speed up the distributed learning process as it was shown in [59]. Data reduction is among the keys in mining high-dimensional and distributed data [221], [231], [232], [233], [238].

Data reduction is also called editing, prototype selecting, condensing, filtering, etc. In all cases, however, the scope of the process depends on the object of the reduction. Data reduction can be achieved by selection of instances, by selection of attributes or by simultaneous reduction in both dimensions [22]. Both problems, i.e. the instance selection problem and the attribute selection problem, are NP-hard [95], [127] and can be classified as the NP-complete. This was proved through the transformation from the subset selection problem which is known to be NP-complete [95].

Since the instance selection and attribute selection are known to belong to the NP-hard problem class, none of the approaches proposed so far (see, for example, [171], [199], [215], [216]) can be considered superior, guaranteeing satisfactory results in terms of the learning error reduction or increased efficiency of the learning process. While there exists an abundance of methods for finding prototypes (see note in [21]), a method superior in certain domains is inferior in others [118]. Hence, searching for robust and efficient approaches to data reduction is still a lively field of research.

This section focuses on data reduction which might be also referred to as the prototype selection. Firstly, the data reduction problem formulation is proposed. Next, the section contains an overview of data reduction algorithms and discusses basic approaches to data reduction including those proposed by the author.

4.2   Problem Formulation

The data reduction process aims at identifying and eliminating irrelevant and redundant information, and finding patterns or regularities within certain attributes, allowing to induce the so-called prototypes or reference vectors. A lot of research work confirms that data reduction through instance or attribute or instance and attribute selection can play a pivotal role in building robust learning models [22], [66], [97], [124], [135], [215]. From the findings of the above mentioned authors it is clear that data reduction should be perceived as a key to reinforce the learning process.

The data reduction algorithms can be divided into two categories: prototype selection and prototype extraction. Prototype selection is a technique of choosing a subset of reference vectors from the original set, also by reduction of attributes, whereas prototype extraction means the construction of an entirely new set of instances, smaller, in respect to its dimensionality, than the original dataset. Prototype extraction can also include the process of feature construction, where decreasing the number of attributes is carried-out by creating new features on the basis of some transformation of original attributes [21]. The aim of both techniques is to find out or construct a subset of prototypes representing the original training set in such a manner that the performance of a classifier built on the set of prototypes is better or at least not worse than a classifier built on the original dataset [155]. More often the data reduction techniques are seen as a key to the problem of the so-called "curse of dimensionality" [207].

This work focuses on the prototype selection under the assumption that data reduction is carried-out in the attribute or instance space or in both of these spaces simultaneously. The author considers the data reduction problem as a problem of finding the optimal subset of prototypes, where the optimal set is defined with respect to the particular induction algorithm. Hence, the definition of the data reduction problem can be formalized as follows:

Definition 5. Given a learning algorithm L, and a dataset D with attributes described by attribute set A, the optimal prototype dataset, S_{opt}, is a subset of the dataset D, where each example is described by set of $A' \subset A$, such that the performance criterion of the learning algorithm L is maximized.

The performance criteria used in data reduction include, for example, the accuracy of classification, the complexity of the hypothesis, the classification cost of a classification error and many others (see [118], [137], [224]).

In general, the problem of finding an optimal subset of prototypes is NP-hard. This sentence is true since the instance selection and attribute selection are known to belong to the NP-hard problem class as it has been mentioned in the previous subsection. From the practical point of view, it means that the data reduction problems are solved using approximation algorithms, which is a standard approach for solving the NP-hard optimization problems.

Based on the above it can be observed that a good set of prototypes has the following properties:

- Firstly, the cardinality of the reduced dataset is smaller that the cardinality of the original, non-reduced dataset.

- Secondly, the reduced dataset assures maximum or acceptable classification quality criterion or criteria with respect to the classifier induced using such reduced dataset.

Thus, the data reduction process can be seen as a means to achieve one of the following goals:

- Reducing original dataset to maximize classification quality criterion or criteria.
- Finding the smallest set of prototypes that assures an acceptable value of the performance criterion used.
- Finding the Pareto-optimal compromise between the dataset compression rate and the value of the quality criterion.

Without the loss of generality, the data reduction problem can be formally defined under the assumption that the data reduction goal is to reduce the original dataset with a view to maximize the classification accuracy. Thus, the following inequality holds: $|S| < |D|$. Similarly, with respect to attribute space, the following inequality holds: $|A'| < |A|$ also. Ideally $|S| << |D|$ and $|A'| << |A|$. In such case the instance reduction rate and the attribute reduction rate can be computed, respectively, as $R_D = \frac{|D|-|S|}{|D|}$ and $R_A = \frac{|A|-|A'|}{|A|}$. Both rates are often shown in percentages (see, for example, [118]).

With respect to the problem of learning from data, when data reduction process is carried-out, the task of learner L is to output the hypothesis $h \in H$ that optimizes performance criterion F using dataset S which is a subset of the set D, such that $|S| < |D|$ (ideally $S = S_{opt}$), where each example $x \in S$ is described by a set A' of m attributes, where $m < n$.

When the data reduction is considered with respect to physically distributed repositories then, finally, sets $D_1, \ldots, D_K$ are replaced by the reduced datasets $S_1, \ldots, S_K$ of local patterns such that $\forall_{i=1,\ldots,K} S_i \subset D_i$. Thus, the goal of data reduction is to find subset S_i from given D_i. In such case, the task of the distributed learner L_d is to output a hypothesis $h \in H$ optimizing F using operations allowed by Z and using datasets $S_1, \ldots, S_K$, such that $\forall_{i:i=1,\ldots,K} S_i \subset D_i$.

Additionally, the following properties of the distributed reduced datasets can be formulated:

- The reduced datasets are heterogeneous, when the reduction is carried-out in both dimensions, i.e. through instance and attribute selection. In such case $A'_{i:i=1,\ldots,K}$ denotes the set of the selected instances which values are stored at sites $1, \ldots, K$ respectively, where $\forall_{i:i=1,\ldots,K} A'_i \subset A_i$ and $\exists_{i,j:i,j=1,\ldots,K} A'_i \neq A'_j$. When the distributed, non-reduced datasets are homogenous the following property holds: $\forall_{i:i=1,\ldots,K} A_i = A$, where A denotes the set of attributes of the non-reduced datasets. Thus it is also true that $\forall_{i:i=1,\ldots,K} A'_i \subset A$.
- The reduced datasets are homogenous, when the data reduction is carried-out through instance selection. In such case the reduced datasets $S_1, \ldots, S_K$

have the same set of attributes A and the following properties can be observed: $S_\Sigma = \bigcup_{i=1}^{K} S_i$, where S_Σ denotes the set of prototypes that can be obtained by merging prototypes from the reduced, distributed data sets.

- The reduced datasets are heterogeneous, when the data reduction is carried-out through instance selection and when the distributed, non-reduced datasets are inherently heterogeneous. In such case the selected prototypes from a heterogeneous sets $A_1, \ldots, A_K$, i.e. $\exists_{i,j:i,j=1,\ldots,K} A_i \neq A_j$.
- The reduced datasets are heterogeneous, when the data reduction is carried-out through attribute selection. In such case each one reduced data set $S_{i:i=1,\ldots,K}$ has the set of attributes $A'_{i:i=1,\ldots,K}$ such that $\forall_{i:i=1,\ldots,K} A'_i \subset A_i$ and $\exists_{i,j:i,j=1,\ldots,K} A'_i \neq A'_j$. When the distributed, non-reduced datasets are homogenous the following property holds: $\forall_{i:i=1,\ldots,K} A_i = A$.

4.3 Techniques and Algorithms for Data Reduction

4.3.1 State-of-the-Art Review

As it has been mentioned, data reduction can be carried-out in the attribute or instance space or in both of these spaces simultaneously. As it has been established in [34], [51], [143], [216], [225], such reduction can result in:

- Increasing capabilities and generalization properties of the classification model
- Reducing space complexity of the classification problem
- Decreasing the required computational time
- Diminishing the size of the formulas or decision and expression trees obtained by an induction algorithm on the reduced datasets
- Speeding up the knowledge extraction process.

Usually, instance selection algorithms are based on distance calculation between instances in the training set [215]. Methods based on other approaches, known as instance-based methods, remove an instance if it has the same output class as its k nearest neighbors, assuming that all neighborhood instances will be, later on, correctly classified [215]. Both approaches have several weaknesses. They often use distance functions that are inappropriate or inadequate for nominal attributes [45], [215]. Besides, there is a need to store all the available training examples in the model. To eliminate the above requirements, several approaches have been proposed, including, for example, the Condensed Nearest Neighbor (CNN) algorithm [97], the Instance Based learning algorithm 2 (IB2) [2], the Instance Based learning algorithm 3 (IB3) [2], the Selective Nearest Neighbor (SNN) algorithm [171], the Edited Nearest Neighbor (ENN) algorithm [216], the family of Decremental Reduction Optimization Procedures (DROP1-DROP5) [216] and the instance weighting approach [225]. Methods belonging to the other group (e.g.: the family of four instance reduction algorithms denoted respectively IRA1-IRA4 [51], the All k-NN method [199]) try to eliminate unwanted training examples using some removal criteria that need to be fulfilled. The same principle has been mentioned in [222]. The authors of the above paper conclude that if many instances of the same class are found in an area, and when the area does not include instances from the other classes, then an unknown instance can be correctly classified when only selected prototypes from such area are used.

The above reasoning results also in approaches, where the instance situated close to the center of a cluster of similar instances should be selected as a prototype (see, for example, [6] and [215]). Such an approach requires using some clustering algorithms like, for example, k-means or fuzzy k-means algorithm [78], [144]. These algorithms generate cluster centers which are later considered to be the centroids and the reduced dataset is produced. In such an approach, a good reduced dataset can be obtained if the centroids are "good" representatives of clusters in the data [135]. It must be also noted that the quality of the selected centroids depends on the structure of such clusters and best results can be expected in the case when they have the Gaussian distribution property. Furthermore, another constraint on clustering approach is the dimensionality of the dataset. When the number of attributes is large, the quality of the selected centroids tends to become poor. It means that the approach for instance selection based on the clustering should be robust independently of the structure and dimensionality of the data [135], [215], [216], [225]. It can be also noted that the above discussed approaches more often are proposed as a technique for the prototype extraction i.e. a technique that is used to construct an entirely new set of instances smaller, with respect to its dimensionality, than the original dataset [135].

In the IRA family of algorithms, prototypes are selected from clusters of instances and each instance has a chance to be selected as the prototype [51]. Another approach is to consider the so-called candidate instances situated close to the center of clusters and then to select the prototypes using the classification accuracy as a criterion [92].

Instance selection can also be carried-out through sampling of data [218]. Sampling is a well-known statistical technique that "*selects a part from a whole to make inferences about the whole*" [93]. Different versions of sampling-based prototype selection, including random sampling, stratified sampling, clustering sampling, inverse sampling and others, are proposed and discussed in [140], [143], [153]. In [34] the so called stratified strategy, as a variant of sampling technique, was proposed. In this case the prototypes are selected from strata using evolutionary algorithm, assuming that data are divided into disjoint strata with equal class distribution.

Local search heuristics and metaheuristics, like for example tabu search, simulated annealing, genetic algorithms or evolutionary algorithms, seem to be a practical approach to solving the instance selection problem taking into account the fact that the instance selection belongs to the class of NP-hard problems (see, for example, [104], [135], [179], [185], [222]).

In [75] the selection of the relevant data is seen as the process of looking for prototypes that can be used to construct prototype-based rules.

In the literature various hybrid data reduction methods have been also proposed. Such methods are expected to boost the effectiveness of the instance selection processes. Examples include a combination of CNN and ENN, and boosting or bootstrap approach [153]. Learning Vector Quantization (LVQ), a supervised learning algorithm [128], is yet another approach to improve instance selection algorithms. LVQ is used to create new prototypes rather than to select some of the existing instances as prototypes. In [106] the conjunction of the LVQ with some instance selection algorithms is discussed. The hybrid approach can be also helpful when the imbalanced datasets are observed. In such case, the class imbalance problem through modifying the data distribution can help the real-life data mining applications [209].

Attribute selection methods based on enumeration understood as a review of all possible subset of attributes lead directly to finding the best one. This class of methods includes branch and bound, beam search, exhaustive search or best first search. Unfortunately, these algorithms are very time consuming and hence, in majority of cases, not feasible.

Another kind of algorithms attempting to remove the irrelevant attributes use the idea of enumeration and evaluation of the attribute subsets. Examples include FOCUS [4] and RELIEF [122]. The first one tries to identify the subset of attributes that is sufficient to re-construct the hypothesis correctly i.e. the subset containing no such two instances that have the same values for all attributes and conflicting class labels. The approach also belongs to the class of the instance-based learning. The second one first assigns weights to attributes and next evaluates the subsets of attributes based on the calculation of differences between them. Such procedure is very time consuming and in majority of cases not feasible. Another example is the Winnow system, able to adjust attribute weights depending on the fact that a false positive or a false negative classification decisions are discovered during the learning [210].

Two other approaches, called Decision Independent Correlation (DIC) and Decision Dependent Correlation (DDC), remove both irrelevant and redundant attributes by using independent and dependent correlation measurements have been investigated. In [69] it has been shown, that both assure better performance, in terms of computational time and accuracy, than the FCBF (Fast Correlation Based Filter) algorithm based on a predominant correlation concept to identify relevant and redundant attributes [225].

The attribute ranking mechanism for attribute selection has been proposed in [101]. Other attribute selection strategy based on rough sets theory has been investigated in [17], [208], where additionally particle swarm optimization (PSO) can be applied to find the optimal attribute subsets.

Evaluation of attributes and their selection is considered to be an important step in the process of inducing decision trees [165]. For example, the ID3 algorithm induces decision tree considering the most relevant attributes, i.e. only those which are required to completely classify the training set. All other attributes are removed. A similar approach is used within C 4.5 and CART algorithms (see [28], [166]).

Evaluation of attributes can be also based on statistical methods where each attribute is evaluated independently. Most often used statistical measure for an independent attribute selection is the correlation coefficient (see, for example, [66]). Another approach is to evaluate attributes using the multiple correlation coefficient [52], the Pearson χ^2 test [23] or the Kolmogorov-Smirnov test [24]. Among statistical techniques for attribute selection also Principle Component Analysis (PCA) or Independent Component Analysis [133] were used, though they are rather dedicated for feature construction.

Other approaches for attribute selection attempt to evaluate and rank some subsets of attributes that were generated by heuristics or metaheuristics such as random search, particle swarm, ant colony, genetic or evolutionary search procedures [52], [72], [91], [115], [208]. All attribute selection methods that have been proposed so far, try to find the best subset of attributes satisfying certain criterion. Among the criteria used one can observe the following: classifier error rate, information entropy, dependence measure, consistency measure or distance measure. Extensive overviews of the attribute selection approaches can be found in [66], [120], [127], [168], [239].

In case of the simultaneous reduction in both of the discussed dimensions, that is instance and attribute spaces, some sophisticated heuristics or random search techniques are used. Example heuristic approach to the data reduction can be found in [168], where the algorithm for attribute selection called Subset selection using Case-based Relevance APproach (SCRAP) and the Learning Algorithm using SEarch Ring (LASER) for instance selection are combined. The SCRAP is a sequential search filter, while the LASER is an embedded instance selection method. Raman [168] also showed that such combination can yield a substantial improvement of the prediction accuracy of the learner when compared to the case where only one dimension is reduced. In [179] a random hill climbing algorithm with mutation is proposed for selecting the most accurate prototype set. The algorithm uses the problem representation where both - the instances and attributes are stored in a single binary string. The length of such string depends on the number of bits required to represent the required set of prototypes and on the number of attributes. Within such representation the i-th bit shows whether to include or not to include in the reduced dataset the corresponding instance or the corresponding attribute. The search is carried-out using the mutation mechanism over the binary string in question. Each mutation move changes the composition of instances or attributes and at each iteration of the algorithm only one bit is muted. The idea of data reduction by the genetic algorithm is discussed in [174]. In their approach each solution is described by two chromosomes, one representing the selected instances and the other representing the selected attributes. Each chromosome consists of integers which point to the selected instances or to the selected attributes. Such encoding is more flexible in the domain with many instances as opposed to the binary chromosome representation proposed in [136].

Yet another approach to data reduction was proposed in [61], where data reduction in both discussed dimensions is integrated with the learning process. The above concept is further elaborated and extended in Section 4.4. Similar ideas were also investigated in [3], [22], [31], [176]. Integration of the data reduction with the learning process may require introduction of some adaptation mechanisms as exemplified by the idea of learning classifier systems [31]. Unfortunately, integration of the data reduction and classifier construction stages leads to a considerable enlargement of the decision space and hence the computational complexity of the problem. One possible way of dealing with such complexity proposed in [61] is discussed in Section 4.4. Considering that attribute and instance selection are themselves computationally difficult, obtaining effective solutions in case of the discussed integrative approaches, requires the application of some sophisticated metaheuristics and local search random techniques executed, preferably, in the parallel computational environments.

4.3.2   Taxonomies of Data Reduction Algorithms

The instance selection methods can be classified on the basis of several different criteria. Raman and Ioerger in [168] point out, that the instance selection methods can be grouped into three classes - filter methods, wrapper methods, and embedded methods. The filtering is based on random search, random sampling or genetic algorithms. In this case the selected instances are tested with a view to deciding whether they come from the same distribution as the original entry dataset and whether the current reduced dataset contains sufficient information. The wrapper methods include boosting, where the distribution of the data is modified [168], [209]. The windowing technique [166] belongs also to the wrapper group methods. Lazy learners, like the k nearest neighbors' method, belong to the embedded methods. This category of methods has the example selection strategy embedded in their learning scheme [168].

Wilson and Martinez [215] suggested that the instance selection methods can be categorized into incremental search, decremental search and batch search. The incremental search begins with an empty set of prototypes S and adds each instance to S if it fulfills some criteria (example approaches include: CNN, the IB family, SNN). The decremental search begins with $S = D$, and successfully removes instances from S (example approaches include: ENN, the DROP family). In [93] the decremental search methods are referred to as the condensation algorithms. Finally, in the batch search mode, instances fulfilling the removal criteria are removed at one go (example approaches include: kNN based methods, the IRA family, Random Mutation Hill Climbing [179]).

Bezdek and Kuncheva [21] group the instance selection into three categories: condensation, error-edition and search methods. The object of the condensation methods is to find a consistent reference set. The original condensation method is CNN. The error-edition methods base on the assumption that points from different classes that are close to apparent boundaries between them contain "noise" and should be removed from the original dataset. This category includes, for example, the DROP algorithm family. The last category includes search methods that can achieve the same goal by the criterion-driven combinational optimization. This group of methods includes: local search heuristics, tabu search, and metaheuristics like for example particle swarm optimization, simulated annealing, genetic algorithm or evolutionary algorithm (see, for example, [135], [155], [179], [185]).

The attribute selection approaches can be grouped into three classes. Two main ones include filter and wrapper methods. The third approach comes under the umbrella of the so-called ensemble methods [73].

The filter methods choose the preferred attribute set optimizing some assumed evaluation function like, for example, distance, information value, dependency or consistency. Evaluation based on information measure helps to select these attributes which inclusion assures the greatest information gain [66]. A distinctive feature of the filter methods is that they remove the irrelevant attributes before the data is presented to the learning algorithm [168]. This, however, means that the selected subset of attributes may not actually fit the learning method used. This class of methods includes, for example, RELIEF, FOCUS, DIC, DDC and FCBF algorithms.

The wrapper methods use the learning algorithm performance as the evaluation function and the classifier error rate is considered as the attribute selection criterion. The evaluation is usually done by estimating the classification accuracy obtained by classifier induced based on the selected subset of attributes. The methods of this class are more complex than filter class methods and hence are computationally more costly. They are also more accurate in comparison to filter methods and provide a better classification accuracy on unseen data. Among this class of methods are: hill-climbing, best-first search [127] and several approaches based on a random or genetic search.

The wrapper methods carrying-out the sequential search can be further divided into three following groups: sequential forward selection, sequential backward selection and bi-directional search. The first group includes methods which start with all attributes and successfully eliminate the ones that do not improve the performance measure. The second group starts with an empty set of attributes and successfully adds the one improving best the performance measure. In bi-directional search both schemas are integrated [168].

Finally, another type of the attribute selection method is called the embedded attribute selection. In this case, the selection process is carried-out within the classification algorithm itself. This category of methods is represented, for example, by the decision tree algorithms. Other example of the embedded method is Recursive Feature Elimination (RFE) with the attribute selection process embedded within the Support Vector Machines [73].

In [66] attribute selection strategies, which can be used within wrapper or filter methods, are divided into three following groups: complete, heuristic and random. Complete approach is based on the exhausting search over competing candidate subsets. Examples of such an approach are branch and bound, and beam search. Heuristic approaches, in each iteration, consider all attributes that remained as candidates for selection to be incorporated to the final attribute subset. Examples of such approaches include RELIEF and FOCUS algorithms. Random methods select randomly and iteratively candidate subsets.

All types of the algorithms discussed above can also be classified as deterministic or non-deterministic. In deterministic ones the final number of selected prototypes of attributes is controlled and determined by the user [118].

4.4 Approaches to Data Reduction

As it was mentioned in the previous subsection, various data reduction methods have been so far proposed in the literature. The aim of this subsection is to discuss properties of several basic approaches to data reduction evaluating their features with a view to propose own alternative solutions. First, the approaches based on similarity measures are considered, next the integrated data reduction is investigated and, finally, the multi-objective data reduction is suggested.

4.4.1 Approaches Based on Similarity Measures

Defining similarity measures plays the key role in different areas, including machine learning. In [164] it was mentioned that: "*Similarity is fundamental for learning, knowledge and thought, for only our sense of similarity allows us to order things into kinds so that these can function as stimulus meanings. Reasonable expectation depends on the similarity of circumstances and on our tendency to expect that similar causes will have similar effects.*" Similarity is thus fundamental in making predictions, as it happens in the case of machine learning.

In the literature similarity measures are classified into two different categories. The first is related to the kind of knowledge representation to which they are applied. In such case it is possible to distinguish measures applied to attribute vectors or to instances [170]. The second is related to the way in which the similarity is computed. With respect to the second category it is possible to distinguish, among others, measures based on geometric models, feature matching, semantic relations, information content (for the review see [173]).

One of the areas of machine learning where defining similarity measures plays a vital role is the data reduction. Among similarity-based data reduction methods there are, among others, instance-based methods and clustering methods. These methods are, in general, a generalization of the minimal distance methods.

Instance-based methods compute the similarity between instances and use a value of the similarity to determine the output class of the new instance. In general, it is assumed that similar instances belong to the same class. It should be noted that instance-based methods store instances while generalizing. The algorithms of this class are also referred to as the memory-based learning algorithms [215]. One of the most straightforward instance-based algorithms is the nearest neighbor algorithm described briefly in Section 2.4.

The basic disadvantage of the nearest neighbor algorithm and, in general, the instance-based approaches is that they have large storage requirements, because they store all the available training examples in the model. Secondly, they are slow during execution, because all of the training instances must be considered in order to classify each new instance. The nearest neighbor algorithm is also very sensitive to noise that can be present within the training set. In such case the accuracy of kNN can dramatically decrease [215]. The accuracy of kNN can be also degraded with the introduction of irrelevant attributes [215]. To eliminate the above weakness several approaches have been proposed. Although the main aim of these approaches is to improve the quality of datasets, the result of their application is the reduction of the training dataset. A well known example of such an approach resulting in removing part of the instances from the training set is the Condensed Nearest Neighbor algorithm [97]. The CNN is considered as a basic data reduction schema. The pseudo-code of the CNN algorithm is shown as Algorithm 3.

Algorithm 3. *The CNN algorithm*

Input: D -the original training set containing instances with known class labels.
Output: S - the reduced dataset.
1. Set $S := \emptyset$.
2. Select randomly one example from D belonging to each class $c_{l:l=1,...,k}$ and add selected examples to S.
3. Select randomly an example x from D and set $D := D \backslash \{x\}$.
4. Using the examples in S assign a class to x based on majority vote.
5. If x is misclassified then add an example x to S.
6. If $D \neq \emptyset$ then goto 3.
7. Return S.

The CNN is a very simple approach deciding which instances are to be kept in the reduced dataset and which should be discarded. The algorithm makes use of the similarity between concepts i.e. between an instance class from the non reduced dataset D and instance classes from the reduced set S (see, for example, the discussion of different conceptual similarity measures in [64]).

The CNN data reduction algorithm assures that all instances from the original training set are classified correctly, though such an approach does not guarantee the minimal reduced set. Another disadvantage of the CNN is its sensitivity to the noise which could be present in the training set. Unfortunately, the learning process based on such reduced training set may result in a very poor accuracy [216]. Several other algorithms for instance selection have been proposed as an extension of the CNN. For example, in the SNN every member of the original training set must be closer to a member of the reduced set of the same class than to any other member of the training set (instead of the reduced set) from a different class.

Another example of the instance selection algorithm is the ENN algorithm. The ENN, in comparison to CNN, starts with $S = D$ and then, in each iteration, an instance is removed from S if it does not agree with the majority of its nearest neighbors. Typically, the number of neighbors is equal to 3 but can be also set by its user [216]. The pseudo-code of the ENN algorithm is shown as Algorithm 4.

Algorithm 4. *The ENN algorithm*

Input: D -the original training set containing examples with known class labels; k- the number of neighbors (a user-defined constant).
Output: S - the reduced dataset.
1. Set $S := D$.
2. Set $j := 1$.
3. Select randomly example x_j from S.
4. Run kNN algorithm for the number of neighbors equal to k and classify the example x_j.
5. If an example x_j is classified incorrectly then $S := S \setminus \{x_j\}$.
6. If $j \leq N$, where N is the number of examples within S, then set $j := j+1$ and goto 3.
7. Return S.

It has been also observed that all the above algorithms are sensitive to noise and they are computationally complex [216]. The accuracy of the instance-based learning algorithms can be improved through instance weighting. Such an approach assigns weight to each instance based on its ability to reliably predict the class of the unseen instances. Unreliable instances are treated as the noise. The approach based on the instance weighing has been proposed in [177].

In [2] it has been pointed out that the instance selection algorithms select instances which can be situated as border points of the decision boundaries or as central points of the decision boundaries. In this case a decision boundary is understood as a partition in N-dimensional space that divides the space into two or more decision spaces. It means that the classifier classifies all instances on one side of the decision boundary as belonging to one class and all instances on the other side as belonging to the other class (see also [21] and [215]).

In [2] it is pointed out that the noises tend to settle down at the border points. Thus, these algorithms which select reference instances from the border points are sensitive to removing the noise. Examples of the robust algorithms performing well in the presence of the noises include the DROP family algorithms. One of them, known as DROP3, uses a noise-filter pass in the reduced dataset that is done using a rule similar to ENN and where instances misclassified by their k nearest neighbors are removed. It means that DROP3 removes noisy instances as well as close to border points and central points of the decision boundaries. Modified DROP3, known as the DROP4 algorithm, contains an implementation of one additional rule requiring to remove an instance if it does not hurt the classification of other instances [216].

It has been also observed that the selection of the internal points of the decision boundaries may not affect the decision boundaries as much as the selection of the border points. Thus, the selection of the border points requires careful attention, since decision boundary lies between two nearest instances of different classes [225]. The motivation for selecting internal points can be found in [184], where instance selection method has been proposed for the case-based reasoning.

As it has been already mentioned in the previous subsection, the k-means clustering algorithm can be used to produce clusters from which, in the next step, prototypes are selected. Selection of prototypes from clusters is one of the promising approaches to obtain "good" representatives of such clusters [50].

The author proposes using k-means clustering algorithm for instance selection that differs from the approaches reported in the literature by the property of being able to produce the reduced dataset having identical class distribution as the original dataset. The approach assumes that the clusters of data instances are produced separately for each class. It follows that the number of clusters for each class must be calculated in advance. Since the approach is expected to produce the final prototype set with the property of having identical class distribution as the original dataset, a procedure deciding on the number of clusters for each class needs to be defined. A detailed pseudo-code of such procedure, denoted NCC (Number of Clusters Calculation), is shown as Algorithm 5. The proposed prototype selection algorithm based on k-means clustering is shown as Algorithm 6.

Algorithm 5. *The NCC procedure*

Input: D - the original training set containing examples with known class labels; t - predefined number of clusters (a user-defined constant).
Output: p - the vector containing the number of clusters for each class.
1. Map input vectors from D belonging to the class $c_{l:l=1,...,k}$ into disjoint subsets D_l.
2. Calculate the cardinality of D_l denoted as $card(D_l)$.
3. Set $M := \max card(D_l)$.
4. Set $p := [p_l : l = 1, ..., k]$, where $p_l = \frac{card(D_l)}{M} \cdot t$.
5. Round elements of p to the nearest integer.
6. Return p.

Algorithm 6. *k-means for the prototype selection*

Input: D - the original training set containing examples with known class labels; t - predefined number of clusters (a user-defined constant).
Output: Clusters from which prototypes will be selected.
1. Set $p := NCC(D, t)$, where p is a vector that contains number of clusters for each class.
2. Map randomly examples from D belonging to the class $c_{l:l=1,...,k}$ into clusters D_l.
3. Map examples from D_l into p_l disjoint clusters using k-means.
4. Let $Y_{p_l}^{(l)}$ $(l = 1, ..., k)$ denote the obtained clusters such that $\forall_l$ and $\forall_{i \neq j:i,j=1,...,p_l} Y_i^{(l)} \cap Y_j^{(l)} = \emptyset$, where $D = \bigcup_{l=1}^{k} \bigcup_{i=1}^{p_l} Y_i^{(l)}$, and where the total number of clusters $t^* = \sum_{l=1}^{k} p_l$.

Next, from obtained sets $Y_1^{(l)}, \ldots, Y_t^{(l)}$ the prototypes can be selected using a dedicated heuristic or metaheuristic procedure.

Although several weaknesses of k-means have been observed (see, for example, [27]) this procedure has been proposed as an alternative approach to obtain clusters of the potential prototypes. The complexity of the above clustering procedure depends on the time complexity of the k-means and steps included within the NCC procedure. K-means spends most of the time on computing vector distances and is linear in all its relevant factors, i.e. iterations, number of clusters, number of instances and dimensionality of the space [145]. The overall complexity of the discussed procedure is $O(N \log N) + O(ItnNk)$, where I is the number of iterations of k-means, t is the predefined number of clusters, k is the cardinality of the set of decision classes, N denotes the number of instances and n is the number of attributes [49].

Although the stratification does not belong to the similarity-based methods, it is often considered as a variant of clustering. The approach assumes that instances are selected from strata which in fact, are subsets of the original training dataset. The stratification strategy has been used to the prototype selection by Cano et al. in [34], where the combination of stratification strategy and evolutionary algorithm was proposed. The basic idea of the stratification strategy is to divide the initial dataset into disjoint strata of equal size with equal class distribution. Using the proper number of strata can reduce significantly the size of sets from which the selection is carried-out. The detailed pseudo-code of the stratification-based instance clustering is shown as Algorithm 7.

Algorithm 7. *Stratification-based instance clustering*

Input: D - the original training set containing examples with known class labels; t - predefined number of clusters (a user-defined constant).

Output: Subsets of D from which prototypes can be selected.

1. Map randomly examples from D into t disjoint strata with equal size and with equal class distribution.

2. Let $Y_1, \ldots, Y_t$ denote the obtained sets such that $D = \bigcup_{i=1}^{t} Y_i$ and $\forall_{i \neq j: i, j = 1, \ldots, t} Y_i \cap Y_j = \emptyset$.

From the obtained sets (strata) prototypes are selected using a dedicated heuristic or metaheuristic algorithm. The most time consuming part of the above approach is the mapping process aiming at conserving the equal class distribution within subsets. The procedure has the complexity $O(Nkt) + O(N \log N)$, where N denotes the number of instances, k is the cardinality of the set of decision classes and t is the number of cluster (strata).

The approach proposed in [34] assumes random division of the dataset into disjoint strata independently for each class. However, assuming that one prototype is selected from each cluster (strata), the number of strata has a direct influence on the final number of prototypes. Since the stratification strategy is expected to produce the final prototype set with the property of having identical class distribution as the original dataset, the NCC procedure deciding on the number of clusters for each class is suggested. This results in modification of the original stratification approach of [34]. In the modified approach steps 1, 2 and 4 are identical as in the Algorithm 6. Step 3 is defined as mapping randomly input vectors from D_l into p_l disjoint strata. Finally, the prototypes are selected from the obtained clusters (strata).

The accuracy of many similarity-based methods is highly sensitive to the definition of the distance function. Among approaches to reduce this sensitivity are attribute selection or attribute weighting. The review of attribute selection and attribute weighting with respect to the accuracy of instance-based approaches can be found in [25]. The attribute weighting proposed for the collaborative filtering is discussed in [225]. In [225] it is also pointed out that the attribute weighting method can reduce the above mentioned sensitivity through parameterizing the distance function with attribute weights.

Another approach to eliminate sensitivity to the choice of the distance function is to use an appropriate type of distance (similarity) measure minimizing the discussed sensitivity. Among the available and widely used distance measures one can mention the Minkovsky, Mahalanobis, Chebychev, Quadratic, Chi-square, Value Difference Metric (VDM), Minimum Risk Metric, Disccretized Value Difference Metric and many others. Most often used measures are these reviewed and discussed in [75], [216]. Out of the variety of distance measures the Euclidean distance function is the most popular. It is defined as:

$$E(x_1, x_2) = \sqrt{\sum_{i=1}^{n}(x_{1,i} - x_{2,i})^2}, \tag{7}$$

where x_1 and x_2 are input vectors and n is the number of attributes.

The Euclidean distance function is especially useful in case of the continuous attributes. When dealing with the nominal attributes, the VDM measure, based on calculation of the differences between posterior probabilities, is often used. Here, probabilities are calculated using the statistics derived from the training set. In case the dataset has a mixed attribute types it is necessary to converse the nominal attribute values to the numerical ones. Another possibility is to use the heterogeneous distance function such as, for example, HVDM, which is a heuristic measure obtained by combining the Euclidean and the VDM measures [75], [216].

Another worry with using similarity measures is the manner in which values of the different attributes are scaled. In the ideal case contributions from different types of attributes are scaled to be combined in the optimal way. In the majority of papers, scaling of attributes by normalization or z-score standardization is a common approach helping to reduce the influence of the outliers. When the distance functions are based on the probability difference metrics for both discrete and continuous attributes, then the problem is the estimation of probability for continuous attributes. In such case, values of the continuous attributes require discretization prior to the calculation of the respective probabilities. Example of the distance function with discretization is the Discretized Value Difference Metric [214]. Problems of scaling attribute values involving different types of attributes were also discussed in [75].

One of the author's contributions is to propose a new similarity measure together with the family of instance reduction algorithms based on this measure. The idea was first presented in [51] and the discussed family of the similarity-based algorithms for instance selection was denoted as IRA (Instance Reduction Algorithms). In the discussed approach it is proposed to reduce the original dataset through calculating for each instance from the dataset the value of its similarity coefficient and then grouping instances into clusters consisting of instances with identical values of this coefficient, selecting the representation of instances for each cluster and removing the remaining instances. The selected reference vectors, i.e. the representation of instances, are considered as the reduced training set. Algorithms belonging to the IRA family differ between themselves in a manner how the reference instances are chosen from clusters produced using the proposed similarity coefficient. Moreover, the IRA family algorithms assume that the number of selected instances is determined by the value of the representation level, V, which is set arbitrarily by the user. Clearly such a decision has a direct influence on the size of the reduced dataset [54].

In [54] the family of four instance reduction algorithms denoted respectively IRA1-IRA4 have been validated and the obtained results were compared with several well-known data reduction approaches (i.e. CNN, ENN, SNN, IB2, IB3, DROP1-DROP5). Fig. 1-2 present experiment results obtained by the kNN classifier and the decision-tree classifier (C 4.5), where IRA1-IRA4 have been validated and where the experiment involved tree datasets from UCI Machine Learning Repository including: Wisconsin breast cancer, Cleveland heart diseases and credit approval [7]. The results are averaged over benchmark instances. In case of the IRA family algorithms the reduced datasets have been generated with the representation levels set, respectively, to 1, 2, 3, 4 and 10. In Fig. 1-2 the horizontal axis ($|S|/|D|$) shows the percentage of compression of the training set, where 100% represents the whole training set. The vertical axis ($\Delta\eta$) corresponds to accuracy changes depending on instance selection algorithm. The level $\Delta\eta = 0\%$ is defined by the accuracy obtained by the respective classification algorithm trained on the original, that is not reduced, training set.

Computational experiment results discussed in the following chapters show that using IRA algorithms can result in reducing the number of instances and still preserving the quality of the data mining results. It will be also demonstrated that in some cases reducing the training set size can increase the efficiency of

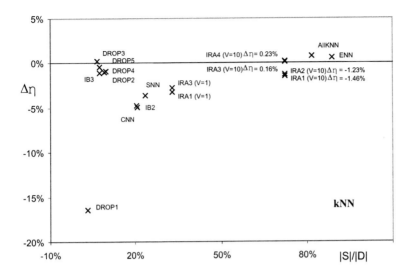

Fig. 1. Performance of the IRA family of the data reduction algorithms versus the competitive algorithms performance. Results obtained using the kNN classifier ($\Delta\eta = 0\%$ corresponds to accuracy 87.42%) - source [54].

the supervised learning. A distinctive feature of the IRA approach, as compared with others reported in the literature, is that the clusters are produced basing on the measure of the similarity between instances where the similarity coefficient values are derived from the overview of all instances within the training set.

All further versions of the IRA-based algorithm, originally presented in [51], base on the assumption that the number of prototypes is determined by the number of produced clusters (see, for example, [57], [58], [61]). Additionally, originally the IRA family of algorithms has been proposed for the two-classes classification problems. In [61] the IRA approach has been extended to the multi-class problems.

To describe the proposed approach in a formal manner, the following notation needs to be introduced. Let x denote a training example, N - the number of instances in the original training set D and n - the number of attributes. Total length of each instance (i.e. training example) is equal to $n+1$, where the element numbered $n + 1$ contains the class label. The class label of each example can take any value from the finite set of class labels $C = \{c_l : l = 1, \ldots, k\}$, which has cardinality k. Also, let $X = \{x_{ij} : i = 1, \ldots, N; j = 1, \ldots, n + 1\}$ denote the matrix of $n + 1$ columns and N rows containing values of all instances from D. The pseudo-code of the procedure producing clusters of instances is shown as Algorithm 8.

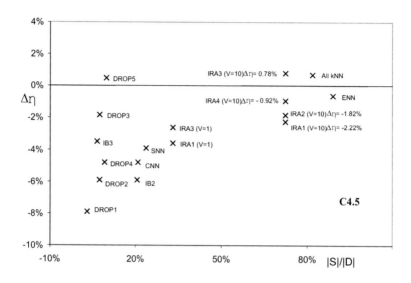

Fig. 2. Performance of the IRA family of the data reduction algorithms versus the competitive algorithms performance. Results obtained using the C 4.5 classifier ($\Delta\eta = 0\%$ corresponds to accuracy 86.02%) - source [54].

Algorithm 8. *The cluster producing procedure based on the similarity coefficient values*

Input: X - the matrix containing values of all instances from D.
Output: Clusters from which prototypes will be selected.
1. Transform data examples: each $\{x_{ij}\}$ for $i = 1, \ldots, N$ and $j = 1, \ldots, n$ is normalized into interval $[0, 1]$ and then rounded to the nearest integer, that is 0 or 1.
2. Calculate values:

$$s_j = \sum_{i=1}^{N} x_{ij}, \quad where \quad j = 1, \ldots, n. \tag{8}$$

3. For examples from X, belonging to the class c_l, (where $l = 1, \ldots, k$), calculate the value of its similarity coefficient I_i:

$$\forall_{x:x_{i,n+1}=c_l} I_i = \sum_{j=1}^{n} x_{ij}s_j, \quad where \quad i = 1, \ldots, N. \tag{9}$$

4. Map examples from X with the same value of similarity coefficient I_i into clusters.
5. Let $Y_1, \ldots, Y_t$ denote the obtained clusters such that $D = \bigcup_{i=1}^{t} Y_i$ and $\forall_{i \neq j:i,j=1,\ldots,t} Y_i \cap Y_j = \emptyset$.

Next, from subsets $Y_1, \ldots, Y_t$ the prototypes could be selected and the reduced training set S could be produced, where initially $S = \emptyset$. The selection is based on the following rules:

- If $|Y_i| = 1$ then $S := S \cup Y_i$, where $i = 1, \ldots, t$.
- If $|Y_i| > 1$ then $S := S \cup \{x_i\}$, where x_i is a reference instance selected from the cluster Y_i. It is assumed that the reference instances are selected using some specialized heuristic or metaheuristic algorithm. In Section 5 such a highly effective algorithm is proposed.

The basic idea of the above presented procedure is mapping the data into disjoint subsets, where the number of subsets is determined by the value of the similarity coefficient. In this case, all the required procedure operations include data transformation, calculation of the similarity coefficient values and vectors mapping. Hence, the overall time complexity of the approach is $O(nN) + O(N \log N)$.

Applying the above IRA algorithm can result in substantial reduction of the training set size as compared with the original data set. One of the author's theses is that reducing the training dataset using the IRA approach can still preserve the features of the analyzed data. Intuitively, this can be observed in the case of Example 1.

Example 1. In Fig. 3 the distribution of values of the sepal length and width from the Iris problem from the UCI Machine Learning Repository [7] consisting originally of 150 instances is shown and compared with their distribution obtained after applying Algorithm 8 and reducing the number of instances from 150 to 11.

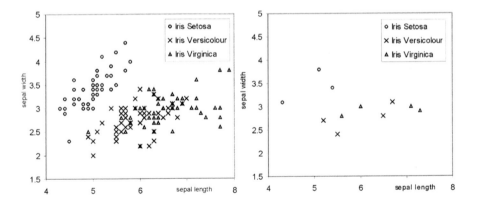

Fig. 3. Initial distribution of values of attributes "sepal length" and "sepal width" from the Iris problem (on the left) and their final distribution after reduction of the number of instances (on the right)

4.4.2   Integrating Data Reduction with Learning Classifiers

It is generally accepted that the improvement of the quality of machine learning tools can be achieved through the integration of the data reduction with the learning process stage [3], [22], [31]. Such integration allows to introduce some adaptation mechanisms into the learning process [31]. Integrated adaptive classifiers should possess two important features:

- Integration, at least partial, of data reduction and learning stages.
- The existence of the positive feedback whereby more effective data reduction leads to a higher learning accuracy, and in return, higher learning accuracy results in even more effective data reduction.

Traditional learning process is known to be a sequential one, in which stages or steps do not overlap. Traditional approach to learning classifiers does not include neither integration nor adaptation procedures. In Fig. 4 the idea of traditional versus integrated and adaptive approaches to constructing machine classifiers is shown.

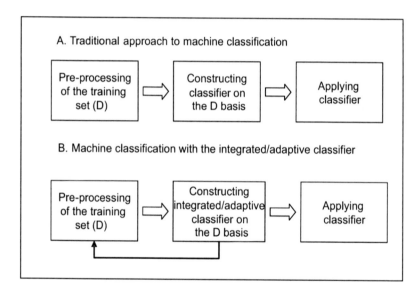

Fig. 4. Traditional versus integrated/adaptive approach to constructing machine classifiers

Within the traditional model of learning (scheme A in Fig. 4), attribute and instance selection processes are not integrated with the classifier learning. Training set thus produced forms the approximation space which is not adaptable. In other words, the approximation space used for the purpose of the classifier construction remains constant. In such case the machine classification problem can be defined as follows: given the approximation space in the form of the training set produced at the pre-processing stage, construct a classifier which performs best from the point of view of the performance criterion used. It should also be noted that the approximation space is a universal tool for describing the concepts of the set of examples U [181].

The situation changes with the introduction of the integrated and adaptive learning (scheme B in Fig. 4). In such case some processes within the pre-processing stage, like instance selection and/or attribute selection can be integrated with the construction of the classifier, which allows for introducing the adaptability of the approximation space. Thus, the machine learning problem can be formulated as follows: construct hypothesis which performs best from the point of view of the performance criterion by finding the representation of the approximation space and, at the same time, deciding on the classifier features.

In [182] the adaptability has been considered with respect to a parameterized approximation space. Assume the goal of learning from examples is to find a hypothesis h that is a good approximation of the target concept and where the learner used to produce h requires setting of some parameters decisive from the point of view of its performance. Let parameters g describe the way the training set should be transformed before training. Thus, it can be said that the goal of learning from examples is to find a hypothesis $h = L(D, g)$ where parameters g affect the learning process and influence the performance measure f. In such case the learning task takes the following form:

$$h = \arg \max_{h \in H, g \in G} f(h = L(D, g)), \qquad (10)$$

where G is the parameter space.

Unfortunately, the integration of the pre-processing and learning stages leads to a considerable extension of the decision space at the classifier construction phase. From the practical point of view, it means that the learning process is realized in hypothesis space H and parameter space G. Moreover, both - attribute selection and instance selection are computationally difficult, as it has been mentioned before, and of course the resulting problem of constructing the integrated and adaptive classifier is also computationally difficult.

The author, following his earlier observation [57] suggests the following integration schemes:

- Integration of the instance selection with the learning process stage - the approach allows to construct a classifier and, at the same time, to modify the approximation space obtained from the training set by changing the way instances are represented or simply by selecting instances (scheme C in Fig. 5). Modified approximation space allows to improve the classifier performance. Additionally, such schema allows other data improvement mechanisms, like attribute selection, at the pre-processing stage (scheme D in Fig. 5).
- Integration of attribute selection with the learning process stage - this allows to construct the classifier and, at same time, to modify the approximation space obtained from the training set by selecting a subset of attributes

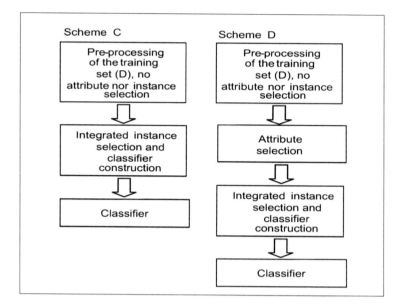

Fig. 5. Machine classification with the integrated instance selection and classifier construction without (Scheme C) and with (Scheme D) attribute selection

(scheme E in Fig. 6). Modified approximation space allows to improve the classifier performance. Additionally, such schema allows other data improvement mechanisms, like instance selection, at the pre-processing stage (scheme F in Fig. 6).

- Integration of both: instance and attribute selection, with the learning process stage - instances and attributes are selected iteratively while constructing the classifier (scheme G in Fig. 7).

Section 6 presents the results of the computation experiment carried-out to validate the above presented integration schemes.

4.4.3 Multi-objective Prototype Selection

Several useful machine learning tools and techniques, as for example neural networks, support vector machines or statistical methods do not provide explanations on how they solve problems. In some application areas like medicine or safety assurance this may cause some doubts or even lower the trust of the users. In such case the users may prefer techniques where the process of knowledge extraction from data is easier to comprehend. An obvious approach would be using the methods leading to the extraction of some logical rules representing the knowledge about the phenomenon at hand. Extracting precise, reliable, useful and easy to comprehend rules from datasets is not a trivial task [75], [187].

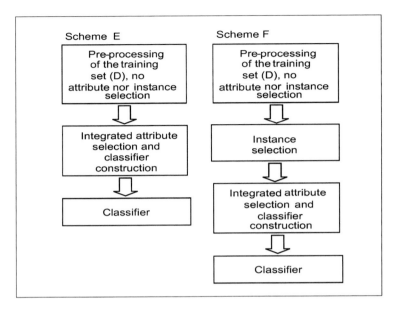

Fig. 6. Machine classification with the integrated attribute selection and classifier construction without (Scheme E) and with (Scheme F) instance selection

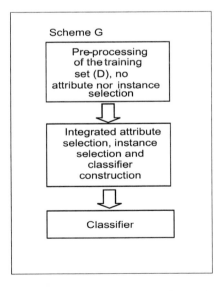

Fig. 7. Machine classification with the integrated attribute selection, instance selection and classifier construction

A well known and popular approach to rules generation is applying decision trees. Unfortunately, in the case of large datasets the resulting decision tree might become very complex, making it difficult to understand and evaluate by a human being. One possible way to overcome the problem is to select a set of prototypes as an input to the decision tree generating algorithm, producing then, so-called, a prototype-based model [75]. It is expected that the prototype selection may bring about several benefits including, beyond increased quality of generalization, decreased requirements for storage and computational resources - which have been pointed out in the previous subsections, easier to comprehend set of rules and increased simplicity of the extracted knowledge.

Selecting prototypes through data reduction can be seen as a multiple-objective problem. The resulting set should be evaluated not only in terms of generalization (classification) quality of the prototype model, but also in terms of the resulting number of rules, their complexity, data compression level, computational time required etc.

One way to obtain a solution to the multi-objective optimization problem is using a weighted-sum objective function. Such an approach has been proposed in [33], [135]. For example, in [33] the evolutionary stratified instance selection algorithm with a weighted-sum objective function was proposed. The proposed evolutionary algorithm aimed at maximizing the classification accuracy associated with the reduced dataset and, at the same time, minimizing the number of instances within the reduced dataset. In this case the weights value in the fitness function was set to 0.5. In [135] the genetic algorithm was proposed to obtain a solution to the multi-objective optimization problem in which classification accuracy and compression rate calculated with respect to both dimensions i.e. the attribute and instance space were maximized.

In [33] it was observed that different datasets represent different classification problems with different degrees of difficulties. Moreover, the authors [33] conclude that, from the practical point of view, without using domain knowledge, it is difficult to determine the appropriate weight values in the weighted-sum approach. It means that the classifier performance might be sensitive to weight values.

The multi-objective data reduction problem is also seen as a multi-objective optimization problem which solution is a non-dominated (or Pareto-optimal) set of reference vector sets.

In general, the multiple-objective optimization problem can be formulated as follows [105]:

$$max\{z_1, \ldots, z_J\} = max\{f_1(s), \ldots, f_J(s)\} \tag{11}$$

or

$$min\{z_1, \ldots, z_J\} = min\{f_1(s), \ldots, f_J(s)\} \tag{12}$$

where $s \in S$ and solution $s = [s_1, \ldots, s_l]$ is a vector of decision variables, S is the set of feasible solutions and z is a vector of objective functions $z_{j:j=1,\ldots,J}$. When the decision variables are discrete the multiple-objective optimization problem becomes the multiple-objective combinational optimization problem.

The image of a solution s in the objective space is a point $z^* = [z_1^*, \ldots, z_J^*]$, where $z_j^* = f(s_j)$, where $j = 1, \ldots, J$.

Point z dominates z', if, for maximization case, $z_j \geq z_j'$ (for each j) and $z_j > z_j'$ for at least one j, and vice versa for minimization problem.

A solution $s \in S$ is Pareto-optimal, if there is no $s' \in S$ that dominates s. A point being an image of a Pareto-optimal solution is called non-dominated. The set of all Pareto-optimal solutions is called the Pareto-optimal set. The image of the Pareto-optimal set in objective space is called the non-dominated set.

Further details in respect to the multiple-objective optimization can be found, for example, in [105].

Multiple-objective approach to prototype selection in the form of the intelligent multi-objective evolutionary algorithm IMOEA was proposed by [46]. IMOEA has been implemented to obtain solutions maximizing the classification accuracy and minimizing number instances and attributes used as prototypes.

Following the idea of [56] the author proposes to construct the set of non-dominated solutions - in this case the set of the selected reference vectors maximizing classification accuracy and data compression level, at the same time minimizing the number of rules and the length of rules obtained from the decision tree induced from the reduced dataset. Section 5.5 provides details on the algorithm generating a non-dominated (or Pareto-optimal) set of reference vector sets.

5 Population-Based Multi-agent Approach to Data Reduction and Distributed Learning

5.1 Introductory Remarks

Techniques used to solve difficult combinatorial optimization problems have evolved from constructive algorithms to local search techniques, and finally to population-based algorithms. Population-based methods have become very popular. They provide good solutions since any constructive method can be used to generate the initial population, and any local search technique can be used to improve each solution in the population. Moreover, population-based methods have the additional advantage of being able to combine good solutions in order to get possibly better ones. The basic idea behind this way of finding solutions is that good ones often share parts with optimal ones

Population based methods are optimization techniques inspired by the natural evolution processes. They handle a population of individuals that evolves with the help of information exchange procedures. However, each individual may also evolve independently and during the process periods of cooperation alternate with periods of self-adaptation. Among the best-known population-based methods are evolutionary algorithms.

Since the publication of Goldberg seminal work [85] different classes of evolutionary algorithms have been developed including genetic algorithms, genetic programming, evolution strategies, differential evolution, cultural evolution, co-evolution and population learning algorithms. Subsequent studies of the social behavior of organisms have resulted in the development of swarm intelligence systems including ant colony optimization and particle swarm optimization [71], [117], [156].

In the recent years technological advances have enabled the development of various parallel and distributed versions of the population based methods. At the same time, as a result of convergence of many technologies within computer science such as object-oriented programming, distributed computing and artificial life, the agent technology has emerged [8]. An agent is understood here as any piece of software that is designed to use intelligence to automatically carry-out an assigned task, mainly retrieving and delivering information.

Tweedale and co-authors [205] outline an abridged history of agents as a guide for the reader to understand the trends and directions of future agent design. This description includes how agent technologies have developed using increasingly sophisticated techniques. It also indicates the transition of formal programming languages into object-oriented programming and how this transition facilitated a corresponding shift from scripted agents (bots) to agent-oriented designs, which is best exemplified by multi-agent systems (MAS). A MAS tries to solve complex problems with entities called agents, using their collaborative and autonomous properties.

During the last few years a number of significant advances have been made in both the design and implementation of autonomous agents. A number of agent-based approaches have been proposed for solving different types of optimization problems [8], [146], [157]. Paradigms of the population-based methods and multiple agent systems have been, during the mid nineties, integrated within the concept of the asynchronous team of agents (A-Team), originally introduced by Talukdar [194]. Some recent developments in the field of implementation and application of the A-Team concept have been reviewed in [111].

Machine learning is concerned with the design and development of algorithms that allow computers to evolve solutions to a wide range of problems based on empirical data. Since 1976 when Holland proposed Learning Classifier Systems [102] the idea of applying machine learning techniques which combine evolutionary computing, reinforcement learning, supervised learning and heuristics to produce adaptive systems has been gaining a growing interest from the machine intelligence research community.

The section focuses on the application of the A-Team approach to solving the problem of effectively learning classifiers from the reduced and distributed data. Because both tasks, i.e. learning from data, including distributed learning, and data reduction are computationally hard, it is justified to relay on heuristics and approximation algorithms. One possible approach is to take advantage of the robustness and flexibility of the population based methods combined with efficiency of the multi-agent systems integrated within the A-Team concept.

The basic assumption behind the proposed population-based multi-agent approach to learning from data is that the data are reduced through the prototype selection. The approach solves the problem of deriving the classification model by integrating data reduction and learning stages using the advantages of the A-Team capabilities including the inherent adaptation mechanism. The approach is based on designing and running a set of agents which process the local data and communicate results to other agents controlling and managing the learning process.

The section contains a description of the A-Team architecture including its main features, explains the proposed agent-based framework for learning classifiers from the reduced and distributed data, and gives descriptions of the suggested agent-based algorithms for data reduction and for multi-objective prototype selection.

5.2   A-Team Concept and Its Implementation

5.2.1   A-Team Concept

A-Team is a multi agent architecture which has been proposed in several papers of S.N. Talukdar and co-authors [191], [192], [193], [194], [195], [196]. It has been shown that the A-Team framework enables users to easily combine disparate problem solving strategies, each in the form of an agent, and enables these agents to cooperate to evolve diverse and high quality solutions [169]. According to [192] an asynchronous team is a collection of software agents that cooperate to solve a problem by dynamically evolving a population of solutions. As [169] observed, agents cooperate by sharing access to populations of candidate solutions. Each agent works to create, modify or remove solutions from a population. The quality of the solutions gradually evolves over time as improved solutions are added and poor solutions are removed. Cooperation between agents emerges as one agent works on the solutions produced by another. Within an A-Team, agents are autonomous and asynchronous. Each agent encapsulates a particular problem-solving method along with the methods to decide when to work, what to work on and how often to work. The main design issues are the structure of the network and the complement of agents.

A-Team architecture could be classified as a software multi-agent system that is used to create software assistant agents [154]. According to [19] an asynchronous team (A-Team) is a network of agents (workers) and memories (repositories for the results of work). It is possible to design and implement A-Teams which are effective in solving hard computational problems. An overview of some recent successful implementations can be found in [12] and [111].

A formal definition of an A-Team was offered in [194]. An A-Team is a set of autonomous agents and a set of memories, interconnected to form a strongly cyclic network, that is, a network in which every agent is in a closed loop. As a consequence, an A-Team can be visualized as a directed hypergraph called a data flow. Each node represents a complex of overlapping memories and each arc represents an autonomous agent. The results or the trial-solutions accumulate in the memories (just as they do in the blackboards) to form populations (like those in genetic algorithms). These populations are time varying. The ground principle of the asynchronous teams rests on combining algorithms, which alone could be inept for the task, into effective problem-solving organizations [194]. Talukdar [196] proposed the grammar to provide means for constructing all asynchronous teams that might be used in solving a given instance of a family of off-line problems. In other words, the grammar constructively defines the space that must be searched if an asynchronous team that is good at solving the given problem-instance is to be found. The primitives of the grammar are:

- Sharable memories, each dedicated to a member of the family-of-problems, and designed to contain a population of trial-solutions to its problem.
- Operators for modifying trial-solutions.
- Selectors for picking trial-solutions.
- Schedulers for determining when selectors and operators are to work.

It should be also noted that several related agent-based architectures have been proposed in parallel to the emergence of A-Teams. One of them is the blackboard architecture enabling cooperation among agents, called knowledge sources, by sharing access to a common memory and allowing agents to work on different parts of the problem [47]. The key difference is that A-Teams do not have a central scheduler responsible for sequencing agent invocations. The blackboard architecture contains three principal components:

- A central, globally accessible, hierarchically organized database called the blackboard that contains the results of applying problem-solving knowledge.
- A set of knowledge sources representing the available problem solving knowledge.
- A scheduler implementing problem solving strategies through analyzing the state of the solution and the available knowledge.

Another related concepts are architectures of evolutionary (EMAS) and co-evolutionary (CoEMAS) systems. The main idea of evolutionary multi-agent system is the modeling of evolution process in multi-agent system (MAS). In opposition to classical evolutionary algorithms, in EMAS there is no centralized algorithm which manipulates the whole population. All agents are independent and make their own decisions, particularly these concerning reproduction and death. Co-evolutionary multi-agent systems (CoEMAS) allow co-evolution of several, different (usually two) species of agents. One of them represents solutions. The goal of the second is to cooperate (or compete) with the first one in order to enforce the population of solutions and to locate the solution of the problem. The overview of these and other architectures can be found in [111].

5.2.2   A-Team Implementation
Population-based multi-agent algorithms for learning classifiers from the reduced and distributed data discussed in the next part of the subsection has been

implemented using a specialized middleware platform allowing for an easy A-Team implementation. The above middleware platform is called JADE-Based A-Team Environment (JABAT). Its subsequent versions, developed with the participation of the author, were proposed in [11],[13], [60], [112]. The platform offers a generic A-Team architecture allowing users to execute the population learning algorithm with some default or user-defined optimization procedures implemented as agents within an asynchronous team of agents.

In the discussed population-based multi-agent approach multiple agents search for the best solution using local search heuristics and population based methods. The best solution is selected from the population of potential solutions which are kept in the common memory. Specialized agents try to improve solutions from the common memory by changing values of the decision variables. All agents can work asynchronously and in parallel. During their work agents cooperate to construct, find and improve solutions which are read from the shared common memory. Their interactions provide for the required adaptation capabilities and for the evolution of the population of potential solutions.

The main functionality of the agent-based population learning approach includes organizing and conducting the process of searching for the best solution. This process involves a sequence of the following steps:

- Generation of the initial population of solutions to be stored in the common memory.
- Activation of optimizing agents which apply solution improvement algorithms to solutions drawn from the common memory and store them back after the attempted improvement applying some user defined replacement strategy.
- Continuation of the reading-improving-replacing cycle until a stopping criterion is met. Such a criterion can be defined either or both as a predefined number of iterations or a limiting time period during which optimizing agents do not manage to improve the current best solution. After the computation has been stopped the best solution achieved so far is accepted as the final one.

To implement the agent-based population learning algorithm one has to set and define the following:

- Solution representation format
- Initial population of individuals
- Fitness function
- Improvement procedures
- Replacement strategy implemented for managing the population of individuals.

Further details on implementation of A-Teams using JABAT can be found in [11], [12] and [14].

5.3   Agent-Based Framework for Learning Classifiers from the Reduced and Distributed Data

5.3.1   Main Features of the Proposed Approach

One of the author's main hypotheses is that learning classifiers from the reduced and distributed data through constructing and using an A-Team architecture is an effective approach assuring, on average, better performance than the existing methods. The following arguments justify formulating the above hypothesis:

- As it has been already observed in earlier sections, data reduction and learning classifier from distributed data are computationally difficult combinatorial optimization problems. The proposed approach, integrating features such as: heuristics like evolutionary computation [147], local search algorithm [84], population learning algorithm [110], have the ability to solve such combinatorial optimization problem.
- In case of the distributed data, the data reduction is carried-out in parallel at each separated site. The multiple-agent systems and the A-Team concept may be superior to other distributed learning approaches with respect to ability of cooperation, coordination and scalability when multiple agents search, in parallel at the local level, for the best combination of instances.

The proposed approach, denoted as LCDD (Learning Classifiers from Distributed Data), involves two stages (also called levels), both supported by collaboration between agents:

- Local stage, in which the selection of prototypes from the distributed data takes place (A-Teams are used to select prototypes by instance selection and/or removing irrelevant attributes).
- Global stage, consisting of pooling of the selected prototypes and producing the global learning model.

The approach allows also to deal with several data reduction subproblems solved in parallel. At the local level, that is, at the distributed data sources, agent-based population learning data reduction algorithms are executed in parallel.

At the local level the proposed solution provides instance and attribute reduction capabilities integrated with the classifier learning process. It is expected that such an integration guarantees a high probability of getting the best set of prototypes for producing the global learning model at the global level.

An important feature of the LCDD approach is A-Teams ability to select instances and attributes in cooperation between agents thus assuring a homogenous set of prototypes at the global level. In this case, the instance selection is carried-out independently at each site through applying the agent-based population search but the attribute selection is managed and coordinated through the process of interaction and collaboration between agents.

All the required steps of the proposed approach are carried-out by program agents of the four following types:

- Global level manager - agent responsible for managing the process of distributed learning
- Optimizing agent - agent containing an implementation of some improvement algorithm
- Solution manager - agent responsible for managing the population of solutions
- Attribute manager - agent responsible for the attribute selection coordination.

Basic functionality of the proposed architecture integrating agents of the above types is shown on the use case diagram in Fig. 8. Agents roles are described in a detailed manner in the following section.

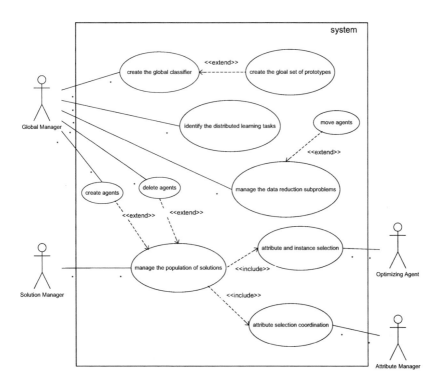

Fig. 8. Use case diagram of the framework for distributed learning

5.3.2 Agents Solving the Distributed Data Reduction Problem

Data reduction is carried-out, in parallel, separately for each distributed data site. Data reduction, carried-out at a site, is an independent process which can be seen as a part of the distributed data learning. Each data reduction subproblem is solved by two main types of agents responsible for instance and/or attribute selection, namely a solution manager and a set of optimizing agents. Each optimizing agent is an implementation of some improvement algorithm, and the problem of data reduction at local sites is solved by an A-Team, that is a team of optimizing agents executing the solution improvement algorithms, supervised by the solution manager.

The solution manager is responsible for organizing the data reduction process at a local site through managing the population of solutions called individuals and updating them when appropriate. During the data reduction process the solution manager continues reading individuals (solutions) from the common memory and storing them back after attempted improvement until a stopping criterion is met. During this process the solution manager keeps sending randomly drawn individuals (solutions) from the common memory to optimizing agents. Each optimizing agent tries to improve the quality of the received solution and afterwards sends back the improved solution to the solution manager, which, in turn, updates common memory, replacing a randomly selected individual with the improved one.

The improvement algorithms for data reduction used by optimizing agents are described in Section 5.4.

5.3.3   Agent Responsible for Coordinating the Attribute Selection

While data reduction is carried-out independently at each site, solutions themselves cannot be seen as independent. The outcomes of the data reduction at local sites influence the overall quality of the distributed learning. Hence, some form of the coordination between solutions at local sites is required. Such coordination is possible by introducing the attribute manager. His role is to coordinate the attribute selection. The attribute manager agent is also responsible for the final integration of attributes selected locally by optimizing agents. The attribute manager actions include receiving candidate attributes from solution mangers, overseeing all data reduction subproblems and deciding on the common set of attributes to be used at both the local and the global levels. The final attribute set is called a winning set of attributes.

The attribute manager performs its tasks in collaboration with solution managers supervising data reduction processes at local sites. Such collaboration involves information exchange and decision making. Each solution manager, after having supervised a prescribed number of iterations within the data reduction process at a local site is obliged to send to the attribute manager a set of the candidate attributes together with the quality measure (fitness) of the respective solution. Such a set contains attributes from the current best local solution. The fitness is calculated as the estimated classification accuracy of the classifier induced from the reduced dataset at the local site. The number of iterations carried-out by a local A-Team is a parameter set by the user. One iteration cycle covers all A-team activities between the two successive replacements of a single solution from the common memory by the improved one received from an optimizing agent.

Having received all candidate attributes from local sites the attribute manager decides on the winning set of attributes. Its decision is based on a predefined strategy selected from the set of possible strategies by the user. Once the winning set of attributes has been chosen the attribute manager passes the outcome of its decision to all solution managers, whose role now is to update the respective individuals by correcting accordingly the structure of attributes in the strings representing solutions in the current population.

The simplest strategy for deciding on the winning set of attributes is to accept all attributes that have been proposed at the local level. In such case the procedure of updating attributes is equivalent to adding to each string representing the best solution at a local site the numbers of attributes that have been selected from the best solutions at other sites. Another strategy for deciding on the winning set of attributes is the attribute voting. In such case the winning set contains attributes that have been proposed by the majority of the local level solutions. Functional interactions between agents used for solving the distributed data reduction problem with the attribute selection coordination are shown in the sequence diagram in Fig. 9.

5.3.4 Agent Responsible for Managing the Process of Distributed Learning

The parallel process of data reduction at sites is managed by the global manager, which is activated as the first one within the learning process. Its role is to manage all stages of the learning process. As the first step the global manager identifies the distributed learning task that is to be coordinated and allocates optimizing agents to the local sites using the available agent migration procedure. Then the global manager initializes parallel execution of all subtasks, that is data reduction processes at local sites. The agent migration procedure has been described in details in [12] and [63].

When all the subtasks have been completed, solutions from the local levels are used to produce the global solution. Producing it requires that the global manager is equipped with skills needed to induce the global classifier. When the prototypes obtained from local sites are homogenous, i.e. when the prototypes are described by the same set of attributes (i.e. $\forall_{i,j:i,j=1,...K} A_i = A_j$), then the local prototypes are integrated and the global manager creates the global classifier (meta-classifier), using some machine learning algorithm. When the local level solutions are represented by heterogeneous set of prototypes then the global classifier can be induced by applying one of the possible meta-classifier strategies described in Section 6.2.

5.3.5 Remark on the Computational Resources Requirements

The proposed approach in terms of computational resources requirements is more effective than transferring all distributed datasets to a central site and than carrying-out data reduction and classifier learning. The effectiveness of the

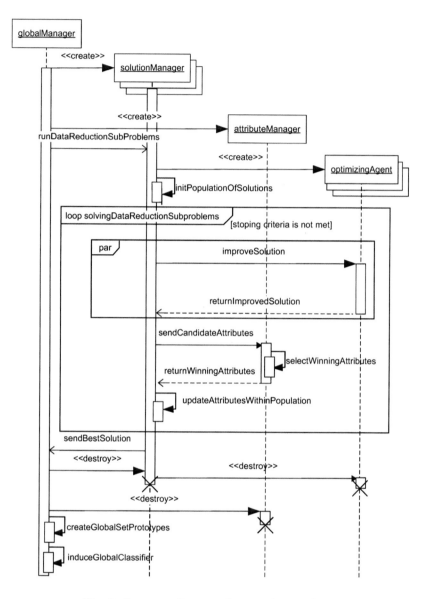

Fig. 9. Sequence diagram of agents interactions

proposed approach, can be contributed to the possibility of replacing a large sample with several smaller ones. Since the complexity of both - data reduction and machine learning predominantly depends on the number of instances and attributes at hand, the total computational resources requirements in case of the proposed approach are smaller than in case of the centralized data, no matter which method is used to induce classifier. Obviously, also the overall communication costs of the proposed approach are lower than in case of the centralized approach where all data are moved into a centralized location.

5.4   Agent-Based Algorithm for Data Reduction

In this subsection the agent-based algorithm for data reduction in both dimensions i.e. the instance and attribute spaces is proposed. The algorithm provides data reduction capabilities integrated with the learning classifier process. The combination can be used as a tool for data reduction in case of both - the distributed and centralized datasets.

The basic assumptions behind the proposed agent-based data reduction approach are following:

- A solution is represented as a string consisting of two parts. The first contains the numbers of instances selected as prototypes and the second - the numbers of attributes chosen to represent the dataset.
- Instances are selected from clusters of instances.
- To induce clusters an arbitrary procedure can be implemented. Nevertheless, further on the procedure proposed as Algorithm 8 is used.
- Prototype instances are selected from clusters through the population-based search carried-out by the optimizing agents.
- Attributes are selected through the population-based search.
- Initially, potential solutions are generated by random selection of a single instance from each cluster and by random selection of the attribute numbers.
- Attributes are later adjusted by the attribute manager with a view to find the best combination and, at the same time, to unify the set of selected attributes at a global level.

A solution representation example is shown below:

Example 2. Solution representation.
A feasible solution s is represented by a string consisting of the numbers of the selected reference instances and the numbers of selected attributes. The first t numbers represent the instance numbers from the reduced data set D, where t is a number of clusters of potential reference instances. The value of t is calculated at the initial phase of the population generation, where, at first, the clusters of instances are identified through applying the clustering procedure. Thus, the first t numbers refer to the respective reference instances from each cluster. In such a representation each cluster is represented by a single instance. The second part of the solution is a string containing the numbers of the selected attributes. It has a length of minimum 1 and maximum n. Assume that the number of instances in the original data set is 15, numbered from 1 to 15, and there are 6 attributes numbered from 1 to 6. Let the considered string representing the solution be: $s = [4, 7, 12, 1, 2, 4, 5, 6]$ with $t = 3$, where t determines the number of clusters in s, thus:

- The first 3 positions indicate the numbers of the reference instances that represent three clusters ($s_1 = 4$ is the number of vector selected to represent the first one, $s_2 = 7$ the second one and $s_3 = 12$ the third one).
- s_i, for $i \in \{4, 5, 6, 7, 8\}$, represents the number of the selected attribute. In the example attributes numbered 1, 2, 4, 5 and 6 were selected.

To solve the data reduction problem, the following four types of optimizing agents carrying-out different improvement procedures have been implemented:

- Local search with the tabu list for instance selection
- Simple local search for instance selection
- Local search with the tabu list for attribute selection
- Simple local search for instance and attribute selection.

The first procedure - local search with tabu list for instance selection, modifies a solution by replacing a randomly selected reference instance with some other randomly chosen reference instance thus far not included within the improved solution. The modification takes place providing the replacement move is not on the tabu list. After the modification, the move is placed on the tabu list and remains there for a given number of iterations. The computational complexity of the above procedure is linear. Hence, time required for computation depends on the size of the tabu list.

The second procedure - simple local search for instance selection, modifies the current solution either by removing the randomly selected reference instance and by adding some other randomly selected reference instance thus far not included within the improved solution. The computational complexity of the local search procedure is $O(1)$. Hence, time required for computation is independent of the data size.

The third procedure - local search with tabu list for attribute selection, modifies a solution by replacing a randomly selected attribute with some other randomly selected attribute thus far not included within the current solution, providing the move is tabu active and not on tabu list. The computational complexity of the search procedure with tabu list for attribute selection is linear. Hence, time required for computation depends only on the size of the tabu list.

The remaining procedure - local search for instance and attribute selection, modifies a solution by replacing a randomly selected instance with some other randomly chosen instance thus far not included within the solution and by adding a new attribute so far not included within the solution or by removing a randomly selected attribute from the solution and where both parts of the solution are modified with identical probability. The computational complexity of the local search procedure is independent of the number of instances and attributes, and is $O(1)$.

The above procedures used by the respective agents are shown as algorithms 9, 10, 11 and 12, respectively.

Algorithm 9. *Local search with tabu list for instance selection*

Input: s - individual representing a solution encoded as the string defined in Section 4.2;
L - list of the problem instance numbers not in s; t - number of clusters in s; $T = \emptyset$ -
tabu list; x - number of iterations a move remains on the tabu list.
Output: *solution* - the improved individual encoded as a string defined in Section 4.2.
1. Set k by drawing it at random from $\{1, 2, .., t\}$.
2. Identify r which is an instance number representing the kth cluster.
3. If $(r \in T)$ then goto 9.
4. Set r' by drawing it at random from L.
5. Replace an instance numbered r by an instance numbered r' within the kth cluster
of s thus producing individual s'.
6. Calculate fitness of s'.
7. If $(s'$ is better then $s)$ then $(s := s'$ AND r replaces r' in L AND r is added to $T)$.
8. Remove from T instances numbers staying there for x iterations.
9. If (!terminating condition) then goto 1.
10. *solution* := s.

Algorithm 10. *Local search for instance selection*

Input: s - individual representing a solution encoded as the string defined in Section 4.2;
L - list of the problem instance numbers not in s; t - number of clusters in s.
Output: *solution* - the improved individual encoded as a string defined in Section 4.2.
1. Set k by drawing it at random from $\{1, 2, .., t\}$.
2. Identify r which is an instance number representing the kth cluster.
3. Set r' by drawing it at random from L.
4. Replace an instance numbered r by an instance numbered r' within the kth cluster
of s thus producing individual s'.
5. Calculate fitness of s'.
6. If $(s'$ is better then $s)$ then $(s := s'$ AND r replaces r' in $L)$.
7. If (!terminating condition) then goto 1.
8. *solution* := s.

Algorithm 11. *Local search with tabu list for attribute selection*

Input: s - individual representing a solution encoded as the string defined in Section 4.2;
M - list of the attribute numbers in s; M' - list of the attribute numbers not in s; $T = \emptyset$
- the tabu list; x - number of iterations a move remains on the tabu list.
Output: *solution* - the improved individual encoded as a string defined in Section 4.2.
1. Set f by drawing it at random from M.
2. If $(f \in T)$ then goto 8.
3. Set f' by drawing it at random from M'.
4. Replace f by f' in s thus producing s'.
5. Calculate fitness of s'.
6. If $(s'$ is better then $s)$ then $(s := s'$ AND update M and M' AND add f to $T)$.
7. Remove from T attribute numbers staying there for x iterations.
8. If (!terminating condition) then goto 1.
9. *solution* := s.

Algorithm 12. *Local search for instance and attribute selection*

Input: s - individual representing a solution encoded as the string defined in Section 4.2;
L - list of the problem instance numbers not in s; M - list of the attribute numbers in s; M' - list of the attribute numbers not in s.
Output: *solution* - the improved individual encoded as a string defined in Section 4.2.
1. Set i:=0.
2. Set h by drawing it at random from $\{0, 1\}$.
3. If $((i \bmod h)$ is not 0) then goto 14.
4. Set d by drawing it at random from $\{0, 1\}$.
5. If $(d$ is not 0) then goto 10.
6. Set f' by drawing it at random from M'.
7. Add f' to s producing s'.
8. Calculate fitness of s'.
9. If $(s'$ is better then s) then $(s := s'$ AND update M and M' AND goto 20).
10. Set f by drawing it at random from M.
11. Remove f from s producing s'.
12. Calculate fitness of s'.
13. If $(s'$ is better then s) then $(s := s'$ AND update M and M' AND goto 20).
14. Set k by drawing it at random from $\{1, 2, .., t\}$.
15. Identify r which is an instance number representing the kth cluster.
16. Set r' by drawing it at random from L.
17. Replace an instance numbered r by an instance numbered r' within the kth cluster of s thus producing individual s'.
18. Calculate fitness of s'.
19. If $(s'$ is better then s) then $(s := s'$ AND r replaces r' in L).
20. If (!terminating condition) then $(i := i + 1$ AND goto 3).
21. *solution* := s.

In each of the above cases the modified solution replaces the current one if it is evaluated as a better one. Evaluation of the solution is carried-out by estimating classification accuracy of the classifier, which is constructed taking into account the instances and the attributes as indicated by the solution. Since the computational complexity of the above search procedures is linear, the computational complexity of the fitness evaluation is not greater than the complexity of the classifier induction,

If, during the search, an agent has successfully improved the received solution then it stops and the improved solution is transmitted to the solution manager. Otherwise, agents stop searching for an improvement after having completed the prescribed number of iterations.

5.5   Agent-Based Multiple-Objective Data Reduction

As it has been already observed the data reduction can be seen as the multi-objective optimization problem which solution is a non-dominated (or Pareto-optimal) set of prototypes. It is proposed to apply the agent-based search for solving the multiple-objective data reduction problem under the assumption that data reduction is carried-out in the instance dimension only.

In this case a feasible solution consists of the list of the selected references instances from the original data set and the values of the cost factors corresponding respectively to the criteria that are used to evaluate reference instances. The solution manager manages the population of solutions, which in the initial phase is generated randomly. It is also assumed that the instances are selected from the initially produced clusters. The initial population is generated with assurance that it consists of solutions with different number of reference instances in each cluster. This makes the approach different from the one proposed in the Subsection 5.4. Moreover, the solution manager, after adding to the population a solution received from the optimizing agent, overwrites and updates the set of potentially Pareto-optimal solutions.

To solve the discussed multiple objective problem two types of agents representing different improvement procedures have been implemented. Both procedures aim at improving current solution through modification and exchange of the reference instances in different clusters. After having received a solution to be improved an optimizing agent generates random vector of weights Λ. It is used to obtain the normalized linear scalarizing function $\phi(z, \Lambda)$, which, in turn, is used to evaluate potential solutions and where weighted linear scalarizing functions are defined as:

$$\phi(z, \Lambda) = \sum_{j=1}^{J} \lambda_j z_j, \tag{13}$$

where $\Lambda = [\lambda_1, \ldots, \lambda_J]$ is a weight vector such that $\lambda_j \geq 0$ and $\sum_{j=1}^{J} \lambda_j = 1$ and where z is a vector of objective functions.

The first optimization agent - random local search with tabu list (in short: RLS), modifies the current solution by removing the randomly selected reference instance from the randomly chosen cluster and replacing it with some other randomly chosen instance thus far not included within the improved solution. The modification takes place providing the replacement move is not on the tabu list. After the modification the move is placed on the tabu list and remains there for a given number of iterations. This number depends on the cluster size and decreases for smaller clusters. The modified solution replaces the current one if it is evaluated as a better one using the current normalized function $\phi(z, \Lambda)$. The computational complexity of the whole procedure is $O(N)$, where N denotes the number of training instances in the corresponding site.

The second optimization agent - incremental/decremental local search (in short: IDLS), modifies the current solution either by removing the randomly selected reference instance from the randomly chosen cluster or by adding some other randomly chosen instance thus far not included within the improved solution. Increasing or decreasing the amount of reference vectors within clusters is a random move executed with equal probabilities. The computational complexity of the incremental/decremental local search procedure is independent of the data size and is $O(1)$.

Pseudo-codes showing both types of the discussed optimization agents are shown as Algorithm 13 and 14.

Algorithm 13. *Random local search*

Input: s - individual representing a solution consists of the list of the selected references instances;
L - list of the problem instance numbers not in s; t - number of clusters in s; $T = \emptyset$ - tabu list; q - number of iterations a move remains on the tabu list.
Output: *solution* - the improved individual.
1. Draw at random the weight vector Λ.
2. Set k by drawing it at random from $\{1, 2, \ldots, t\}$.
3. Identify r which is an instance number representing the kth cluster.
4. If $(r \in T)$ then goto 9.
5. Set r' by drawing it at random from L.
6. Replace the instance numbered r by the instance numbered r' within the kth cluster of s thus producing individual s'.
7. Calculate fitness of s' on $\phi(z, \Lambda)$.
8. If $(s'$ is better on $\phi(z, \Lambda)$ then $s)$ then $(s := s'$ AND r replaces r' in L AND the move is added to $T)$.
9. Remove from T moves staying there for q iterations.
10. If (!terminating condition) then goto 2.
11. *solution* := s.

Algorithm 14. *Incremental/decremental local search*

Input: s - individual representing a solution consists of the list of the selected references instances;
L - list of the problem instance numbers not in s; t - number of clusters in s; $T = \emptyset$ - tabu list; q - number of iterations a move remains on the tabu list.
Output: *solution* - the improved individual.
1. Draw at random a weight vector Λ.
2. Set u, as a parameter determining decremental/incremental phase, by drawing it at random from $\{0, 1, \ldots, q\}$.
3. Set $i := 0$.
4. Set k by drawing it at random from $\{1, 2, \ldots, t\}$.
5. If $((i \bmod u)$ is equal to 0) then goto 12.
6. Set d by drawing it at random from $\{0, 1\}$.
7. If $(d$ is not equal to 0) then goto 10.
8. Set r' by drawing it at random from L.
9. Add r' to s AND update L AND goto 12.
10. Select randomly r which is an instance number representing the kth cluster.
11. Remove r from s AND add r to L.
12. Select randomly r which is an instance number representing the kth cluster.

13. Set r' by drawing it at random from L.

14. Replace an instance numbered r by an instance numbered r' within the kth cluster of s thus producing individual s'.

15. Calculate fitness of s' on $\phi(z, \Lambda)$.

16. If (s' is better on $\phi(z, \Lambda)$ then s) then ($s := s'$ AND r replaces r' in L).

17. Set $i := i + 1$.

18. If (!terminating condition) then goto 4.

19. *solution* $:= s$.

6   Computational Experiments

This section contains the results of several computational experiments carried-out with a view to evaluate the performance of the proposed approach. In particular, the reported experiments aimed at evaluating:

- Quality of classifiers induced from the set of prototypes selected by the proposed algorithms.
- Quality of the global classifiers induced form the set of prototypes selected at each of the autonomous distributed sites.
- Relationship between the clustering procedure used for data reduction and the classifier performance.
- Relationship between the quality of clusters and the classifier performance.
- Relationship between the data integration strategy and the classifier performance.
- Effectiveness of the proposed approach for the multi-objective data reduction.
- Relationship between the strategy of the prototype selection and the classifier performance.

The computational experiments have been conducted to evaluate the proposed approach to the data reduction with respect to the distributed and non-distributed learning classifiers problems.

6.1   Evaluation of the Agent-Based Data Reduction Approach

6.1.1   Selection from Clusters

The approach to data reduction proposed in Section 5 is based on the assumption that instances are selected from clusters by the A-Team executing the population learning algorithm. Clusters are produced at the first stage of data reduction using a dedicated clustering procedure. This part of the chapter aims at investigating experimentally how the choice of the clustering procedure and the quality of the produced clusters influence the classifier performance. Experiments have been carried-out under the assumption that the data reduction covers only the instance selection. In the reported experiment the following approaches to the instance selection from clusters are considered:

- Selection based on the k-means clustering algorithm using Algorithm 6.
- Selection based on the stratification-based instance clustering using Algorithm 7.
- Selection based on the similarity coefficient, where the clusters are produced using Algorithm 8.
- Selection based on the modified stratification-based instance clustering algorithm discussed in Section 4.4.

The experiment involved several benchmark classification problems. Datasets for each problem have been obtained from the UCI Machine Learning Repository [7]. They include: Cleveland heart disease, credit approval, Wisconsin breast cancer, sonar problem, adult and Intelligence Customer [197]. The characteristics of these datasets are shown in Table 1.

Table 1. Instances used in the reported experiment

Size of the dataset	Dataset name	Number of instances	Number of attributes	Number of classes	Reported classification accuracy
small	heart	303	13	2	90.00% [66]
	sonar	208*	60	2	97.1% [66]
medium	credit	690	15	2	86.9% [66]
	cancer	699	9	2	97.5% [6]
large	adult	30162	14	2	84.46% [6]
	customer	24000	36	2	75.53% [179]

* - The data set consists of 104 training and test instances.

Each benchmarking problem has been solved 30 times and the reported values of the quality measure have been averaged over all runs. The quality measure in all cases was the correct classification ratio calculated using the 10-cross-validation approach, where at first the available dataset was randomly partitioned into training and test sets in approximately 9/10 and 1/10 proportions. In the second step each training dataset was reduced using the proposed approaches.

For the algorithm based on the modified stratification and the k-means clustering the reduction was carried-out for several different numbers of clusters. These values influenced the total number of clusters as calculated by the Number of Clusters Calculation (NCC) procedure (see Algorithm 5) and hence also the final number of the selected prototypes. The values of the initial parameter of the NCC procedure and the total numbers of produced clusters with the respective final number of the selected prototypes are shown for each considered dataset in Table 2.

In case of the stratification algorithm, the numbers of the considered strata are shown in Table 3. Recall that, in this algorithm, the number of strata (clusters) also defines the number of prototypes in the final reduced training set.

Table 2. Average number of clusters calculated by the NCC procedure for different values of the input parameter (the respective number of prototypes is shown in brackets)

Dataset	Number of clusters and the respective number of prototypes				
NCC parameter	**10**	**20**	**30**	**40**	**50**
heart	18.4 (18)	36.9 (36)	55.2 (55)	73.6 (73)	92.1 (92)
sonar	19 (19)	38 (38)	57 (57)	76 (76)	95 (95)
NCC parameter	**20**	**40**	**60**	**80**	**100**
credit	36.1 (36)	72.1 (72)	108.2 (108)	144.3 (144)	180.2 (180)
cancer	30.6 (30)	61.1 (61)	91.7 (91)	122.1 (122)	152.8 (152)
NCC parameter	**50**	**100**	**150**	**200**	**250**
customer	94.3 (94)	192.1 (192)	287.6 (283)	382.5 (382)	456.8 (456)
adult	73.3 (73)	134.3 (134)	211.4 (211)	272.1 (272)	351.4 (351)

Table 3. Number of clusters for the stratification algorithm

Dataset	The number of clusters
heart, sonar	20, 40, 60, 80, 100
credit, cancer	35, 65, 95, 135, 165
customer, adult	80, 150, 230, 300, 400

All the above input parameters have been set in the way assuring comparability with respect to the number of the selected prototypes. In case of the clustering algorithm based on the similarity coefficient the resulting numbers of clusters are shown in Table 4.

Table 4. Average number of clusters produced by the algorithm using the similarity coefficient (the average number of the selected prototypes is shown in brackets)

Dataset	heart	sonar	credit	cancer	customer	adult
Average number of clusters	162.5 (162)	94 (94)	184.5 (184)	133.9 (133)	172.3 (172)	431.3 (431)

All optimization agents were running for 100 iterations. The common memory size was set to 100 individuals. The number of iterations and the size of the common memory was set arbitrarily. The process of searching for the best solution stopped earlier than after 100 iterations in case there was no improvement of the best solution during 3 minutes of computation. The values of these parameters have been set out arbitrarily at the fine-tuning phase. The starting points of the k-means procedure have been chosen randomly. The number of iterations in the k-means procedure was set arbitrarily to 100.

In the first part of the reported experiment the prototypes from training sets were selected. Subsequently, the reduced training sets were used to induce classifiers. The following machine learning algorithms for inducing classifiers have been used: C 4.5 classifier with pruned leaves [166], support vector machine (WLSVM) [79] and 1NN, kNN, Bayes Network implemented in the WEKA library [219].

Experiment results in terms of the correct classification ratio for each of the considered case are shown in Tables 5-10 where the following cases are covered:

- Results obtained using full datasets
- SC - results obtained using the reduced training sets produced through selection based on the similarity coefficient
- SS - results obtained using sets of prototypes produced through selection based on the stratification strategy (these results are shown for several variants of the number of strata)
- MSS - results obtained using the set of prototypes produced through selection based on the modified stratification-based instance clustering strategy (these results are shown for several variants of the number of strata)
- kCA - results obtained using the set of prototypes produced through selection based on the k-means clustering (these results are shown for several variants of the number of clusters).

Additionally, Tables 5-10 show the average percentage of the retained instances in the training sets as well as the correct classification ratio averaged over all classifiers used in each case.

From Tables 5-10 it is clear that, for the considered datasets, the agent-based prototype selection assures better classification accuracy as compared with the case when a classifier is induced using an original, non-reduced dataset. It is also evident that the choice of the instance reduction algorithm, and specifically the underlying clustering algorithm, has an impact on the classification accuracy. The above conclusion holds true for all the considered datasets apart from the WLSVM classifier. In case of WLSVM, the data reduction results in the deterioration of the classification accuracy. This can be observed in case of the two considered classification problems. However, when the results for the considered classifiers are compared, it can be observed that the data reduction increases quality of their performance. When the parameters are carefully selected, the WLSVM is outperformed by all remaining classifiers. The experiment results indicate also that there is no single winning classifier although the C 4.5 has been significantly better than others especially when the dataset is huge.

To confirm the above the two-way analysis of variance (ANOVA) with the following null hypotheses has been carried-out:

I: The choice of the prototype selection procedure does not influence the classifier performance.
II: The choice of the classifier does not influence the classification accuracy.
III: There are no interactions between both factors (i.e. the choice of the prototype selection procedure and the choice of the classifier type).

Table 5. Experiment results for the heart dataset (in %)

Reduction method	label	1NN	10NN	Bayes Network	WLSVM	C 4.5	$|S|/|D|$	Average
Full dataset	(a)	77.23	80.86	83.50	80.53	77.89	100%	80.00
SC	(b)	84.00	**85.67**	87.33	87.00	**91.21**	53%	**87.04**
SS, t=20	(c)	75.32	82.10	81.43	84.21	80.66	7%	80.74
SS, t=40	(d)	79.66	78.43	83.50	80.30	82.66	13%	80.91
SS, t=60	(e)	82.54	77.32	81.46	80.14	84.10	20%	81.11
SS, t=80	(f)	80.18	81.02	82.54	82.66	88.00	26%	82.88
SS, t=100	(g)	82.43	80.40	84.21	82.86	85.33	33%	83.05
MSS, t=10	(h)	**91.00**	83.32	**90.67**	83.33	80.91	6%	85.85
MSS, t=20	(i)	90.00	81.33	88.67	80.30	85.33	12%	85.13
MSS, t=30	(j)	89.67	82.00	89.67	86.00	87.67	18%	87.00
MSS, t=40	(k)	87.33	83.32	88.00	84.67	88.00	24%	86.26
MSS, t=50	(l)	84.67	**85.67**	86.00	82.33	91.11	30%	85.96
kCA, t=10	(m)	87.67	82.52	88.00	84.67	82.00	6%	84.97
kCA, t=20	(n)	88.33	82.67	88.00	**88.33**	85.67	12%	86.60
kCA, t=30	(o)	90.00	84.43	87.33	81.67	87.67	18%	86.22
kCA, t=40	(p)	88.33	85.00	88.33	85.00	88.00	24%	86.93
kCA, t=50	(r)	87.33	82.33	87.00	87.33	90.00	30%	86.80

Source: own computations.

Table 6. Experiment results for the sonar dataset (in %)

Reduction method	label	1NN	10NN	Bayes Network	WLSVM	C 4.5	$|S|/|D|$	Average
Full dataset	(a)	94.23	75.00	73.08	**72.12**	74.04	100%	77.69
SC	(b)	94.23	75.00	75.00	40.38	**83.65**	90%	73.65
SS, t=20	(c)	90.32	72.43	70.54	49.32	80.43	19%	72.61
SS, t=40	(d)	87.64	74.67	72.23	50.46	77.43	38%	72.49
SS, t=60	(e)	89.65	72.32	73.08	52.34	76.32	58%	72.74
SS, t=80	(f)	89.06	74.08	72.41	40.15	79.04	77%	70.95
SS, t=100	(g)	91.20	71.07	72.48	40.15	80.30	96%	71.04
MSS, t=10	(h)	89.42	71.85	80.62	54.65	78.02	18%	74.91
MSS, t=20	(i)	92.15	73.88	79.73	58.45	77.20	37%	76.28
MSS, t=30	(j)	91.08	73.04	76.92	58.45	73.49	55%	74.60
MSS, t=40	(k)	93.12	74.88	71.15	60.06	76.37	73%	75.12
MSS, t=50	(l)	91.15	75.96	75.96	62.54	68.91	91%	74.91
kCA, t=10	(m)	80.77	70.19	80.77	58.43	79.17	18%	73.87
kCA, t=20	(n)	86.06	77.64	79.81	60.67	77.24	37%	76.28
kCA, t=30	(o)	91.35	**79.09**	80.69	59.40	75.96	55%	77.30
kCA, t=40	(p)	**95.67**	73.04	**80.77**	65.90	82.69	73%	**79.61**
kCA, t=50	(r)	94.32	72.53	77.09	61.34	83.54	91%	77.76

Source: own computations.

Table 7. Experiment results for the credit dataset (in %)

Reduction method	label	1NN	10NN	Bayes Network	WLSVM	C 4.5	$|S|/|D|$	Average
Full dataset	(a)	82.46	86.38	75.36	85.22	84.93	100%	82.87
SC	(b)	83.33	88.70	75.22	85.94	**90.72**	27%	84.78
SS, $t=35$	(c)	80.89	83.21	79.45	78.89	80.12	5%	80.51
SS, $t=65$	(d)	83.45	84.32	77.49	77.43	80.45	9%	80.63
SS, $t=95$	(e)	83.09	83.98	76.60	80.43	82.60	14%	81.34
SS, $t=135$	(f)	84.15	84.56	72.34	81.43	82.31	20%	80.96
SS, $t=165$	(g)	83.87	86.07	77.56	80.77	81.68	24%	81.99
MSS, $t=20$	(h)	83.55	88.99	79.71	82.26	84.67	5%	83.83
MSS, $t=40$	(i)	82.57	88.84	75.94	84.23	88.47	10%	84.01
MSS, $t=60$	(j)	82.16	89.42	76.62	83.80	89.46	16%	84.29
MSS, $t=80$	(k)	84.72	**90.72**	77.39	82.51	88.89	21%	84.85
MSS, $t=100$	(l)	85.84	89.71	76.88	85.51	90.12	26%	85.61
kCA, $t=20$	(m)	86.99	87.83	84.64	**89.71**	87.12	5%	87.26
kCA, $t=40$	(n)	88.26	88.70	78.39	87.25	88.99	10%	86.32
kCA, $t=60$	(o)	86.52	88.41	**86.38**	85.65	90.14	16%	**87.42**
kCA, $t=80$	(p)	**90.72**	88.41	75.94	83.51	90.29	21%	85.77
kCA, $t=100$	(r)	87.55	88.26	85.36	82.93	89.57	26%	86.73

Source: own computations.

Table 8. Experiment results for the cancer dataset (in %)

Reduction method	label	1NN	10NN	Bayes Network	WLSVM	C 4.5	$|S|/|D|$	Average
Full dataset	(a)	95.71	96.71	96.00	**95.57**	94.57	100%	95.71
SC	(b)	96.86	**97.43**	**96.87**	90.59	**97.44**	19%	**95.84**
SS, $t=35$	(c)	96.32	92.43	88.32	86.76	94.54	5%	91.67
SS, $t=65$	(d)	95.21	93.21	90.15	85.65	94.32	9%	91.71
SS, $t=95$	(e)	96.54	94.60	92.43	89.88	96.21	14%	93.93
SS, $t=135$	(f)	95.32	93.53	94.20	87.57	93.80	19%	92.88
SS, $t=165$	(g)	95.87	95.93	92.62	87.65	96.03	24%	93.62
MSS, $t=20$	(h)	98.01	95.09	93.44	90.01	94.95	4%	94.30
MSS, $t=40$	(i)	97.86	95.72	92.15	87.29	95.72	9%	93.75
MSS, $t=60$	(j)	**98.43**	96.29	91.01	87.01	96.44	13%	93.84
MSS, $t=80$	(k)	**98.43**	96.01	94.15	87.15	95.44	17%	94.24
MSS, $t=100$	(l)	98.29	96.58	93.01	87.44	96.61	22%	94.39
kCA, $t=20$	(m)	97.32	94.83	94.54	88.30	95.71	4%	94.14
kCA, $t=40$	(n)	97.33	95.02	95.04	89.20	94.43	9%	94.20
kCA, $t=60$	(o)	97.77	96.97	92.15	87.54	95.09	13%	93.90
kCA, $t=80$	(p)	97.68	97.10	93.30	90.23	96.14	17%	94.89
kCA, $t=100$	(r)	98.33	96.51	94.54	89.65	95.57	22%	94.92

Source: own computations.

Table 9. Experiment results for the customer dataset (in %)

Reduction method	label	1NN	10NN	Bayes Network	WLSVM	C 4.5	$|S|/|D|$	Average
Full dataset	(a)	62.92	64.30	50.96	59.83	73.32	100%	61.76
SC	(b)	67.32	70.78	58.25	**64.21**	72.43	0.72%	66.60
SS, $t=80$	(c)	58.29	59.21	58.42	50.19	57.32	0.33%	56.69
SS, $t=150$	(d)	58.00	59.46	57.63	52.34	60.32	0.63%	57.55
SS, $t=230$	(e)	58.38	60.79	59.71	52.78	57.43	0.96%	57.82
SS, $t=300$	(f)	60.08	62.17	58.92	52.50	61.54	1.25%	59.04
SS, $t=400$	(g)	60.83	63.08	61.13	54.05	63.54	1.67%	60.53
MSS, $t=50$	(h)	61.29	69.21	58.42	50.19	66.29	0.39%	61.08
MSS, $t=100$	(i)	68.00	69.46	57.63	52.34	69.25	0.80%	63.33
MSS, $t=150$	(j)	68.38	68.79	59.71	52.78	70.29	1.20%	63.99
MSS, $t=200$	(k)	70.08	70.17	58.92	52.50	69.46	1.59%	64.23
MSS, $t=250$	(l)	71.83	70.08	61.13	54.05	71.52	1.90%	65.72
kCA, $t=50$	(m)	62.45	68.32	67.54	61.40	74.29	0.39%	66.80
kCA, $t=100$	(n)	68.32	70.43	68.32	60.43	**77.25**	0.80%	68.95
kCA, $t=150$	(o)	71.34	72.63	68.65	62.40	74.29	1.20%	69.86
kCA, $t=200$	(p)	70.94	71.54	**69.43**	**64.21**	73.58	1.59%	69.94
kCA, $t=250$	(r)	**72.50**	**73.05**	68.05	64.06	75.17	1.90%	**70.57**

Source: own computations.

Table 10. Experiment results for the adult dataset (in %)

Reduction method	label	1NN	10NN	Bayes Network	WLSVM	C 4.5	$|S|/|D|$	Average
Full dataset	(a)	79.58	80.20	73.80	62.00	82.43	100%	75.60
SC	(b)	82.43	85.00	**76.67**	69.43	85.21	1.43%	79.75
SS, $t=80$	(c)	76.35	75.85	70.53	65.06	77.61	0.27%	73.08
SS, $t=150$	(d)	77.65	75.79	71.15	65.44	77.40	0.50%	73.49
SS, $t=230$	(e)	76.76	75.77	72.43	67.47	79.37	0.76%	74.36
SS, $t=300$	(f)	77.42	75.42	70.43	65.21	80.36	0.99%	73.77
SS, $t=400$	(g)	75.75	75.11	72.83	67.79	81.16	1.33%	74.53
MSS, $t=50$	(h)	78.92	78.95	74.73	67.04	82.17	0.24%	76.36
MSS, $t=100$	(i)	80.17	80.50	75.36	68.14	82.58	0.44%	77.35
MSS, $t=150$	(j)	79.07	81.02	73.88	67.07	84.33	0.70%	77.07
MSS, $t=200$	(k)	77.80	82.15	76.53	68.95	85.12	0.90%	78.11
MSS, $t=250$	(l)	79.89	73.95	74.50	68.39	85.92	1.16%	76.53
kCA, $t=50$	(m)	80.06	80.64	73.25	71.74	84.53	0.24%	78.04
kCA, $t=100$	(n)	79.43	81.96	75.81	70.50	85.32	0.44%	78.60
kCA, $t=150$	(o)	82.64	83.33	74.71	**72.42**	86.40	0.70%	79.90
kCA, $t=200$	(p)	83.15	84.05	75.74	71.87	**87.43**	0.90%	80.45
kCA, $t=250$	(r)	**85.29**	**85.29**	75.36	71.25	87.09	1.16%	**80.86**

Source: own computations.

The analysis has been carried-out at the significance level of 0.05. In Table 11 the ANOVA analysis results are shown. The summary results presented in Table 11 confirm that the choice of the classifier has an influence on the classification accuracy. On the other hand the reduction of the training set through retaining prototype instances only increases the classifier performance in a statistically significant manner. An interaction effect between both considered factors can not be excluded.

Table 11. The ANOVA analysis results

Problem	Main effect A/ H_0 Accepted	Main effect B/ H_0 Accepted	Interaction effect/ H_0 Accepted
heart	-	-	-
sonar	Yes	-	Yes
credit	-	-	-
cancer	Yes	-	Yes
customer	-	-	-
adult	-	-	-

Taking into account the fact that the quality of the prototype selection can depend on the choice of the cluster producing procedure it has been decided to use the non-parametric Friedman test [81] to check whether particular prototype selection procedures are equally effective independently of the kind of the problem being solved.

The above test is based on weights (points) assigned to prototype selection algorithms used in the experiment. To assign weights, the 17 point scale has been used with 17 points for the best and 1 point for the worst algorithm. The test aimed at deciding among the following hypotheses:

- H_0 - zero hypothesis: prototype selection algorithms are statistically equally effective regardless of the kind of the problem being solved.
- H_1 - alternative hypothesis: not all working strategies are equally effective.

The analysis has been carried-out at the significance level of 0.5. The respective value χ^2 statistics with 17 algorithms and 6 considered problems is 72.8 and the value of χ^2 distribution is equal to 26.3 for 16 degrees of freedom. Thus, it can be observed that not all algorithms are equally effective regardless of the kind of the problems being solved. In Fig. 10-12 average weights for each prototype selection algorithm, are shown.

From Fig. 10-12, one can observe that the best results have been obtained by prototype selection algorithm based on the k-means clustering (see cases labeled as: 'm', 'n', 'o', 'p', 'r'), especially in case of larger datasets and high-dimensional datasets like the 'sonar' one. The comparable results have been obtained by prototype selection algorithm based on the similarity coefficient (see case labeled as 'b'). This algorithm is also very effective independently of the data size and dimensionality of the dataset. Both algorithms outperform other approaches and this observation also holds true for the case of classifiers induced from the full datasets. The worst results have been produced by the prototype selection algorithm based on the stratification strategy. However, the modified stratification strategy definitely improves the results.

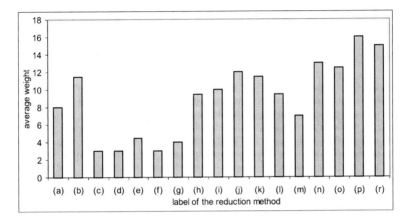

Fig. 10. The average Friedman test weights for small-size datasets

The proposed algorithms are also competitive in comparison to other approaches to instance selection which can be concluded from the data shown in Table 12.

The experiment results allow to observe that the number of produced clusters also influences the classifier performance. Hence, it is reasonable to assume that the number of prototypes selected in the process of data reduction can influence the classifier performance. This means that the choice of the input parameter t value is an important decision. This observation holds true for selection based on the stratification strategy - SS, selection based on the modified stratification-based instance clustering strategy - MSS, and selection based on the k-means clustering - kCA.

The above observations lead to the following two questions:

- How does the number of clusters influence the classification accuracy?
- How does the quality of the clusters influence the quality of the selected prototypes and, in consequence, the classifier performance?

From the computational experiment results it can be observed that there is an interdependence between the number of selected prototypes and the classification accuracy. Its nature seems to vary depending on the dataset size. For instance, for a small and middle size datasets, when the number of the selected prototypes

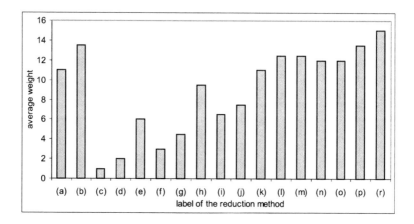

Fig. 11. The average Friedman test weights for medium-size datasets

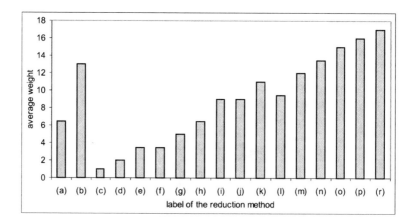

Fig. 12. The average Friedman test weights for large-size datasets

Table 12. Comparison of different data reduction approaches (I - instance selection only; N - no data reduction applied)

Reduction method	type	Accuracy of classification in %					
		heart	sonar	credit	cancer	customer	adult
SC	I	**91.25**	94.23	**90.72**	97.44	72.43	85.21
kCA	I	90.00	**95.67**	**90.72**	98.33	**77.25**	**87.43**
MSS	I	91.11	93.12	**90.72**	**98.43**	71.83	85.92
SS	I	85.33	91.20	86.07	96.54	63.54	81.16
CNN [216]	I	73.95	74.12	77.68	95.71	60.43*	71.72*
SNN [216]	I	76.25	79.81	81.31	93.85	-	-
ENN [216]	I	81.11	81.79	84.49	97.00	70.65*	82.09*
3STAR [236]	I	-	73.84	86.32	-	-	-
DROP 5 [216]	I	79.84	79.88	83.91	95.71	-	-
PSO [155]	I	-	-	-	96.6	-	-
GA [155]	I	-	-	-	95.4	-	-
C 4.5 [104]	N	77.8	76.9	85.5	94.7	-	-
k-NN [216]	N	81.19	58.8	84.78	96.28	-	-
BayesNet [74]	N	83.6	90.4	82.9	96.7	-	-
SVM [74]	N	81.5	76.9	-	96.9	-	-
MLP+BP [74]	N	81.3	90.4	84.6	96.7	-	-

* - Source: own computation.

increases, the accuracy remains at a certain level or can even decrease. In case of large-size datasets, the accuracy increases together with the increasing number of the selected prototypes. On the other hand, this may suggest that the relationship between the accuracy and the number of prototypes selected by a data reduction algorithm depends on the problem domain. Such conclusion was also formulated in the study dedicated to other prototype selection methods [118].

To identify the influence of the quality of clusters on the classifier performance the silhouette technique has been used. The silhouette validation technique [189] calculates the silhouette width for each instance, average silhouette width for each cluster and overall average silhouette width for the total dataset. In details, the silhouette width $s(x_i)$ of the instance x_i is defined as:

$$s(x_i) = \frac{b(x_i) - a(x_i)}{\max\{a(x_i), b(x_i)\}}, \tag{14}$$

where $a(x_i)$ is the average distance of x_i to all other instances of the cluster A to which it belongs and where $a(x_i)$ is computed as:

$$a(x_i) = \frac{1}{|A| - 1} \sum_{j \in A, j \neq i} d(x_i, x_j). \tag{15}$$

$b(x_i)$ denotes the lowest average distance of x_i with the data of another single cluster, that is expressed as:

$$b(x_i) = \min_{C \neq A} d(x_i, C), \tag{16}$$

where C is any cluster different from A and $d(x_i, C)$ is the average distance of x_i to all instances of C, that is calculated as:

$$d(x_i, C) = \frac{1}{|C|} \sum_{j \in C} d(x_i, x_j). \tag{17}$$

Using the silhouette-based approach each cluster can be represented by the silhouette width, which is based on the comparison of its tightness and separation. The average silhouette width, also called the silhouette coefficient, could be used for evaluation of the clustering quality. The silhouette value lies between -1 and 1. The higher the coefficient value the better quality of the cluster has been obtained.

To analyze the relationships between the number of clusters, the quality of clustering and the classifier performance, the values of the silhouette coefficient versus the values of the input parameter t have been recorded. Based on the above observations, it can be concluded that the clusters produced by applying selection method using the k-means algorithm have the highest value of the silhouette coefficient. This coincides with the fact that classifiers induced from prototypes obtained by applying selection method based on the k-means clustering (kCA) are the best performers among SS, MSS and kCA approaches.

It can be also observed that the reduction technique based on the similarity coefficient (SC) produces very good results independently of the dataset. For the comparable instance reduction rate, SC seems better in terms of the classification accuracy than other approaches. This again coincides with a high value of the silhouette coefficient characterizing clusters produced within the SC approach as shown in Table 13. The above observation supports the claim that the value of the similarity coefficient can be used as an important indicator in search for a partition of instances into clusters from which the prototypes are to be selected.

The reported computational experiment shows that the proposed agent-based population algorithm combined with clustering procedures is an effective instance reduction tool contributing to achieving higher quality of machine classification. The approach has been validated experimentally. The validating experiment results allow to draw the following conclusions:

- Learning from prototypes obtained within the data reduction process can produce better results than learning from a full dataset.
- Agent-based approach to prototype selection extends the family of data reduction techniques adding an effective and useful alternative.

- In the data reduction based on clustering, the choice of clustering procedure is a critical factor from the point of view of the classification accuracy.
- In the data reduction based on clustering using stratification and k-means approaches, selection of the number of clusters has an influence on classification accuracy and data reduction rate. In case of the small and middle size datasets it was observed that when the number of clusters increases the accuracy remains at a certain level or can even decrease. In case of the large datasets it was observed that the accuracy increases together with the increasing number of the selected prototypes.
- Instance selection based on the clustering method using the similarity coefficient approach assures better quality of learning in comparison to cases where instances are selected based on clustering using stratification or k-means approaches. It is also competitive in comparison to other data reduction approaches so far proposed in the literature, with respect to the benchmark classification datasets.
- Clustering quality measured by the silhouette coefficient is positively correlated with the quality of classifier learning from the reduced dataset produced through data selection from clusters.

Table 13. Silhouette width and average accuracy of classification (in %) shown with respect to comparable number of clusters)

Algorithm		heart	sonar	credit	cancer	customer	adult
SC	silhouette width	-0.19	-0.11	-0.07	0.11	-0.13	-0.08
	average accuracy	87.04	73.65	84.78	95.84	66.60	79.75
SS	silhouette width	-0.42	-0.31	-0.43	-0.34	-0.28	-0.52
	average accuracy	83.04	71.04	81.99	92.88	57.55	74.53
MSS	silhouette width	-0.34	-0.25	-0.18	-0.32	-0.27	-0.47
	average accuracy	85.96	74.91	85.61	94.24	63.33	76.53
kCA	silhouette width	-0.11	-0.24	-0.08	-0.16	-0.12	-0.27
	average accuracy	86.80	77.76	86.73	94.89	68.95	80.86

Source: own computations.

6.1.2 Integration Schemes

Another hypothesis formulated in Section 4 was that integration of the data reduction with the classifier learning process can improve the classifier performance. The computation experiment, discussed in this part of the chapter, aimed at evaluating the influence of the choice of the integration schema on the classifier performance. The aim of the computation experiment was also to compare the performance of different integration schemas and to evaluate to what extent the proposed approach could contribute towards increasing the classification accuracy of the classifier induced from the set of prototypes selected by applying an agent-based population learning algorithm.

The experiment results discussed in the previous subsection show that the instance selection based on the clustering method using the similarity coefficient approach assures a very good quality of learning. Consequently, the present experiment has been carried-out using the agent-based algorithm with the implementation of the similarity coefficient clustering procedure. The considered algorithm has been named IDR (*Integrated Data Reduction*).

Classification accuracy of the classifier obtained using the agent-based approach for data reduction (i.e. using the set of prototypes, found by simultaneously selecting reference instances and removing irrelevant attributes, and by the integration of data reduction with the learning model) has been compared with:

- Results obtained by machine classification without the integrated data reduction, that is using a full dataset.
- Results obtained by machine classification with different integration and reduction schemes.

To validate the proposed approach several benchmark classification problems have been considered. They include: heart, credit, cancer and sonar problem. The characteristics of these datasets are shown in Table 1.

Each benchmarking problem has been solved 30 times and the reported values of the quality measures have been averaged over all runs. The quality measure in all cases was the correct classification ratio calculated using the 10-cross-validation approach. All optimization agents have been allowed to continue iterating until 100 iterations have been performed. The common memory size was set to 100 individuals. The number of iterations and the size of the common memory have been set out arbitrarily at the fine-tuning phase. The whole process of searching for the best solution stops when there are no improvements of the best solution during the last 3 minutes of computation.

The experiment results are shown in Table 14. These results have been obtained by using the: C 4.5 classifier without pruned leaves and with pruned leaves [166], support vector machine (WLSVM) [79] and 1NN, kNN, Bayes Network implemented in WEKA library [219]. Further, the results in Table 14 are presented for the following cases:

- Case A: results obtained by machine classification using the full dataset.
- Case B: results obtained by machine classification with attribute selection at the pre-processing stage.
- Case C: results obtained by machine classification with the integrated instance selection and without attribute selection at the pre-processing stage.
- Case D: results obtained by machine classification with the integrated instance selection and with attribute selection carried-out at the pre-processing stage.
- Case E: results obtained by machine classification with the integrated attribute selection and with instance selection carried-out at the pre-processing stage.
- Case F: results obtained by machine classification with the integrated instance and attribute selection.

Table 14. Accuracy (%) of classification results obtained for different learning schemes

Classifier Problem	1NN	10NN	Bayes Network	WLSVM	C 4.5 (pruned)	C 4.5 (unpruned)
Case A: no data reduction applied						
cancer	95.71	96.71	96.00	**95.57**	94.57	95.00
credit	82.46	86.38	75.36	85.22	84.93	83.19
heart	77.23	80.86	83.50	80.53	77.89	76.90
sonar	94.23	75.00	73.08	**72.12**	74.04	74.04
average	87.41	84.74	81.98	83.36	82.86	82.28
Case B: attribute selection at the pre-processing stage						
cancer	94.57	95.00	96.00	95.14	94.43	94.43
credit	79.57	84.64	84.93	85.51	77.25	74.78
heart	71.95	80.53	80.53	80.86	79.87	79.54
sonar	79.33	81.25	61.54	73.08	72.10	71.23
average	81.35	85.35	80.75	83.65	80.91	79.99
Case C: integrated instance selection, no attribute selection						
cancer	96.86	97.43	96.87	90.59	97.44	**98.43**
credit	83.33	88.70	75.22	**85.94**	90.72	90.43
heart	84.00	85.67	87.33	87.00	91.21	**92.42**
sonar	94.23	75.00	75.00	40.38	83.65	83.65
average	89.61	86.70	83.61	75.98	90.76	91.24
Case D: integrated instance selection, attribute selection carried-out at the pre-processing stage						
cancer	94.15	96.15	96.72	74.49	95.15	95.44
credit	75.22	72.61	77.54	64.49	81.88	81.16
heart	83.33	87.00	86.00	87.00	85.00	85.67
sonar	76.32	72.31	63.56	71.23	82.02	81.72
average	82.26	82.02	80.95	74.30	86.01	86.00
Case E: integrated attribute selection, instance selection carried-out at the pre-processing stage						
cancer	89.31	94.73	75.16	73.64	95.01	86.45
credit	69.28	61.30	69.71	59.57	81.32	76.71
heart	75.04	81.33	76.00	83.00	81.67	81.33
sonar	74.02	79.32	71.65	65.86	78.43	76.43
average	76.91	79.17	73.13	70.52	84.11	80.23
Case F: integrated instance and attribute selection						
cancer	**98.15**	**98.29**	**98.15**	88.01	**98.15**	97.94
credit	**87.68**	**89.57**	85.22	85.51	**92.61**	**90.87**
heart	**88.67**	**89.33**	**89.33**	90.00	93.00	92.17
sonar	**95.19**	82.69	80.77	72.08	87.50	**88.85**
average	92.42	89.97	88.37	83.90	92.81	92.45

Source: own computations.

In all cases shown in Table 14, the non-integrated attribute selection was carried-out at the pre-processing stage using the *wrapper* technique [66]. The non-integrated instance selection was based on the selection of reference vectors as proposed in [51]. In all the remaining cases the results shown in Table 14 were obtained applying the proposed approach described in Section 5.4.

From Table 14 it is clear that the proposed agent-based integrated data reduction technique is competitive with respect to classification accuracy in comparison to the traditional approach. Moreover, it is also competitive if compared with other classifiers and other approaches to data reduction. This can be concluded from data shown in Table 15, where the results obtained by using the fully integrated approach (case F in Table 14) are compared with the best classification results reported in the literature. The column $|S|/|D|$ in Table 15 shows what percentage of instances from the original training set has been retained by the respective reduction algorithm. The column *type* in Table 15 indicates the type of data reduction applied. In particular, this column contains the following notation:

"I" - the data reduction has been carried-out applying only instance selection.
"F" - the data reduction has been carried-out applying only attribute selection.
"IF" - the data reduction has been carried-out applying simultaneous instance and attribute selection,
"N" - no data reduction applied.

Results obtained during the experiment and presented in Tables 14-15 show that the integration of both, that is instance and attribute reduction, with learning classifier assures a very good quality of solutions in case of the analyzed benchmark classification problems.

It can be observed that the proposed approach guarantees also quite a satisfactory reduction of the original dataset. In case of all of the considered problems integrating instance and attribute selection with the learning process have increased the classification accuracy as compared with the accuracy obtained by training the classifier using the original full dataset. This observation holds true independently from the machine learning tool. Gains in classification accuracy seem to be quite substantial.

It is worth noting that classifiers induced using the original training sets produce for the set of investigated benchmark problems, the average classification accuracy of 82.86% and 82.28%, using C 4.5 with pruned and unpruned leaves, respectively, while the proposed approach to integration instance and attribute reduction with learning classifier assures the average accuracy of 92.81% and 92.45%, respectively. In case of the *sonar* problem, which is considered to be a difficult classification problem, the improvement is even more spectacular (from the average accuracy of 74.04% to the accuracy of 88.85%, for C 4.5, when integration instance and attribute selection with classifier construction is applied). The experiment results also show that the proposed approach to attribute

Table 15. Performance comparison of different classifiers and data reduction algorithms

Reduction method	type	cancer Accur.	$\frac{|S|}{|D|}$	heart Accur.	$\frac{|S|}{|D|}$	credit Accur.	$\frac{|S|}{|D|}$	sonar Accur.	$\frac{|S|}{|D|}$
IDR+C 4.5	IF	98.15%	19%	**93.0%**	53%	**92.61%**	30%	87.58%	90%
IDR+10NN	IF	**98.29%**	19%	89.33%	53%	89.57%	30%	82.69%	90%
IDR+1NN	IF	98.15%	19%	88.67%	53%	87.68%	30%	**95.19%**	90%
IDR+WLSVM	IF	95.57%	19%	80.53%	53%	85.22%	30%	72.12%	90%
IDR+BayesNet	IF	96.0%	20%	83.5%	60%	75.36%	30%	73.08%	90%
SC	I	97.44	19%	91.25	53%	90.72	27%	94.23	90%
CNN [216]	I	95.71%	7.09%	73.95%	30.84%	77.68%	24.22%	74.12%	32.85%
SNN [216]	I	93.85%	8.35%	76.25%	33.88%	81.31%	28.38%	79.81%	28.26%
IB2 [216]	I	95.71%	7.09%	73.96%	30.29%	78.26%	24.15%	80.88%	33.87%
IB3 [216]	I	96.57%	3.47%	81.16%	11.11%	85.22%	4.78%	69.38%	12.02%
DROP3 [216]	I	96.14%	3.58%	80.84%	12.76%	83.91%	5.96%	78%	26.87%
RMHC [179]	IF	70.9%	7%	82.3%	3%	-	-	-	-
GA-KJ [174]	IF	95.5%	33.4%	74.7%	33.1%	-	-	55.3%	52.6%
1NN+RELIEF [168]	IF	72.12%	100%	77.85%	100%	79.57%	100%	-	-
IB3+RELIEF [168]	IF	73.25%	100%	79.94%	100%	71.75%	100%	-	-
ID3+FSS [126]	F	94.53%	100%	-	-	-	-	-	-
ID3 [74]	N	94.3%	100%	-	-	-	-	-	-
C 4.5+BFS [74]	F	95.28%	100%	-	-	-	-	-	-
C 4.5 [104]	N	94.7%	100%	77.8%	100%	85.5%	100%	76.9%	100%
k-NN [216]	N	96.28%	100%	81.19%	100%	84.78%	100%	58.8%	100%
BayesNet [74]	N	96.7%	100%	83.6%	100%	82.9%	100%	90.4%	100%
SVM [74]	N	96.9%	100%	81.5%	100%	-	-	76.9%	100%
MLP+BP [74]	N	96.7%	100%	81.3%	100%	84.6%	100%	90.4%	100%

reduction results in better classification accuracy as compared to the accuracy obtained through applying the wrapper technique.

To reinforce the above observations, the experiment results, shown in Table 14, have been used to perform the two-way analysis of variance. The following null hypothesis were formulated:

I. The choice of the integration scheme does not influence the classifier performance.
II. The choice of the classifier type does not influence the classification accuracy.
III. There are no interactions between both factors (i.e. the choice of the integration scheme and the choice of the classifier type).

It was established that with the degree of confidence set at 95%, hypothesis II. and III. hold true. However, hypothesis I. should be rejected. Table 16 includes, as the analysis of variance summary, the ANOVA F test values. In addition, Tukey test confirmed that in case of the integrated approach there are no statistically significant differences between mean performances obtained using different classifiers.

On the other hand, the experiment results show that the data reduction can result in a decreased complexity and size of the decision tree as compared with the decision tree constructed using a full, non-reduced dataset. This can be concluded from results presented in Table 17, where the average number of rules and the average size of the decision tree are shown. It is clear that the proposed approach results in decreasing the complexity of knowledge representation as well as in a reduction of computation time required. This remains true not only for decision trees but also for other machine learning techniques.

Table 16. The ANOVA F test values summary table

Problem	df	credit	cancer	heart	sonar	F_{crit}
Main effect A	5	5.93683	6.86430	5.16468	7.08378	2.22267
Main effect B	5	1.62890	1.93260	2.03260	1.95232	2.22267
Interaction effect	20	0.46085	0.70185	0.42165	0.23422	1.51666

Table 17. Average number of rules and average size of the decision tree

Algorithm	C 4.5 - pruned leaves					C 4.5 - unpruned leaves				
Cases	A	B	C	D	E	A	B	C	D	E
Problem	Average number of rules									
credit	12.0	36.0	16.4	15.5	10.5	54.0	75.0	24.5	15.4	13.9
cancer	15.0	8.0	8.2	2.3	6.5	20.0	19.0	12.8	2.7	7.7
heart	17.0	11.0	17.6	8.7	11.5	44.0	26.0	23.8	8.4	14.3
sonar	8.0	10.0	9.0	16.0	11.0	8.0	12.0	10.0	14.0	11.4
	Average size of the tree									
credit	23.0	71.0	31.8	30.0	20.0	107.0	149.0	48.0	29.8	26.8
cancer	29.0	15.0	15.4	3.6	12.0	39.0	37.0	24.6	4.4	14.3
heart	33.0	21.0	34.3	16.4	22.0	87.0	35.0	46.6	15.8	27.6
sonar	15.0	20.0	17.0	19.0	21.0	15.0	25.0	19.0	17.0	21.8

Source: own computations.

The proposed solution has been implemented using the multi-agent paradigm. The main principles behind such approach include population-based computations, A-Team based search for optimal solutions and the proposed similarity factor as a tool for selecting reference instances. Combining the above into an adaptive classification system has resulted in constructing an effective and dependable classification tool. Validating experiment results enable us to draw the following further conclusions:

- Reducing training set size still preserves knowledge content of the analyzed data.
- Integration of the preprocessing stage with learning classifier assures better results than a non-integrated solution.
- The choice of the data integration scheme may significantly influence classifier performance.
- The choice of the classifier is not a decisive factor from the point of view of performance of the integrated classifier.

6.1.3 Multiple-Objective Data Reduction

The agent-based approach proposed in Section 5.5 has been used for the multiple-objective data reduction problem. The main aim of the experiment has been to evaluate the usefulness and effectiveness of the agent-based approach in solving the problem of multiple-objective data reduction under the assumption that data reduction is carried-out in the instance dimension only. The agent-based algorithm has been implemented using the similarity coefficient approach, described in Section 4 as the clustering procedure and optimizing agents proposed in Section 5.5 and denoted, respectively, RLS (Random Local Search with tabu list) and IDLS (Incremental/Decremental Local Search). The experiment aimed at establishing experimentally how different strategies of selecting and using optimizing agents affect the computation results.

The proposed approach has been used to solve four classification problems - heart, credit, cancer and sonar problem, which characteristics are shown in Table 1.

The experiment plan has been based on the 10-cross-validation approach. Each thus obtained training set D has been then reduced to a subset S containing reference instances. Each reference instances set has been, in turn, used to produce a decision tree. This has been evaluated from the point of view of the four objective functions, where each of the functions corresponds to one of the following goals:

- Classification quality - the objective function f_1 that should be maximized.
- Data compression level - the objective function f_2 that should be minimized.
- Number of rules - the objective function f_3 that should be minimized.
- Length of rules - the objective function f_4 that should be minimized.

Each decision tree was created using only the instances in S and each C 4.5 classifier was trained without pruned leaves.

For each benchmarking problem the experiment has been repeated 50 times and the reported values of the quality measures have been averaged over all runs. All optimization agents have been allowed to continue iterating until 100 iterations have been performed. The common memory size was set to 100 individuals. The number of iterations and the size of the common memory have been set out arbitrarily at the fine-tuning phase.

In order to evaluate the resulting Pareto-optimal sets approximations two quality measures have been used. The first measure is the average of the best values of weighted Tchebycheff scalarizing function over a set of systematically generated normalized weight vectors. In general, the weighted Tchebycheff scalarizing function is an example of scalarizing function calculating distances between z_j and z_j^0, where z_j and z_j^0 are vectors of objective functions and where z^0 is called a reference point [105]. The function is defined as follows:

$$\phi_\infty(z, z^0, \Lambda) = \max_j \{\lambda_j(z_j^0 - z_j)\}. \tag{18}$$

The set of such weight vectors is denoted and defined as:

$$\Psi_s = \{\Lambda = [\lambda_1, \ldots, \lambda_J] \in \Psi | \lambda_j \in \{0, \frac{1}{\kappa}, \frac{2}{\kappa}, \ldots, \frac{\kappa - 1}{\kappa}, 1\}\}, \tag{19}$$

where Ψ is the set of all normalized weight vectors and κ is a sampling parameter. Finally, the first quality measure is calculated in the following way:

$$R(A) = 1 - \frac{\sum_{\Lambda \in \Psi_s} \phi_\infty^*(z^0, A, \Lambda)}{|\Psi_s|}, \tag{20}$$

where $\phi_\infty^*(z^0, A, \Lambda) = min_{z \in A}\{\phi_\infty(z, z^0, \Lambda)\}$ representing the best value achieved by function $\phi_\infty(z, z^0, \Lambda)$ on the set A, where A is composed of mutually nondominated points. Before calculating the value of this measure the reference point z^0 composed of the best attainable objective function values was set as an ideal point.

The second quality measure is the coverage of the two approximations of the nondominated set and is defined as:

$$C(A, B) = \frac{|\{z'' \in B\}| \exists z' \in A : z' \succ z''|}{|B|}, \tag{21}$$

where the value $C(A, B) = 1$ means that all points in B are dominated by or are equal to some points in A. The value $C(A, B) = 0$ means that no point in B is covered by any point in A.

Experiment results for different combinations of optimization agents averaged over all benchmark datasets and instances are shown in Table 18. Values of the R measure have been calculated with the sampling parameter κ set to 100 and 5 for the bi-objective and four-objective cases, respectively.

The results of the Pareto-optimal set approximations using the R measure indicate that each combination of agents produces similar results. There are no statistically significant differences between average values of the R measure for all investigated combination of agents.

The results of the Pareto-optimal set approximations using the C measure indicate that IDLS produces a better coverage then RLS and RLS+IDLS better coverage than either RLS or IDLS. This observation holds true for all the investigated cases i.e. multi-objective optimization with two and four objectives, and is independent on the dimensionality of problems. Thus RLS+IDLS

Table 18. Performance of different agent combinations measured using average values of C and R

Objectives	C measure and standard deviations						R measure and standard deviations		
	C(RLS, IDLS)	C(IDLS, RLS)	C(RLS +IDLS, RLS)	C(RLS, RLS +IDLS)	C(RLS +IDLS, IDLS)	C(IDLS, RLS +IDLS)	RLS	IDLS	RLS+IDLS
f_1, f_2, f_3, f_4	0,464	0,618	0,862	0,208	0,760	0,328	0,858	0,857	0,859
	±0, 12	±0, 073	±0, 149	±0, 084	±0, 254	±0, 11	±0, 003	±0, 003	±0, 002
f_1, f_2	0,361	0,798	0,735	0,430	0,867	0,422	0,732	0,732	0,734
	±0, 172	±0, 155	±0, 087	±0, 096	±0, 153	±0, 183	±0, 004	±0, 004	±0, 003
f_1, f_3	0,523	0,728	0,827	0,390	0,824	0,435	0,959	0,961	0,959
	±0, 103	±0, 052	±0, 158	±0, 139	±0, 084	±0, 194	±0, 003	±0, 003	±0, 007

Source: own computations.

generates the best approximation of the Pareto-optimal (non-dominated set). a pair-wise comparison of average It has been also confirmed that the following inequalities:

- $C(IDLS, RLS) > C(RLS, IDLS)$,
- $C(RLS + IDLS, RLS) > C(RLS, RLS + IDLS)$,
- $C(RLS + IDLS, IDLS) > C(IDLS, RLS + IDLS)$.

are statistically significant for all instances.

In Fig. 13 and 14 example Pareto fronts obtained from classifying a single instance of each of the considered problem types are shown.

In Fig. 15 example approximations of the Pareto-optimal sets produced by different combination of agents for an instance of the four-objective selection of the reference vector problem are shown.

The focus of this part of the chapter is however not on the efficiency of the agent based approach but rather on the methodology of dealing with the multiple-objective selection of reference vectors through employing a team of agents. It has been shown that there exist adequate methodology and suitable tools allowing to obtain a good approximation of the Pareto-optimal solutions to the problems of the discussed type. The proposed method and tools can be used to design customized machine learning and data mining systems corresponding better to the user is requirements and needs. The approach allows also for a discovery of interactions between composition of various vector selection optimization procedures and a quality of generalization measured using multiple

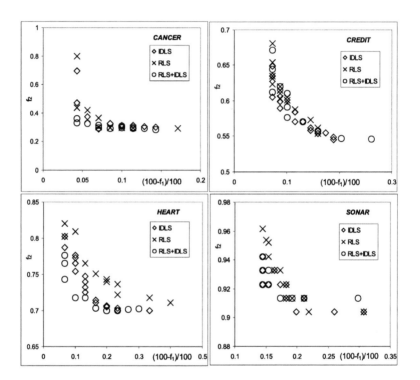

Fig. 13. Example Pareto fronts - instances of the bi-objective optimization (f_1 and f_2)

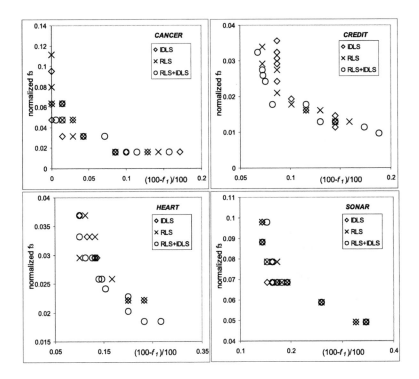

Fig. 14. Example Pareto fronts - instances of the bi-objective optimization (f_1 and f_3)

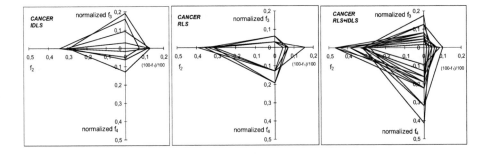

Fig. 15. Example approximations of Pareto-optimal sets - an instance of the four-objective optimization problem

criteria. Such knowledge can be used for evaluation and selection of optimization agents and procedures.

6.2 Evaluation of the Agent-Based Algorithms for Learning Classifiers from the Distributed and Reduced Data

The computation experiments described in this part of the chapter deal with distributed learning with data reduction carried-out at separated sites. As it was shown in Section 5, the proposed approach to the distributed learning uses a set of agents which process the local data and communicate the results to other agents controlling and managing the distributed learning process. The aim of the computation experiment was to evaluate several variants of the agent-based architectures for the distributed learning with data reduction.

6.2.1 Cluster-Based Data Reduction

The aim of the computational experiment was to decide to what extent (if any) the proposed approach contributes towards increasing the classification accuracy of the classifier induced from the set of prototypes obtained by the data reduction at the local level where the data are stored. The computational experiment focused on evaluating the agent-based approach for distributed learning under the assumption that data reduction is carried-out in the instance dimension only and where the prototypes are selected from the generated clusters. The computational experiment was also expected to clarify how the choice of the clustering procedure for the data reduction influences the classification accuracy. In the reported computational experiment the following approaches to instance selection from clusters have been considered:

- Selection based on the k-means clustering algorithm using Algorithm 6.
- Selection based on the similarity coefficient, where the clusters are produced using Algorithm 8.
- Selection based on the modified stratification-based instance clustering algorithm discussed in Section 4.4.

Classification accuracy of the global classifier induced from the set of prototypes obtained using the proposed approach has been compared with:

- Results obtained by pooling together all instances from the distributed databases, without data reduction, into the centralized database.
- Results obtained by applying for data reduction at the local level selected instance-based learning algorithms: IB2 [2], CNN and ENN [216].
- results obtained by applying for data reduction the instance-based learning algorithms integrated with the selection based on clustering and stratification. In this case the instances have been first mapped into subsets using one of the described clustering procedures and next, from thus obtained subsets, the prototypes have been selected using the instance based learning algorithm.

In the reported experiment generalization accuracy has been used as the performance criterion. The learning tool used at the global level was C 4.5 algorithm [166]. The C 4.5 algorithm has been also used to evaluate the prototype selection by the agent-based population learning algorithm.

In the experiment four different datasets: customer, adult, waveform and shuttle have been used. The characteristics of the first two datasets are shown in Table 1. The waveform problem consists of 30000 instances with 21 attributes and 2 classes. The shuttle dataset consists of 58000 instances with 9 attributes and 7 classes.

Each benchmarking problem has been solved 30 times. The quality measure in all cases was the correct classification ratio calculated using the 10-cross-validation approach. At first, the available datasets have been randomly divided into the training and test sets in approximately 9/10 and 1/10 proportions. The second step involved random partitioning of the previously generated training sets into training subsets, each representing a different dataset placed in the separate location. Next, each of the obtained datasets has been reduced. The reduced subsets have been then used to compute the global classifier using the proposed strategies for instance reduction.

The above scheme has been repeated four times, once for each of the investigated partitions of the training set into the distributed database. The original data set was randomly partitioned into, respectively, the 2, 3, 4 and 5 distributed databases of, approximately, a similar size.

Computations have been run with the size of the initial population set to 50. The number of repetitions for each improvement procedure was set to 100. The number of strata and the number of clusters have been set to 50 and 100. The number of iterations I of k-means was set to 100. The values of these parameters have been set arbitrarily at the fine-tuning phase. The starting points of the k-means algorithm have been chosen randomly. The computations have been carried on several PC computers connected within a local area network.

The respective experiment results are shown in Tables 19-20. They represent the averages of all experiments showing the accuracy of classification obtained on the test sets by the C 4.5 classifier induced at the global level.

It should be noted that data reduction at local sites assures, as a rule, better classification accuracy as compared with the case of pooling together all instances from the distributed datasets into a centralized database without data reduction. The above conclusion has been drawn through comparison of the results from Tables 19-20 with the reference results obtained by the C 4.5 classifier for the whole, non-distributed datasets (classification accuracy of 73.32%(+/-1.42), 82.43%(+/-1.03), 71.01%(+/-0.8) and 99.9%(+/-0.03) for customer, adult, waveform and shuttle datasets, respectively). On the other hand, the experiment results show that the choice of the data reduction algorithm can influence the classification accuracy. It can be claimed, based on the presented results, that data reduction carried-out by the agent-based population learning algorithm assures better classification accuracy than data reduction using instance-based learning algorithms.

Table 19. Average classification accuracy (%) for the distributed learning classifier (cases A-H)

Problem	Number of distributed data sources				
	2	3	4	5	average
Case A: Prototype selection based on the similarity coefficient					
customer	68.45	70.40	74.67	75.21	72.18
adult	86.20	87.20	86.81	87.10	86.82
waveform	75.52	77.61	78.32	80.67	78.03
shuttle	99.95	99.92	99.98	99.96	99.95
Case B: Prototype selection based on the stratification strategy; the number of strata - 50					
customer	62.23	64.54	65.23	67.10	64.77
adult	78.02	80.71	81.63	83.90	81.06
waveform	71.23	71.15	73.01	74.67	72.51
shuttle	99.78	99.87	99.91	99.89	99.86
Case C: Prototype selection based on the stratification strategy; the number of strata - 100					
customer	64.43	64.54	66.32	69.43	66.18
adult	78.32	82.30	83.03	85.2	82.21
waveform	72.23	73.15	75.41	74.67	73.86
shuttle	98.93	99.92	99.92	99.95	99.68
Case D: Prototype selection based on k-means clustering algorithm; the number of clusters - 50					
customer	67.23	69.14	72.65	72.13	70.28
adult	84.12	85.12	87.09	87.70	86.00
waveform	74.33	78.54	77.65	81.2	77.93
shuttle	99.94	99.91	99.95	99.98	99.94
Case E: Prototype selection based on k-means clustering algorithm; the number of clusters - 100					
customer	69.33	70.72	72.08	75.32	71.86
adult	85.92	86.25	87.72	87.83	86.93
waveform	74.13	75.9	77.05	80.41	76.87
shuttle	99.94	99.91	99.99	99.95	99.95
Case F: Prototype selection through the CNN algorithm					
customer	56.43	54.45	57.01	60.43	57.08
adult	69.10	70.62	71.72	70.00	70.36
waveform	62.42	63.33	64.90	66.78	64.35
shuttle	97.21	96.67	97.47	97.32	97.17
Case G: Prototype selection through the IB2 algorithm					
customer	55.43	56.45	57.01	56.43	56.33
adult	68.60	69.02	70.12	71.43	69.79
waveform	61.09	62.5	63.12	65.08	62.94
shuttle	98.23	97.3	98.41	98.41	98.08
Case H: Prototype selection through the ENN algorithm					
customer	64.45	66.11	69.10	70.65	67.57
adult	77.12	80.54	80.21	82.09	79.99
waveform	66.04	69.12	72.70	74.32	70.54
shuttle	99.82	99.87	99.85	99.92	99.86

Source: own computations.

Table 20. Average classification accuracy (%) for the distributed learning classifier (cases I-N)

Problem	Number of distributed data sources				
	2	3	4	5	average
Case I: CNN integrated with the k-means algorithm; the number of clusters - 100					
customer	60.20	64.10	65.17	66.53	64.00
adult	71.70	72.04	73.40	74.84	72.99
waveform	69.80	70.41	73.3	74.28	71.94
shuttle	99.81	99.77	99.81	99.81	99.8
Case J: IB2 integrated with the k-means algorithm; the number of clusters - 100					
customer	59.40	61.07	62.00	64.06	61.63
adult	73.03	74.60	74.67	76.13	74.60
waveform	70.30	71.61	72.2	73.02	71.78
shuttle	99.56	99.63	99.75	99.81	99.68
Case K: ENN integrated with the k-means algorithm; the number of cluster - 100					
customer	65.70	66.34	69.16	73.43	68.65
adult	81.32	81.15	83.14	85.04	82.66
waveform	72.10	74.05	76.34	76.60	74.77
shuttle	99.83	99.91	99.87	99.87	99.87
Case L: CNN integrated with the stratification strategy; the number of strata - 100					
customer	59.00	62.03	62.74	63.4	61.79
adult	70.41	72.46	71.44	73.44	71.93
waveform	69.04	70.71	72.23	71.58	70.89
shuttle	99.76	99.85	99.87	99.87	99.84
Case M: IB2 integrated with the stratification strategy; the number of strata - 100					
customer	63.70	69.3	70.2	72.16	68.84
adult	70.03	71.6	73.67	75.13	72.60
waveform	71.30	71.81	73.32	74.10	72.63
shuttle	99.82	99.84	99.92	99.9	99.87
Case N: ENN integrated with the stratification strategy; the number of strata - 100					
customer	66.43	68.54	70.32	71.43	69.18
adult	79.32	83.3	83.02	85.41	82.76
waveform	73.23	73.15	76.41	79.67	75.61
shuttle	99.82	99.89	99.91	99.92	99.88

Source: own computations.

The results of the experiment shown in Tables 19-20 suggest also that the prototype selection based on a similarity coefficient is competitive in terms of classification accuracy as compared with the prototype selection based on clustering with the k-means algorithm and with the stratification strategy. The computation results also show that the number of strata and the number of clusters can influence classification accuracy. For example, the number of clusters and the number of strata set to 100 assure better results as compared with the case where these parameters have been set to 50. However, it should be noted that the quality of the prototype selection based on clustering with the k-means algorithm and with the stratification strategy is limited by the number of strata/clusters. Additionally, the quality of the k-means clustering algorithm can be poor because of the insufficient number of iterations. Also, it often converges to a local minimum and is sensitive to initial starting conditions, which was originally pointed out in [27].

To reinforce the above conclusions, experiment results, shown in Tables 19- 20, have been used to perform the non-parametric Friedman test to decide whether data reduction algorithms are equally effective independently of the kind of the problem being solved. To assign weights required by the test, the 14 point scale has been used with 14 points for the best and 1 point for the worst algorithm. The average classification accuracy for each considered approach to data reduction has been weighted using the above weights. The test aimed at deciding among the following hypotheses:

- H_0 - zero hypothesis: data reduction approaches are statistically equally effective regardless of the kind of problem which instances are being solved.
- H_1 - alternative hypothesis: not all approaches are equally effective.

The analysis has been carried-out at the significance level of 0.05. The respective value of the χ^2 statistics with 14 approaches and 4 instances of the considered problems is 47.2 and the value of χ^2 distribution is equal to 7.81 for 3 degrees of freedom. Thus, it can be observed that not all algorithms are equally effective regardless of the kind of problem which instances are being solved. In Fig. 16 overall total of weights for each data reduction algorithm are compared.

Friedman test results from Fig. 16 and average weighted performance shown in Fig. 17, allow to observe that approaches (cases) A, D, E, K, M and N produced above the average results. The highest score in total and in comparison to each of the analyzed approaches has been obtained by the agent-based prototype selection based on the similarity coefficient. The Friedman test confirms also that data reduction based on clustering algorithms allows to obtain better classification results than those obtained by applying instance based data reduction algorithms. High quality results have been obtained also through integration of the ENN algorithm with the stratification strategy. This confirms the finding that, in general, clustering improves the quality of the selected prototypes.

On the other hand, the data reduction techniques assure good quality classification results achieving, at the same time, high rates of data compression. For instance, pooling of 250 prototypes (i.e. average about 1% of "full datasets"), selected by the algorithm based on the stratified strategy, from five distributed

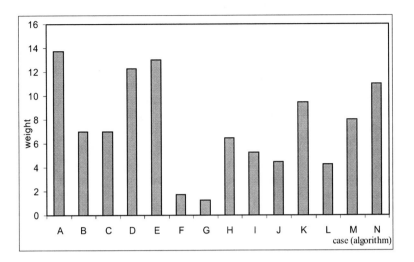

Fig. 16. The total of the Friedman weights for the distributed learning algorithms. Notation A,B,...,N corresponds to the investigated cases as explained in Tables 19-20

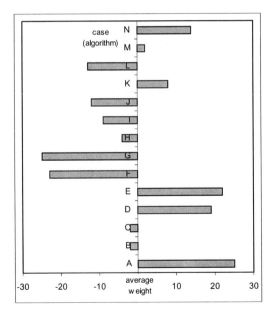

Fig. 17. Average weighted performance of the distributed learning algorithms. Notation A,B,...,N corresponds to the investigated cases as explained in Tables 19-20

datasets, together into the training set, assures classification accuracy of 67.1%, 83.9%, 74.67% and 99.89% for customer, adult, waveform and shuttle respectively. Fig. 18 shows the average percentage of instances retained in the training set by the investigated approaches. The highest compression rates have been obtained using approaches which require partitioning datasets into clusters before selecting prototypes. This conclusion remains true independently of the procedure used to produce clusters. The highest compression rate has been obtained for the data reduction algorithm based on the stratification strategy with the number of strata set at 50. Equally high compression rate and a very good classification accuracy characterized data reduction approach based on the similarity coefficient. It is also reasonable to expect that the data reduction decreases computation time required for machine learning and reduces the cost and time of moving data to the central site where the distributed learning problem is finally solved.

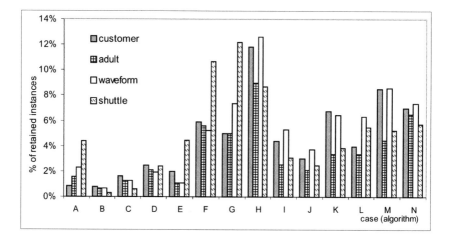

Fig. 18. Percentage of instances retained by the evaluated distributed learning algorithms. Notation A,B,...,N corresponds to the investigated cases as explained in Tables 19-20

To confirm the above conclusion, Fig. 19 shows how the time required for inducing global classifiers, in these cases C 4.5 classifiers, depends on the size of the training set. The learning processes have been run on PC Celeron 1.3GHz, 750MB of main memory. Analyzing Fig. 19, it is evident that time needed for inducing a classifier is reduced when the training set contains prototypes. This conclusion is true for all benchmark datasets. Additionally, Fig. 20 shows the average percentage of instances moved to the central site with respect to the number of sites.

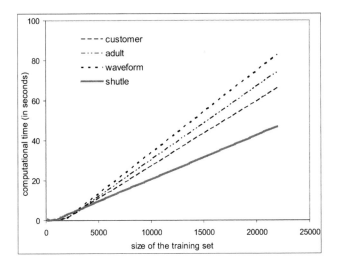

Fig. 19. The trend line of the time needed for inducing C 4.5 classifiers for different sizes of three different prototype sets

Computation experiment has been carried-out with a view to analyze and compare different distributed learning algorithms with data reduction. In all cases it has been assumed that prototypes are selected from clusters by agent-based population algorithms. The results confirmed that the quality of the distributed learning results depends on the algorithm used for the prototype selection. The approach with similarity coefficient used to produce data clusters and select prototypes should be considered as a promising tool for the distributed learning. Its advantage, apart from a good quality of the distributed learning results, is that it does not require to set in advance the number of clusters from which prototypes are selected.

Results also indicate that the proposed agent-based approach for learning classifiers from the reduced and distributed data can effectively achieve the comparable or better performances than a standard approach to the distributed learning when the data are pooled together in a centralized data repository. Computation experiment results confirm also that selected prototypes preserve basic features of the original data.

6.2.2   Strategies for the Prototype Selection in the Distributed Learning

The learning classifier from distributed data approach, proposed in Section 5.3, is dedicated to distributed learning with data reduction. It is assumed that data reduction through instance and attribute selection is carried-out independently at each site by a team of agents. To assure obtaining homogenous prototypes,

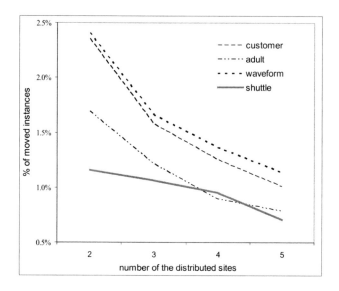

Fig. 20. The average percentage of instances moved to the central site versus the number of the distributed sites in the reported experiment

the attribute selection must be coordinated using a special collaborative strategy. Alternatively, heterogeneous prototypes can be merged to create a compact representation and a special strategy for constructing a combined classifier must be implemented.

The aim of the computational experiment study presented in this subsection was to evaluate to what extent the combiner constructing strategies contribute to increasing classification accuracy of the global classifier induced from the set of prototypes selected at autonomous distributed sites. The experiment was also expected to share some light on how the choice of strategy for deciding on the winning set of attributes can influence the classification accuracy of the global classifier.

In the reported experiment the following combiner constructing strategies have been considered:

- Bagging combiner strategy - this strategy is based on the bagging approach as described in [167]. The bootstrap sample is obtained by uniformly sampling instances from the given reduced dataset S_i with replacement. From each sample set a classifier is induced. This procedure is carried-out independently for each reduced dataset $S_1, \ldots, S_K$, and next the global classifier is generated by aggregating classifiers representing each sample set. The final classification of a new object x is obtained by the uniform voting scheme on h_{ij}, where h_{ij} is a classifier learned on j trial where $j = 1, \ldots, T, i = 1, \ldots, K$ and T is the number of the bootstrap samples. In this case the voting decision for a new object x is computed as:

$$h(x) = \arg\max_{c \in C} \sum_{j=1}^{T} \sum_{i=1}^{K} (h_{ij}(x) = c), \tag{22}$$

where $h(x)$ is the class label predicted for object x by ij-th classifier. The pseudo-code of the bagging is shown as Algorithm 15.

Algorithm 15. *Bagging combiner strategy*

Input: S_i, with N_i examples and correct labels, where $i = 1, \ldots, K$, and integer T specifying the number of bootstrap iterations.
Output: h - classifier.
1. For each separated reduced data set S_i repeat points 2-4.
2. For $j = 1, \ldots, T$ repeat points 3-4.
3. Take sample S_i' from S_i.
4. Generate a classifier h_{ij} using S_i' as the training set.
5. Run x on the input h_{ij}.
6. The classification of vector x is built by voting scheme based on condition (22).

- AdaBoost combiner strategy - this strategy is based on the AdaBoost approach [167]. Weak classifiers are constructed from the reduced datasets. The boosted classifier h is combined from all weak classifiers h_{ij}, which are induced on the j-th boosting trial ($j = 1, \ldots, T$) and based on the i-th reduced dataset ($i = 1, \ldots, K$). In particular, the combined decision is taken through summing up the votes of the weak classifiers h_{ij}. The vote of each h_{ij} is worth $\log(1/\beta_{ij})$ units, where $\beta_{ij} = \varepsilon_{ij}/(1 - \varepsilon_{ij})$ is a correct classification factor calculated from the error ε_{ij} of the weak classifier h_{ij}. Thus, the voting decision for a new object x is computed as:

$$h(x) = \arg\max_{c \in C} \sum_{j=1}^{T} \sum_{i=1}^{K} ((\log \frac{1}{\beta_{ij}}) \cdot h_{ij}(x) = c). \tag{23}$$

The pseudo-code of the AdaBoost is shown as Algorithm 16.

Algorithm 16. *AdaBoost combiner strategy*

Input: S_i, with N_i examples and correct labels, where $i = 1, \ldots, K$, and integer T specifying the number of boosting trials.
Output: h - classifier.
1. For each separated reduced data set S_i repeat points 2-9.
2. Initialize the distribution $w_1(k) := \frac{1}{N_i}$ ($k = 1, \ldots, N_i$) for each example from S_i.
3. For $j = 1, \ldots, T$ repeat points 4-9.
4. Select a training data set S_i' from S_i based on the current distribution.
5. Generate a classifier h_{ij} using S_i' as the training set.
6. Calculate the error of the classifier h_{ij}.
7. If $\varepsilon_{ij} > \frac{1}{2}$ then goto 10.
8. Set β_{ij}.

9. Update the distribution $w_j(k)$ and normalize $w_j(k)$.

10. Run x on the input h_{ij}.

11. The classification of vector x is built by voting scheme based on condition (23).

- Simple voting strategy - at the global level the set of all prototypes from different sites is further reduced in the attribute dimension to obtain prototypes with attributes belonging to the subset of attributes A', where $A' = \bigcup_{i=1}^{K} A_i$. It means that the decision for new object x is computed by the classifier induced from the global set of prototypes $S' = \bigcup_{i=1}^{K} S_i$, where each example is a vector of attribute values with attributes A'. The pseudo-code of the simple voting is shown as Algorithm 17.

Algorithm 17. *Voting strategy*

Input: A_i, S_i and where $i = 1, \ldots, K$.

Output: h - classifier.

1. Create a global set of attributes $A' := \bigcup_{i=1}^{K} A_i$.

2. Based on A' update each S_i by deleting values of attributes not in A'.

3. Create the global set of prototypes $S' := \bigcup_{i=1}^{K} S_i$, where each example is described by the set of attributes A'.

4. Generate a classifier h using S' as the training set.

5. Run x on the input h.

- Hybrid attribute voting strategy - after integrating local level solution attributes are selected independently by two attribute selection techniques i.e. by the forward and backward sequential selection (FSS and BSS) [127]. The 10-cross-validation approach has been used. The learning and the validation sets are obtained by randomly splitting the global set of prototypes. In each of the 10CV runs the attribute selection process is carried-out. The final set of attributes is obtained through the unanimous voting mechanism. The pseudo-code of the hybrid voting is shown as Algorithm 18.

Algorithm 18. *Hybrid attribute voting strategy*

Input: A_i, S_i and where $i = 1, \ldots, K$.

Output: h - classifier.

1. Create a global set of attributes $A' := \bigcup_{i=1}^{K} A_i$.

2. Based on A' update each S_i by deleting values of attributes not in A'.

3. Create the global set of prototypes $S' := \bigcup_{i=1}^{K} S_i$, where each example is described by the set of attributes A'.

4. For ten cross validation iteration repeat points 5-6.

5. Divide S' into the learning and the validating set.

6. Run wrapper approaches and create appropriate attributes sets A_i^{FSS} and A_i^{BSS}, where i is a iteration number of cross validation fold.

7. Create a final set of attributes $A'' := \bigcup_{i=1}^{10} (A_i^{FSS} \cup A_i^{BSS})$.

8. Generate a classifier h using S' as the training set and where prototypes are described by the set of attributes A''.

9. Run x on the input h.

The second considered group of strategies includes strategies for deciding on the winning set of attributes. It has been decided to implement and evaluate the following strategies:

- Static attribute selection
- Dynamic attribute selection.

The respective pseudo-codeds are shown as Algorithms 19 and 20.

Algorithm 19. *Static attribute selection*

1. For each *solution manager* repeat points 2-3.
2. Solve the data reduction subproblem using optimizing agents.
3. Send A_i and β to the attribute manager, where $\beta := f(A_i)$ denote the value of the fitness function and A_i the set of candidate attribute from the best solution, where $i = 1, \ldots, K$.
4. For the *attribute manager* select the winning set
of attributes $A^{win} := \arg\max_{A_i} \sum_{i=1}^{K} \beta(A_i)$.
5. For the *attribute manager* return A^{win} to solution managers.
6. For each *solution manager* repeat points 7-10.
7. Replace attributes from the best solution in the current population by attributes from A^{win}.
8. Solve the instance reduction subproblem using optimizing agents.
9. Select the best solution from the current population.
10. Send the best solution to the global manager.
11. For the *global manager* create the global set of prototypes by integrating local solutions and produce the global classifier.

Algorithm 20. *Dynamic attribute selection*

1. Set the temporary set of attributes $A^{temp} := \emptyset$.
2. For each *solution manager* repeat points 3-7.
3. If (*iteration* is not equal to 1) then goto 5.
4. Solve the data reduction subproblem using all optimizing agents.
5. Solve the data reduction subproblem using only optimizing agents responsible for instance selection.
6. Select the best solution from the current population.
7. Send A_i and β to the attribute manager, where $\beta = f(A_i)$ denote the value of the fitness function and A_i the set of candidate attribute from the best solution, where $i = 1, \ldots, K$.
8. For the *attribute manager* run points 9-15.

9. Select the winning set of attributes $A^{win} := \arg\max_{A_i} \sum_{i=1}^{K} \beta(A_i)$.
10. If ($A^{win} = A^{temp}$ and $random() < 0.5$) then goto 12. else goto 14.
11. Select randomly $\{a\} \subset A^{win}$.
12. Select randomly $\{a'\} \subset A'$, where $A' = (\bigcup_{i \in \{1,...,K\}} A_i)/A^{win}$.
13. Modify the set of winning attributes $A^{win} := (A^{win} \backslash \{a\}) \cup \{a'\}$.
14. Update the temporary set of attributes $A^{temp} := A^{win}$.
15. Return A^{win} to solution managers.
16. For each *solution manager* repeat points 17-18.
17. Replace attributes from the best solution in the current population by attributes from A^{win}.
18. If (!terminating condition) then goto 2.
19. For each *solution manager* repeat points 20-21.
20. Select the best solution from the current population.
21. Send the best solution to the global manager.
22. For the *global manager* create the global set of prototypes by integrating local solutions and produce the global classifier.

Classification accuracy of the global classifiers obtained using the above described strategies has been compared with:

- Results obtained by pooling together, without data reduction, all instances from distributed databases, into the centralized database.
- Results obtained by pooling together all instances selected from distributed databases through the instance reduction only.

Classification accuracy has been used as the performance criterion. The learning tool used was C 4.5 algorithm.

The experiment involved four datasets - customer, adult, waveform and shuttle. The reported computational experiment was based on the 10-cross-validation approach. At first, the available datasets have been randomly divided into training and test sets in approximately 9/10 and 1/10 proportions. The second step involved a random partition of the previously generated training sets into training subsets, each representing a different dataset placed in the separate location. Next, each of the obtained datasets has been reduced. Then, the reduced subsets have been used to compute the global classifier using the proposed strategies. The above scheme was repeated ten times, using a different dataset partition as the test set for each trial.

The experiment has been repeated four times for four different partitions of the training set into a multi-database. The original data set was randomly partitioned into 2, 3, 4 and 5 multi-datasets of approximately similar size.

For the combiner strategy based on bagging, the parameter T (number of bootstraps) was set to 3 and 5. Choosing such small values of T was inspired by good results obtained by Quinlan for the C 4.5 classifier with bagging [167]. In the case of the AdaBoost - based strategy the value of T (number of boosting rounds) was arbitrarily set to 10.

All optimizing agents have been allowed to continue iterating until 100 iterations have been performed. The common memory size was set to 100 individuals. The number of iterations and the size of the common memory had been set out arbitrarily at the fine-tuning phase. The whole process of searching for the best solution stopped when there were no improvements of the best solution during the last 3 minutes of computation.

The experiment has been repeated four times for the four different partitions of the training set into a multi-database. The respective experiment results averaged over 10-cross-validation runs are shown in Tables 21- 22. The results cover several independent cases. In the first case only reference instance selection at the local level has been carried-out, and next, the global classifier has been computed based on the homogenous set of prototypes. The next cases concern the results obtained by applying different strategies for deciding on the winning set of attributes i.e. the strategies for coordination between solutions at local sites, and by applying different strategies for learning combiner classifiers.

It should be noted that data reduction in two dimensions (selection of instances and attributes) assures better results in comparison to data reduction only in one dimension i.e. instance dimension, and that the above conclusion holds true independently of the combiner strategy used at the global level and of the strategy for the winning attribute selection at the local level. It has been also confirmed that learning classifiers from distributed data and performing data reduction at the local level produces reasonable to very good results in comparison to the case in which all instances from distributed datasets are pooled together.

Additionally, it can be observed that combiner strategies produce reasonable to very good results compared with other cases presented in Tables 21- 22. Out of the investigated combiner strategies the strategies based on the simple and hybrid attribute voting have performed best. Second best was the AdaBoost-based strategy, followed by the Bagging-based strategy and the dynamic attribute selection strategy.

Pooling all instances from distributed datasets seems to be the best effective strategy assuring classification accuracy of 73.32%(+/-1.42), 82.43%(+/-1.03), 71.01%(+/-0.8) and 99.9%(+/-0.03) for customer, adult, waveform and shuttle datasets respectively. On the other hand, the global classifier based on instance selection only assures classification accuracy of 75.21%, 87.1%, 80.67% and 99.96%. These results can still be considerably improved using the hybrid attribute voting strategy assuring classification accuracy of 78.15%, 92.48%, 82.04% and 99.25% respectively for the investigated datasets.

However, merging the two strategies as in cases G and J in Tables 21- 22 may further improve the classification accuracy. Based on these results it can be concluded that the best results can be obtained by hybridization of different approaches to distributed learning when data reduction in two dimensions is carried on. In this case the hybridization is understood in the context of applying more than one technique of selecting the final set of attributes or constructing combiner classifiers, or both.

Table 21. Average accuracy (%) of C 4.5 results obtained over the distributed datasets (cases A-G)

Problem	Number of distributed data sources			
	2	3	4	5
Case A: Selection of the reference instances at the local level only				
customer	68.45(+/-0.98)	70.4(+/-0.76)	74.67(+/-2.12)	75.21(+/-0.7)
adult	86.2(+/-0.67)	87.2(+/-0.45)	86.81(+/-0.51)	87.1(+/-0.32)
waveform	75.52(+/-0.72)	77.61(+/-0.87)	78.32(+/-0.45)	80.67(+/-0.7)
shuttle	99.95(+/-0.02)	99.92(+/-0.02)	99.98(+/-0.01)	99.96(+/-0.02)
Case B: Combiner strategy based on the Bagging approach (number of bootstraps equals 3)				
customer	69.67(+/-0.98)	72.13(+/-0.76)	77.36(+/-1.12)	76.13(+/-0.7)
adult	88.34(+/-0.67)	88.86(+/-0.45)	89.15(+/-0.51)	89.17(+/-0.32)
waveform	74.12(+/-0.72)	75.2(+/-0.87)	77.4(+/-0.45)	78.34(+/-0.7)
shuttle	97.43(+/-0.5)	97.41(+/-0.7)	98.82(+/-0.8)	97.91(+/-1.1)
Case C: Combiner strategy based on the Bagging approach (number of bootstraps equals 5)				
customer	69.99(+/-1.34)	72.38(+/-1.12)	77.65(+/-0.97)	77.07(+/-2.03)
adult	87.78(+/-1.67)	88.34(+/-1.3)	89.67(+/-2.5)	88.57(+/-1.45)
waveform	75.23(+/-1.29)	74.67(+/-2.68)	77.87(+/-2.05)	79.23(+/-2.13)
shuttle	97.83(+/-0.6)	97.5(+/-0.8)	98.22(+/-1)	98.36(+/-0.7)
Case D: Combiner strategy based on the AdaBoost approach (number of boosting repetitions equals 10)				
customer	70.05(+/-1.56)	74.78(+/-1.3)	76.23(+/-1.25)	77.41(+/-1.98)
adult	89.64(+/-2.7)	89.28(+/-2.1)	90.23(+/-1.98)	91.78(+/-3.12)
waveform	77.12(+/-2.14)	78.4(+/-1.67)	77.23(+/-3.23)	79.51(+/-2.54)
shuttle	98.05(+/-0.5)	98.42(+/-0.8)	97.85(+/-0.9)	98.1(+/-0.5)
Case E: Combiner strategy based on the simple attribute voting				
customer	69.1(+/-1.43)	73.43(+/-1.01)	75.35(+/-1.23)	77.2(+/-0.74)
adult	88.9(+/-1.98)	87.45(+/-1.21)	91.13(+/-1.58)	91.58(+/-1.1)
waveform	80.12(+/-1.7)	82.46(+/-1.3)	85.04(+/-2.1)	83.84(+/-1.65)
shuttle	98.2(+/-0.5)	98.56(+/-0.5)	98.8(+/-0.3)	99.6(+/-0.2)
Case F: Combiner strategy based on the hybrid attribute voting				
customer	71.02(+/-1.2)	74.53(+/-0.97)	76.85(+/-1.09)	78.15(+/-0.81)
adult	88.24(+/-0.67)	89.47(+/-0.76)	91.87(+/-0.55)	92.48(+/-0.51)
waveform	80.67(+/-0.75)	82.15(+/-0.96)	83.45(+/-0.43)	82.04(+/-1.3)
shuttle	98.11(+/-1.1)	798.5(+/-0.8)	99.35(+/-0.7)	99.25(+/-0.7)
Case G: The AddBoost algorithm applied after the combiner strategy like in case F				
customer	72.13(+/-0.32)	74.84(+/-0.7)	77.21(+/-1.01)	78.32(+/-0.94)
adult	88.67(+/-0.54)	90.02(+/-0.57)	92.6(+/-0.87)	91.34(+/-0.7)
waveform	82.45(+/-0.72)	83.62(+/-0.9)	84.43(+/-0.63)	85(+/-0.62)
shuttle	98.9(+/-0.7)	99.32(+/-0.5)	99.5(+/-0.2)	99.1(+/-0.1)

Source: own computations.

Table 22. Average accuracy (%) of C 4.5 results obtained over the distributed datasets (cases H-J)

Problem	Number of distributed data sources			
	2	3	4	5
Case H: Static attribute selection strategy				
customer	70.12(+/-1.28)	71.22(+/-1.46)	72.1(+/-1.1)	73.21(+/-0.7)
adult	86(+/-1.02)	85.3(+/-1.15)	87.1(+/-0.9)	87(+/-0.9)
waveform	76.12(+/-0.94)	78.2(+/-0.91)	78.32(+/-1)	80.37(+/-1.1)
shuttle	97.54(+/-1.2)	98.3(+/-1.1)	99.1(+/-1)	98.41(+/-1.1)
Case I: Dynamic attribute selection strategy				
customer	71.14(+/-0.38)	72.12(+/-1.1)	73.5(+/-1.3)	74.21(+/-1.3)
adult	87(+/-0.9)	87.1(+/-1.4)	88.56(+/-1.1)	89.15(+/-1.3)
waveform	78.43(+/-1.24)	79.4(+/-1.2)	82.08(+/-0.78)	81.92(+/-1.4)
shuttle	98.43(+/-0.7)	98.5(+/-0.5)	99.5(+/-0.3)	99.5(+/-0.2)
Case J: The AddBoost algorithm applied after the dynamic attribute selection strategy like in case I				
customer	73.16(+/-0.12)	74.14(+/-0.41)	78.51(+/-0.61)	78.32(+/-0.91)
adult	89.62(+/-0.35)	89.62(+/-0.32)	91.92(+/-0.36)	91.1(+/-0.54)
waveform	82.35(+/-0.5)	84.01(+/-0.4)	84.03(+/-0.37)	84.57(+/-0.72)
shuttle	98.73(+/-0.7)	99.5(+/-0.3)	99.9(+/-0.05)	99.6(+/-0.2)

Source: own computations.

To reinforce our conclusions, the experiment results, shown in Tables 21- 22, have been used to perform the one-way analysis of variance (ANOVA), where the following null hypothesis was formulated: the choice of the general strategy, when the data reduction in two dimensions is carried-out, does not influence the classifier performance. It was established, at 5% significance level, that our hypothesis should be rejected in all cases. In addition, the Tukey test has confirmed that in case of attribute selection at the local level there are no statistical differences between mean performance of the attribute selection strategies.

The computation experiment aimed at evaluation of the agent-based algorithm for the distributed learning. It has been assumed that the data reduction is carried-out in two dimensions. Hence, a strategy for constructing the combiner classifier at the global level and a strategy for coordinating attribute selection at the local level are needed. Several strategies of both types have been experimentally evaluated. Experiment results allow to draw the following conclusions:

- Quality of the distributed learning outcome depends on the strategy used for the construction of the combiner classifier.
- Quality of the distributed learning outcome depends also on the approach used to obtain the homogenous prototypes at the global level of distributed learning.
- The collaboration between agents working locally on the data reduction process can improve the distributed learning quality and assure a homogenous set of prototypes obtained from local sites.

- The scope of the reported experiment does not allow to conclude that some of the investigated strategies always outperform the others. However, hybrid attribute voting at the global level or dynamic attribute selection strategy, possibly combined with the AdaBoost algorithm should be seriously considered as a potential winning strategy for solving the distributed learning problems.

7   Conclusions

Learning from multi-databases is considered to be a more complex and difficult task than learning from a single database, and one of the main challenges is to create systems that learn automatically from distributed datasets. Explosion of the quantity of information in databases, technological developments in the field of ICT and especially advance of Internet technologies, together with the ever present quest for achieving a competitive advantage, have recently motivated numerous research teams to seek more effective methods suitable for learning from distributed data. The presented work proposes a novel approach to the supervised distributed machine learning.

The main contribution of the dissertation is to propose a set of procedures for data reduction through simultaneous instance and attribute selection with the cluster-based prototype selection followed by designing and implementing an agent-based framework for learning classifiers from the reduced and distributed data using the paradigms of the asynchronous team of agents and population-based optimization. The approach extends the existing repertoire of methods applicable in the field of the distributed machine learning. According to the author the above supports claiming that main objectives of the research have been attained.

Reaching main objectives required solving several partial problems and reaching partial objectives. Among these the following can be seen as the author's original contribution:

- Analyzing data reduction approaches based on similarity measure.
- Introducing a novel similarity measure together with the family of instance reduction algorithms (IRA family) based on it.
- Incorporating adaptation mechanisms into the learning process by integrating data reduction with learning classifiers and proposing different integration schemes.
- Proposing a family of the agent-based population learning algorithms for data reduction, where the learning process is executed by the asynchronous team of agents, and where the prototype instances are selected from clusters through population-based search and where the population-based approach is also used as a tool to attribute selection. The main feature of the proposed algorithms is their capability to integrate data reduction with learning classifier process.

- Proposing a new algorithm for the multi-objective data reduction problem.
- Analyzing computational complexity of the proposed algorithms.
- Developing an agent-based framework for learning classifiers from the reduced and distributed data and investigating its properties. The main feature of the proposed approach is managing and coordinating the learning process and the data reduction through interactions and collaboration between agents.
- Evaluating different strategies for the prototype selection in the distributed learning.
- Evaluating experimentally different clustering procedures within an agent-based framework and their influence on the accuracy of the respective classifiers.
- Evaluating experimentally different strategies for integration of data reduction with classifier learning.
- Evaluating experimentally the performance of the agent-based algorithms in solving the problem of multi-objective data reduction.
- Evaluating experimentally agent-based algorithms for learning classifiers from the distributed and reduced data considering different data reduction approaches and their influence on the quality of the global classifier induced from the set of prototypes selected at each of the separate distributed sites.

An extensive computational experiment showed that the data reduction based on clustering is an effective tool assuring high quality of the machine classification. The proposed algorithm based on the clustering method using similarity coefficient approach produces, on average, better results than other cluster-based data reduction approaches. It also outperformed in terms of the classification accuracy other approaches based on similarity measures when tested on the identical benchmark datasets.

Important finding obtained through analyzing the computational experiment results is that integrating the process of instance and attribute selection with the classifier constriction phase supports construction of an effective and dependable classification tool. It has been also confirmed that the choice of the integration scheme is a decisive factor influencing the performance of the integrated classifier. Moreover, choosing the right scheme is more important from the point of view of the classifier quality than the choice of the machine learning algorithm used. The computational experiment results confirmed also that an agent and a population-based approach is a suitable tool allowing to obtain a good approximation of the Pareto-optimal front in case of the multi-objective data reduction problem.

Computational experiments involving various A-Teams have shown that it is possible to achieve a synergetic effect from the cooperation of the different types of the optimization agents. Experiments have also shown that such synergetic effect produces good or even very good results while solving difficult data reduction problems.

In view of the above findings it can be finally concluded that the main thesis of the dissertation holds true. The proposed method of solving the distributed learning problem based on data clustering and data reduction schemes integrated with a classifier learning through the population-based family of algorithms, implemented within the A-Team architecture, is an effective and competitive approach to the distributed learning.

The presented results allow to indicate the directions of the further research. The data reduction task has been formulated here in generic terms with instance and feature (attribute) selection only. The approach does not support the prototype extraction as an alternative measure within the data reduction process. As it has been pointed out in Section 4, the prototype extraction may include the process of feature construction and the aim of such process is to find out or construct a new subset of prototypes representing the original training set. Possible extensions include proposing other types of procedures, implemented within an optimizing agents framework, for the prototype extraction. Another extension of the proposed approach is implementing and verifying different strategies for data reduction, where the prototype selection and prototype extraction procedures are integrated. The future research should also examine the influence of the different agent selection scenarios on the learning quality. The future experiments should answer the question whether the selection of optimizing agents and composition of their mix have an impact on efficiency of the agent-based data reduction approach.

The author also believes that the proposed agents' cooperation scheme gives a possibility to develop and implement more advanced strategies for choosing the appropriate winning attribute set shared by all the distributed sites. New strategies based on the fuzzy set theory are currently studied by the author. Evaluating other combiner classifier strategies in terms of classification accuracy is also planned.

Another direction of research will focus on extending the computation experiment to other learning algorithms and to investigate more closely the computational efficiency implications of the investigated approaches to data reduction. This direction allows for extending, modification and theoretical analysis of the proposed cluster-based instance selection procedure based on the similarity coefficient values.

An interesting direction for further research is to establish using formal methods, a theoretical framework for agent-based, multiple-objective optimization of prototype selection including instance and attribute selection and/or extraction. Also, more user friendly tools designed for solving practical multiple objective prototype selection problems should be considered.

The interactive character of the proposed agent-based approach is also well-suitable to tackle classifiers learning from data that change with time. The agent-based approach will be extended to enable solving learning classifiers from the streaming data.

In the future, the cooperative variants of the distributed reduction methods can be developed. They seem worth investigating with a view to further increase the quality of the distributed learning. The additional research could be also undertaken with respect to methods of effectively tuning the population-based search to improve its convergence.

Acknowledgements

The work on this chapter has been partially supported by the Polish Ministry of Science and Higher Education with grant no. N N519 318835 for years 2008-2010 and with grant no. N N519 576438 for years 2010-2013.

References

1. Aha, D.W.: Lazy Learning. Kluwer Academic Publishers, Norwell (1997)
2. Aha, D.W., Kibler, D., Albert, M.K.: Instance-based Learning Algorithms. Machine Learning 6, 37–66 (1991)
3. Aksela, M.: Adaptive Combinations of Classifiers with Application to On-line Handwritten Character Recognition. Department of Computer Science and Engineering. Helsinki University of Technology, Helsinki (2007)
4. Almuallim, H., Dietterich, T.G.: Learning with Many Irrelevant Features. In: Proceedings of Ninth National Conference on Artificial Intelligence, vol. 2, pp. 547–552. AAAI Press, Anaheim (1991)
5. Albashiri, K.A., Coenen, F., Leng, P.: EMADS: An Extendible Multi-agent Data Miner. Knowledge-Based Systems 22, 523–528 (2009)
6. Andrews, N.O., Fox, E.A.: Clustering for Data Reduction: A Divide and Conquer Approach. Technical Report TR-07-36, Computer Science, Virginia Tech. (2007)
7. Asuncion, A., Newman, D.J.: UCI Machine Learning Repository. University of California, School of Information and Computer Science, Irvine, CA (2007), http://www.ics.uci.edu/~mlearn/MLRepository.html (accessed June 24, 2009)
8. Aydin, M.E., Fogarty, T.C.: Teams of Autonomous Agents for Job-shop Scheduling Problems: An Experimental Study. Journal of Intelligent Manufacturing 15(4), 455–462 (2004)
9. Baik, S., Bala, J.: A Decision Tree Algorithm for Distributed Data Mining: Towards Network Intrusion Detection. In: Laganá, A., Gavrilova, M.L., Kumar, V., Mun, Y., Tan, C.J.K., Gervasi, O. (eds.) ICCSA 2004. LNCS, vol. 3046, pp. 206–212. Springer, Heidelberg (2004)
10. Bailey, S., Grossman, R., Sivakumar, H., Turinsky, A.: Papyrus: A System for Data Mining over Local and Wide Area Clusters and Super-clusters. In: Proceedings of ACM/IEEE SC Conference, SC 1999 (1999)
11. Barbucha, D., Czarnowski, I., Jędrzejowicz, P., Ratajczak, E., Wierzbowska, I.: JADE-Based A-Team as a Tool for Implementing Population-based Algorithms. In: Chen, Y., Abraham, A. (eds.) Intelligent Systems Design and Applications, Jinan Shandong, China, pp. 144–149. IEEE, Los Alamitos (2006)
12. Barbucha, D., Czarnowski, I., Jędrzejowicz, P., Ratajczak-Ropel, E., Wierzbowska, I.: e-JABAT - An Implementation of the Web-based A-Team. In: Nguyen, N.T., Jain, L.C. (eds.) Intelligence Agents in the Evolution of Web and Applications. Studies in Computational Intelligence, vol. 167, pp. 57–86. Springer, Heidelberg (2009)
13. Barbucha, D., Czarnowski, I., Jędrzejowicz, P., Ratajczak-Ropel, E., Wierzbowska, I.: Influence of the Working Strategy on A-Team Performance. In: Szczerbicki, E., Nguyen, N.T. (eds.) Smart Information and Knowledge Management. Studies in Computational Intelligence, vol. 260, pp. 83–102. Springer, Heidelberg (2010)

14. Barbucha, D., Czarnowski, I., Jędrzejowicz, P., Ratajczak-Ropel, E., Wierzbowska, I.: JABAT Middleware as a Tool for Solving Optimization Problems. In: Nguyen, N.T., Kowalczyk, R. (eds.) Transactions on CCI II. LNCS, vol. 6450, pp. 181–195. Springer, Heidelberg (2010)
15. Battiti, R., Coalla, A.M.: Democracy in Neural Nets: Voting Schemes for Classification. Neural Network 7(4), 691–707 (1994)
16. Bauer, E., Kohavi, R.: An Empirical Comparison of Voting Classification Algorithhms: Bagging, Boosting and Variants. Machine Learning 36(1-2), 691–707 (1994)
17. Bazan, J., Nguyen, H.S., Nguyen, S.H., Synak, P., Wroblewski, J.: Rough Set Algorithms in Classification Problem. In: Polkowski, L., Tsumoto, S., Lin, T.Y. (eds.) Rough Set Methods and Applications, pp. 49–88. Physica-Verlag, Heidelberg (2000)
18. Bernado-Mansilla, E., Llora, X., Traus, I.: Multi-objective Learning Classifier Systems. In: Jin, Y. (ed.) Multi-Objective Machine Learning. Studies in Computational Intelligence, vol. 16, pp. 261–290. Springer, Heidelberg (2006)
19. Baerentzen, L., Avila, P., Talukdar, S.: Learning Network Designs for Asynchronous Teams. In: Boman, M., Van de Velde, W. (eds.) MAAMAW 1997. LNCS, vol. 1237, pp. 177–196. Springer, Heidelberg (1997)
20. Beck, J.R., Garcia, M.E., Zhong, M.: A Backward Adjusting Strategy for the C4.5 Decision Tree Classifier. Technical Report TR-2007-01. The AMALTHEA REU Program (2007)
21. Bezdek, J.C., Kuncheva, L.I.: Nearest Prototype Classifier Design: An Experimental Study. International Journal of Intelligence Systems 16(2), 1445–1473 (2000)
22. Bhanu, B., Peng, J.: Adaptive Integration Image Segmentation and Object Recognition. IEEE Trans. on Systems, Man and Cybernetics 30(4), 427–444 (2000)
23. Biesiada, J., Duch, W.: Feature Selection for High-Dimensional Data: A Pearson Redundancy Based Filter. Advances in Soft Computing 45, 242–249 (2008)
24. Blachnik, M., Duch, W., Kachel, A., Biesiada, J.: Feature Selection for High-Dimensional Data: A Kolmogorov-Smirnov Class Correlation-Based Filter. In: Proceedings of Symposium on Methods of Artificial Intelligence, Gliwice, Poland, Method of Artificial Intelligence, pp. 33–40 (2009)
25. Blum, A.L., Langley, P.: Selection of Relevant Features and Examples in Machine Learning. Artificial Intelligence 97(1-2), 245–271 (1997)
26. Błażewicz, J.: Złożoność obliczeniowa problemów kombinatorycznych. WNT, Warszawa (1988) (in Polish)
27. Bradley, P.S., Fayyad, U.M.: Refining Initial Points for K-Means Clustering. In: Proceedings of the Fifteenth International Conference on Machine Learning, pp. 91–99 (1998)
28. Breiman, L., Friedman, J.H., Olshen, R.A., Stone, C.J.: Classification and Regression Trees. Wadsworth & Brooks/Cole Advanced Books & Software, Monterey, CA (1984)
29. Brodley, C.E., Friedl, M.A.: Identifying Mislabeled Training Data. Journal of Artificial Intelligence Research 11, 131–167 (1999)
30. Burges, C.J.C.: A Tutorial on Support Vector Machines for Pattern Recognition. Data Mining and Knowledge Discovery 2, 121–167 (1998)
31. Bull, L. (ed.): Learning Classifier Systems: A Brief Introduction, Applications of Learning Classifier Systems. Studies in Fuzziness and Soft Computing. Springer, Heidelberg (2004)
32. Cao, L. (ed.): Agent Data Mining and Multi-agent Integration. Springer, Heidelberg (2009)

33. Cano, J.R., Herrera, F., Lozano, M.: Using Evolutionary Algorithms as Instance Selection for Data Reduction in KDD: An Experimental Study. IEEE Transaction on Evolutionary Computation 7(6), 561–575 (2003)
34. Cano, J.R., Herrera, F., Lozano, M.: On the Combination of Evolutionary Algorithms and Stratified Strategies for Training Set Selection in Data Mining. Applied Soft Computing 6, 323–332 (2004)
35. Caragea, D., Silvescu, A., Honavar, V.: Agents That Learn from Distributed Dynamic Data Sources. In: ECML 2000/Agents 2000 Workshop on Learning Agents, Barcelona, Spain (2000)
36. Caragea, D., Silvescu, A., Honavar, V.: A Framework for Learning from Distributed Data Using Sufficient Statistics and its Application to Learning Decision Trees. International Journal of Hybrid Intelligent Systems 1(1-2), 80–89 (2003)
37. Caragea, D.: Learning Classifiers from Distributed, Semantically Heterogeneous, Autonomous Data Sources. Ph.D. Thesis, Iowa State University, Ames, Iowa (2004)
38. Cichosz, P.: Systemy uczące się. Wydawnictwo Naukowo-Techniczne, Warszawa (2000) (in Polish)
39. Chawla, N., Eschrich, S., Hall, L.O.: Creating Ensembles of Classifiers. In: ICDM 2001, USA, pp. 580–581 (2001)
40. Chawla, N., Moore, T.E., Hall, L.O., Bowyer, K.W., Kegelmeyer, W.P., Springer, C.: Distributed Learning with Bagging-like Performance. Pattern Recognition Letters 24(1-3), 455–471 (2003)
41. Cost, S., Salzberg, S.: A Weighted Nearest Neighbor Algorithm for Learning with Symbolic Features. Machine Learning 10, 57–78 (1993)
42. Castro, J.: Modifications of the Fuzzy ARTMAP Algorithm for Distributed Learning in Large Data Sets. Ph.D. Thesis, University of Central Floryda, Orlando, Florida (2004)
43. Clark, P., Niblett, T.: The CN2 Induction Algorithm. Machine Learning 3, 261–283 (1989)
44. Chan, P.K., Stolfo, S.J.: Experiments on Multistrategy Learning by Meta-Learning. In: Second International Conference on Information and Knowledge Management, pp. 31–45 (1993)
45. Chang, C.L.: Finding Prototypes for Nearest Neighbor Classifier. IEEE Transactions on Computers 23(11), 1179–1184 (1974)
46. Chen, J.H., Chen, H.M., Ho, S.Y.: Design of Nearest Neighbor Classifiers Using an Intelligent Multi-objective Evolutionary Algorithm. In: Zhang, C., Guesgen, H. W., Yeap, W.-K. (eds.) PRICAI 2004. LNCS (LNAI), vol. 3157, pp. 262–271. Springer, Heidelberg (2004)
47. Craig, I.: Blackboard Systems. Alex Publishing Corporation, Norwood (1995)
48. Czarnowski, I.: Zastosowanie algorytmów uczenia populacji do uczenia sieci neuronowych. Ph.D. Thesis, Poznań University of Technology, Poznań (2004) (in Polish)
49. Czarnowski, I.: Prototype Selection Algorithms for Distributed Learning. Pattern Recognition 43(6), 2292–2300 (2010)
50. Czarnowski, I.: Cluster-based Instance Selection for Machine Classification. Knowledge and Information Systems (2010), doi:10.1007/s10115-010-0375-z
51. Czarnowski, I., Jędrzejowicz, P.: An Approach to Instance Reduction in Supervised Learning. In: Coenen, F. (ed.) Research and Development in Intelligent Systems XX, pp. 267–282. Springer, London (2004)

52. Czarnowski, I., Jędrzejowicz, P.: Predicting Glass Manufacturing Quality Using a Hybrid Population Learning and Artificial Neural Network Approach. In: Trappl, R. (ed.) EMCSR 2004, vol. 2, pp. 497–502 (2004)
53. Czarnowski, I., Jędrzejowicz, P.: An agent-based PLA for the cascade correlation learning architecture. In: Duch, W., Kacprzyk, J., Oja, E., Zadrożny, S. (eds.) ICANN 2005. LNCS, vol. 3697, pp. 197–202. Springer, Heidelberg (2005)
54. Czarnowski, I., Jędrzejowicz, P.: Family of Instance Reduction Algorithms Versus Other Approaches. In: Kłopotek, M.A., et al. (eds.) Intelligent Information Processing and Web Mining, Proccedings of the International IIS:IIPWM 2005 Conference, Advances in Soft Computing, pp. 23–30. Springer, Heidelberg (2005)
55. Czarnowski, I., Jędrzejowicz, P.: An Agent-based Approach to ANN Training. Knowledge-Based Systems 19, 304–308 (2006)
56. Czarnowski, I., Jędrzejowicz, P.: An Agent-based Approach to the Multiple-objective Selection of Reference Vectors. In: Perner, P. (ed.) MLDM 2007. LNCS (LNAI), vol. 4571, pp. 117–130. Springer, Heidelberg (2007)
57. Czarnowski, I., Jędrzejowicz, P.: A Framework for Adaptive and Integrated Classification. In: Rutkowski, L., Tadeusiewicz, R., Zadeh, L.A., Zurada, J.M. (eds.) ICAISC 2008. LNCS (LNAI), vol. 5097, pp. 522–532. Springer, Heidelberg (2008)
58. Czarnowski, I., Jędrzejowicz, P.: Data Reduction Algorithm for Machine Learning and Data Mining. In: Nguyen, N.T., Borzemski, L., Grzech, A., Ali, M. (eds.) IEA/AIE 2008. LNCS (LNAI), vol. 5027, pp. 276–285. Springer, Heidelberg (2008)
59. Czarnowski, I., Jędrzejowicz, P., Wierzbowska, I.: An A-Team Approach to Learning Classifiers from Distributed Data Sources. International Journal of Intelligence Information and Database Systems 3(4) (2009)
60. Czarnowski, I., Jędrzejowicz, P., Wierzbowska, I.: A-Team Middleware on a Cluster. In: Håkansson, A., Nguyen, N.T., Hartung, R.L., Howlett, R.J., Jain, L.C. (eds.) KES-AMSTA 2009. LNCS (LNAI), vol. 5559, pp. 764–772. Springer, Heidelberg (2009)
61. Czarnowski, I., Jędrzejowicz, P.: An Approach to Data Reduction and Integrated Machine Classification. New Generation Computing 28, 21–40 (2010)
62. Czarnowski, I., Jędrzejowicz, P.: An Agent-based Framework for Distributed Learning. Engineering Applications of Artificial Intelligence 24, 93–102 (2011), doi:10.1016/j.engappai.2010.07.003
63. Czarnowski, I., Jędrzejowicz, P.: Implementation and Performance Evaluation of the Agent-Based Algorithm for ANN Training. KES Knowledge-Based and Intelligent Engineering Systems 14(1), 1–10 (2010)
64. d'Amato, C.: Similarity-based Learning Methods for the Semantic Web. Ph.D. Thesis, University of Bari, Italy (2007)
65. Dash, D., Cooper, G.F.: Model Aggregating for Prediction with Discrete Bayesian networks. Journal of Machine Learning Research 5, 1177–1203 (2001)
66. Dash, M., Liu, H.: Feature Selection for Classification. Intelligence Data Analysis 1(3), 131–156 (1997)
67. Dam, H.H., Rojanavasu, P., Abbass, H.A., Lokan, C.: Distributed Learning Classifier Systems. In: Bull, L., Ester, G.M., Homes, J. (eds.) Learning Classifier Systems in Data Mining. Studies in Computational Intelligence (SCI), vol. 125, pp. 69–91. Springer, Heidelberg (2008)
68. Dehuri, S., Patnaik, S., Ghosh, A., Mall, R.: Application of Elitist Multi-objective Genetic Algorithm for Classification Rule Generation. Applied Soft Computing 8(1), 477–487 (2008)

69. Deisy, C., Subbulakshmi, B., Baskar, S., Ramaraj, N.: Efficient Dimensionality Reduction Approaches for Feature Selection. In: Proceeding of the International Conference on Computational Intelligence and Multimedia Applications, vol. 2, pp. 121–127 (2007)

70. Diertterich, T.G., Bakiri, G.: Solving Multiclass Learning Problems via Error-correcting Output Codes. Journal of Artificial Intelligence Research 2, 263–286 (1995)

71. Dorigo, M., Maniezzo, V., Colorni, A.: The Ant System: Optimization by a Colony of Cooperating Agents. IEEE Transactions on Systems, Man, and Cybernetics-Part B 26(1), 29–41 (1996)

72. Drozdz, K., Kwasnicka, H.: Feature Set Reduction by Evolutionary Selection and Construction. In: Jędrzejowicz, P., et al. (eds.) KES-AMSTA 2010. LNCS, vol. 6071, pp. 140–149. Springer, Heidelberg (2010)

73. Duangsoithong, R., Windeatt, T.: Relevance and Redundancy Analysis for Ensemble Classifiers. In: Perner, P. (ed.) MLDM 2009. LNCS (LNAI), vol. 5632, pp. 206–220. Springer, Heidelberg (2009)

74. Duch, W.: Results - Comparison of Classification, Nicolaus Copernicus University, http://www.is.umk.pl/projects/datasets.html (accessed June 20, 2010)

75. Duch, W., Blachnik, M., Wieczorek, T.: Probabilistic Distance Measures for Prototype-based Rules. In: Proceeding of the 12th International Conference on Neural Information Processing, pp. 445–450 (2005)

76. Duda, R.O., Hart, P.E., Stork, D.G.: Unsupervised Learning and Clustering, 2nd edn. Pattern Classification. Wiley, New York (2001)

77. Edward, P., Davies, W.: A Heterogeneous Multi-agent Learning System. In: Deen, S.M. (ed.) Special Internet Group on Cooperating Knowledge Based Systems, pp. 163–184 (1993)

78. Eschrich, S., Ke, J., Hall, L.O., Goldgof, D.B.: Fast Accurate Fuzzy Clustering through Data Reduction. IEEE Transactions on Fuzzy Systems 11(2), 262–270 (2003)

79. EL-Manzalawy, Y., Honavar, V.: WLSVM: Integrating LibSVM into Weka Environment (2005), http://www.cs.iastate.edu/~yasser/wlsvm (accessed January 20, 2008)

80. Frawley, W.J., Piatetsky-Shapiro, G., Matheus, C.: Knowledge Discovery in Databases - An Overview. In: Piatetsky-Shapiro, G., Matheus, C. (eds.) Knowledge Discovery in Databases. AAAI/MIT Press (1991)

81. Friedman, M.: The Use of Ranks to Avoid the Assumption of Normality Implicit in the Analysis of Variance. Journal of the American Statistical Association 32, 675–701 (1937)

82. Gallant, S.I.: Perceptron-based Learning Algorithms. IEEE Transactions on Neural Networks 1(2), 179–191 (1990)

83. Gatnar, E.: Podejście wielomodelowe w zagadnieniach dyskryminacji i regresji. Wydawnictwo Naukowo Techniczne PWN, Warszawa (2008) (in Polish)

84. Glover, F.: Tabu Search. Part I and II, ORSA Journal of Computing 1(3) (1990)

85. Goldberg, D.E.: Genetic Algorithms in Search, Optimization, and Machine Learning. Addison-Wesley, Reading (1989)

86. Gordon, D.F., Desjardins, M.: Evaluation and Selection of Biases in Machine Learning. Machine Learning 20, 5–22 (1995)

87. Giannella, C., Liu, K., Olsen, T., Kargupta, H.: Communication Efficient Construction of Decision Trees Over Heterogeneously Distributed Data. In: Fourth IEEE International Conference on Data Mining, pp. 67–74 (2004)

88. Guo, Y., Rueger, S.M., Sutiwaraphun, J., Forbes-Millott, J.: Meta-leraning for Parallel Data Mining. In: Proceedings of the Seventh Parallel Computing Workshop, pp. 1–2 (1997)

89. Guo, G., Wang, H., Bell, D., Bi, Y., Greer, K.: KNN Model-based Approach in Classification. In: Goos, G., Hartmanis, J., van Leeuwen, J. (eds.) CoopIS 2003, DOA 2003, and ODBASE 2003. LNCS, vol. 2888, pp. 986–996. Springer, Heidelberg (2003)

90. Guo, Y., Muller, J.: Multiagent Collaborative Learning for Distributed Business Systems. In: Proceedings of the Third International Join Conference on Autonomous Agents and Multiagent Systems (2004)

91. Gutkin, M., Shamir, R., Dror, G.: SlimPLS: A Method for Feature Selection in Gene Expression-Based Disease Classification. PLoS ONE 4(7), e6416 (2009), doi:10.1371/journal.pone.0006416

92. Grudziński, K., Duch, W.: SBL-PM: Simple Algorithm for Selection of Reference Instances in Similarity Based Methods. In: Proceedings of the Intelligence Systems, Bystra, Poland, pp. 99–107 (2000)

93. Gu, B., Hu, F., Liu, H.: Sampling: Knowing Whole from its Part. In: Liu, H., Motoda, H. (eds.) Instance Selection and Construction for Data Mining, pp. 21–37. Kluwer Academic Publishers, Dordrecht (2001)

94. Hall, L., Chawla, N.V., Bowyer, K.W.: Decision Tree Learning on Very Large Data Sets. In: IEEE SMC Conference, San Diego, California, pp. 2579–2584 (1998)

95. Hamo, Y., Markovitch, S.: The COMPSET Algorithm for Subset Selection. In: Proceedings of The Nineteenth International Joint Conference for Artificial Intelligence, Edinburgh, Scotland, pp. 728–733 (2005)

96. Han, J., Kamber, M.: Data Mining. Concepts and Techniques. Academic Press, San Diego (2001)

97. Hart, P.E.: The Condensed Nearest Neighbour Rule. IEEE Transactions on Information Theory 14, 515–516 (1968)

98. He, H., Garcia, E.A.: Learning from Imbalanced Data. IEEE Transactions on Knowledge and Data Engineering 21(9), 1263–1284 (2009)

99. Ho, T.K.: The Random Subspace Method for Constructing Decision Forests. IEEE Transaction on PAMI 19(8), 832–844 (1998)

100. Ho, T.K.: Data Complexity Analysis for Classifier Combination. In: Kittler, J., Roli, F. (eds.) MCS 2001. LNCS, vol. 2096, pp. 53–67. Springer, Heidelberg (2001)

101. Hu, K., Lu, Y., Shi, C.: Feature Ranking in Rough Sets. Artificial Intelligence Communications 16, 41–50 (2003)

102. Holland, J.H. (ed.): Adaptation, In Rosen & Snell. Progress in Theoretical Biology, vol. 4. Plenum, New York (1976)

103. Howlett, R.J., Jain, L.C. (eds.): Radial Basis Function Networks 1: Recent Developments in Theory and Applications. Studies in Fuzziness and Soft Computing. Physica-Verlag, Heidelberg (2001)

104. Ishibuchi, H., Nakashima, T., Nii, H.: Learning of Neural Networks with GA-based Instance Selection. In: Proceedings of the IFSA World Congress and 20th NAFIPS International Conference, vol. 4, pp. 2102–2107 (2001)

105. Jaszkiewicz, A.: Multiple Objective Metaheuristic Algorithms for Combinational Optimization. Habilitation Thesis 360, Poznań University of Technology, Poznań (2001)

106. Jankowski, N., Grochowski, M.: Instances Selection Algorithms in the Conjunction with LVQ. In: Hamza, M.H. (ed.) Artificial Intelligence and Applications, pp. 209–453. ACTA Press, Innsbruck (2005)

107. Jankowski, N., Grąbczewski, K.: Universal Meta-learning Architecture and Algorithms. In: Duch, W., Grąbczewski, K., Jankowski, N. (eds.) Meta-learning in Computational Intelligence. Studies in Computational Intelligence. Springer, Heidelberg (2009)

108. Jensen, F.V.: Bayesian Networks and Decision Graphs. Springer, Heidelberg (2001)

109. Jelonek, J., Stefanowski, J.: Feature Selection in the n2-classifier Applied for Multiclass Problems. In: Burczyński, T., Cholewa, W., Moczulski (eds.) AI-METH 2002 - Symposium on Methods of Artificial Intelligence, Gliwice, Poland, pp. 197–200 (2002)

110. Jędrzejowicz, P.: Social Learning Algorithm as a Tool for Solving Some Difficult Scheduling Problems. Foundation of Computing and Decision Sciences 24, 51–66 (1999)

111. Jędrzejowicz, P.: A-Teams and their Applications. In: Nguyen, N.T., Kowalczyk, R., Chen, S.-M. (eds.) ICCCI 2009. LNCS(LNAI), vol. 5796, pp. 36–50. Springer, Heidelberg (2009)

112. Jędrzejowicz, P., Wierzbowska, I.: JADE-Based A-Team Environment. In: Alexandrov, V.N., van Albada, G.D., Sloot, P.M.A., Dongarra, J. (eds.) ICCS 2006. LNCS, vol. 3993, pp. 719–726. Springer, Heidelberg (2006)

113. Jędrzejowicz, J., Jędrzejowicz, P.: Cellular GEP-Induced Classifiers. In: Pan, J.-S., Chen, S.-M., Nguyen, N.T. (eds.) ICCCI 2010. LNCS (LNAI), vol. 6421, pp. 343–352. Springer, Heidelberg (2010)

114. Jin, R., Agraval, G.: Communication and Memory Efficient Parallel Decision Tree Construction. In: Third SIAM International Conference on Data Mining, San Francisco, CA (2003)

115. Kabir, M. M., Shahjahan, M., Murase, K.: An Efficient Feature Selection Using Ant Colony Optimization Algorithm. In: Leung, C.S., Lee, M., Chan, J.H. (eds.) ICONIP 2009. LNCS, vol. 5864, pp. 242–252. Springer, Heidelberg (2009)

116. Kargupta, H., Park, B.H., Hershberger, D., Johnson, E.: Collective Data Mining: A New Perspective Toward Distributed Data Analysis. In: Kargupta, H., Chan, P. (eds.) Accepted in the Advances in Distributed Data Mining. AAAI/MIT Press (1999)

117. Kennedy, J., Eberhart, R.: Particle Swarm Optimization. In: Proceedings of IEEE International Conference on Neural Networks, vol. IV, pp. 1942–1948 (1995)

118. Kim, S.W., Oommen, B.J.: A Brief Taxonomy and Ranking of Creative Prototype Reduction Schemes. Pattern Analysis Application 6, 232–244 (2003)

119. Kim, S.G., Woo, K.D., Bala, J., Baik, S.W.: Distributed Data Mining System Based on Multi-agent Communication Mechanism. In: Jedrzejowicz, P., Nguyen, N.T., Howlet, R.J., Jain, L.C. (eds.) KES-AMSTA 2010. LNCS (LNAI), vol. 6071, pp. 100–109. Springer, Heidelberg (2010)

120. Kittler, J.: Feature Selection Algorithms. In: Chen, C.H. (ed.)Pattern Recognition and Signal Processing, pp. 41–60 (1978)

121. Kittler, J., Hatef, M., Duin, R.P.W., Matas, J.: On Combining Classifiers. IEEE Transaction on Pattern Analysis and Machine Intelligence 20(3), 226–238 (1998)

122. Kira, K., Rendell, L.A.: A Practical Approach to Feature Selection. In: Sleeman, D., Edwards, J. (eds.) Proceedings on International Conference on Machine Learning, Italy, pp. 249–256 (1992)

123. Klinkenberg, R.: Learning Drifting Concepts: Example Selection vs. Example Weighting, Intelligent Data Analysis. Incremental Learning Systems Capable of Dealing with Concept Drift 8(3), 281–300 (2004)

124. Kirkpatrick, S., Gelatt, C.D., Vecci, M.P.: Optimisation by Simulated Annealing. Science 220, 671–680 (1983)
125. Klusch, M., Lodi, S., Moro, G.L.: Agent-Based Distributed Data Mining: The KDEC Scheme. In: Klusch, M., Bergamaschi, S., Edwards, P., Petta, P. (eds.) Intelligent Information Agents. LNCS (LNAI), vol. 2586, pp. 104–122. Springer, Heidelberg (2003)
126. Kohavi, R.: A Study of Cross-validation and Bootstrap for Accuracy Estimation and Model Selection. In: Kaufmann, M. (ed.) Proceeding of the 14th International Join Conference on Artificial Intelligence, Montreal, Quebec, Canada, pp. 1137–1145 (1995)
127. Kohavi, R., John, G.H.: Wrappers for Feature Subset Selection. Artificial Intelligence 97(1-2), 273–324 (1997)
128. Kohonen, T.: Learning Vector Quantization for Pattern Recognition. Technical Report TKK-F-A601, Helsinki University of Technology, Espoo, Finland (1986)
129. Kotsiantis, S.B., Zaharakis, I.D., Pintelas, P.E.: Machine Learning: A Review of Classification and Combining Techniques. Artificial Intelligence Review 26(3), 159–190 (2006)
130. Kotsiantis, S.B., Kanellopoulos, D., Pintelas, P.E.: Data Preprocessing for Supervised Leaning. International Journal of Computer Science 1(2), 1306–4428 (2006)
131. Krawiec, K.: Evolutionary Feature Programing. Cooperative Learning for Knowledge Discovery and Computer Vision. Rozprawy 385. Wydawnictwo Politechniki Poznańskiej, Poznań (2004)
132. Krishnaswamy, S., Zaslavsky, A., Loke, S.W.: Techniques for Estimating the Computation and Communication Costs of Distributed Data Mining. In: Sloot, P.M.A., Tan, C.J.K., Dongarra, J., Hoekstra, A.G. (eds.) ICCS-ComputSci 2002. LNCS, vol. 2329, pp. 603–612. Springer, Heidelberg (2002)
133. Krzanowski, W.J.: Principles of Multivariate Analysis: A User's Perspective. Oxford University Press, Oxford (2000)
134. Kubat, M.: Tree Structures of Linear Threshold Units for the Classification of Numeric Examples. Cybernetics and Systems 26(5), 521–533 (1995)
135. Kuncheva, L.I., Bezdek, J.C.: Nearest Prototype Classification: Clustering, Genetic Algorithm or Random Search? IEEE Transaction on Systems, Man and Cybernetics 28(1), 160–164 (1998)
136. Kuncheva, L.I., Jain, L.C.: Nearest-Neighbor Classifier: Simultaneous Editing and Feature Selection. Pattern Recognition Letters 20, 1149–1156 (1999)
137. Kuri-Morales, A.F., Rodriguez-Erazo, F.: A Search Space Reduction Methodology for Data Mining in Large Databases. Engineering Applications of Artificial Intelligence 22(1), 57–65 (2009)
138. Lakshminarayan, K., Harp, S., Samad, T.: Imputation of Missing Data in Industrial Databases. Applied Intelligence 11, 259–275 (1999)
139. Lavesson, N., Davidsson, P.: Evaluating Learning Algorithms and Classifiers. International Journal of Intelligence Information and Database Systems 1(1), 37–52 (2007)
140. Lazarevic, A., Obradovic, Z.: The Distributed Boosting Algorithm. In: Proceedings of the ACM-SIG KDD Internetional Conference on Knowledge Discovery and Data Mining, San Francisco, pp. 311–316 (2001)
141. Lazarevic, A., Obradovic, Z.: Boosting Algorithms for Parallel and Distributed Learning. Distributed and Parallel Databases 11(2), 203–229 (2002)
142. Liu, H., Lu, H., Yao, J.: Identifying Relevant Databases for Multidatabase Mining. In: Proceeding of the Pacific-Asia Conference on Knowledge Discovery and Data Mining, pp. 210–221 (1998)

143. Liu, H., Motoda, H.: Instance Selection and Construction for Data Mining. Kluwer Academic Publishers, Dordrecht (2001)
144. MacQueen, J.B.: Some Methods for Classification and Analysis of Multivariate Observations. In: Proceeding of the 5th Berkeley Symposium on Mathematical Statistics and Probability 1, pp. 281–297. University of California Press, Berkeley (1967)
145. Manning, C.D., Raghavan, P., Schütze, H.: Introduction to Information Retrieval. Cambridge University Press, Cambridge (2008)
146. Marinescu, D.C., Boloni, L.: A Component-based Architecture for Problem Solving Environments. Mathematics and Computers in Simulation 54, 279–293 (2000)
147. Michalewicz, Z.: Genetic Algorithms + Data Structures = Evolution Programs. Springer, Berlin (1996)
148. Michalski, R., Mozetic, I., Hong, J., Lavrac, N.: The Multi-purpose Incremental Learning System AQ15 and its Testing Application to Three Medical Domains. In: Proceedings of the Fifth National Conference on Artificial Intelligence (AAAI 1986), MIT Press, Cambridge (1986)
149. Michalski, R.S., Tecuci, G.: Machine Learning. A Multistrategy Approach, vol. IV. Morgan Kaufmann, San Francisco (1994)
150. Min, F.: Novel Ensemble Learning Based on Multiple Section Distribution in Distributed Environment. Journal of Systems Engineering and Electronics 19(2), 377–380 (2008)
151. Mitchell, T.: Machine Learning. McGraw-Hill, New York (1997)
152. Mitchell, T.: Generalization as Search. Artificial Intelligence 18(2) (1982)
153. Morgan, J., Daugherty, R., Hilchie, A., Carey, B.: Sample Size and Modeling Accuracy of Decision Tree Based Data Mining Tools. Academy of Information and Management Science Journal 6(2), 71–99 (2003)
154. Muller, J.: The Right Agent (architecture) to do The Right Thing. In: Proceedings of the Fifth International Workshop on Agent Theories, Architecture, and Languages, Intelligent Agents V (1998)
155. Nanni, L., Lumini, A.: Particle Swarm Optimization for Prototype Reduction. Neurocomputing 72(4-6), 1092–1097 (2009)
156. Olariu, S., Zomaya, A.Y. (eds.): Handbook of Bioinspired Algorithms and Applications. Chapman & Hall, Boca Raton (2006)
157. Parunak, H.V.D.: Agents in Overalls: Experiences and Issues in the Development and Deployment of Industrial Agent-based Systems. International Journal of Cooperative Information Systems 9(3), 209–228 (2000)
158. Piatti, A.: Learning Under Prior Ignorance. Ph.D. Thesis, University of Logano (2006)
159. Platt, J.C.: Using Analytic QP and Sparseness to Speed Training of Support Vector Machines. In: Kearns, M.S., Solla, S.A., Cohn, D.A. (eds.) Advances in Neural Information Processing Systems. MIT Press, Cambridge (1999)
160. Predd, J.B., Kulkarni, S.R., Poor, H.V.: A Collaborative Training Algorithm for Distributed Learning. IEEE Transactions on Information Theory 55(4), 1856–1871 (2009)
161. Prodromidis, A., Chan, P.K., Stolfos, S.J.: Meta-learning in Distributed Data Mining Systems: Issues and Approaches. In: Kargupta, H., Chan, P. (eds.) Advances in Distributed and Parallel Knowledge Discovery 3. AAAI/MIT Press (2000)
162. Provost, F., Hennessy, D.: Scaling up: Distributed Machine Learning with Cooperation. In: Proceedings of the Thirteenth National Conference on Artificial Intelligence (1996)

163. Pyle, D.: Data Preparation for Data Mining. Morgan Kaufman, San Francisco (1999)
164. Quine, W.V.: Ontological Relativity and Other Essays. Columbia University Press, New York (1969)
165. Quinlan, J.R.: Simplifying Decision Trees. International Journal of Man-Machine Studies 27, 221–234 (1987)
166. Quinlan, J.R.: C4.5: Programs for Machine Learning. Morgan Kaufmann Publishers, San Mateo (1993)
167. Quinlan, J.R.: Bagging, Boosting and C 4.5. In: Proceedings of the Thirteenth National Conference on Artificial Intelligence, pp. 725–730 (1996)
168. Raman, B.: Enhancing Learning Using Feature and Example Selection. Texas A&M University, College Station (2003)
169. Rachlin, J., Goodwin, R., Murthy, S., Akkiraju, R., Wu, F., Kumaran, S., Das, R.: A-Teams: An Agent Architecture for Optimization and Decision-Support. In: Papadimitriou, C., Singh, M.P., Müller, J.P. (eds.) ATAL 1998. LNCS (LNAI), vol. 1555, pp. 261–276. Springer, Heidelberg (1999)
170. Ramon, J.: Clustering and Instance Based Learning in First Order Logic. AI Communications 15(4), 217–218 (2002)
171. Ritter, G.L., Woodruff, H.B., Lowry, S.R., Isenhour, T.L.: An Algorithm for a Selective Nearest Decision Rule. IEEE Transaction on Information Theory 21, 665–669 (1975)
172. Roa, V.S.: Multi Agent-based Distributed Data Mining: An Overview. International Journal of Reviews in Computing 3 (2010)
173. Rodriguez, M.A.: Assessing Semantic Similarity Between Spatial Entity Classes. Ph.D. Thesis, University of Maine (1997)
174. Rozsypal, A., Kubat, M.: Selecting Representative Examples and Attributes by a Genetic Algorithm. Intelligent Data Analysis 7(4), 291–304 (2003)
175. Russell, S., Norvig, P.: Artificial Intelligence: A Modern Approach, 2nd edn. Prentice Hall Series in Artificial Intelligence. Prentice-Hall, Upper Saddle River (2003)
176. Sahel, Z., Bouchachia, A., Gabrys, B., Rogers, P.: Adaptive Mechanisms for Classification Problems with Drifting Data. In: Apolloni, B., Howlett, R.J., Jain, L. (eds.) KES 2007, Part II. LNCS (LNAI), vol. 4693, pp. 419–426. Springer, Heidelberg (2007)
177. Saltzberg, S.: Learning with Nested Generalized Examples. Kluwer, Norwell (1990)
178. Silva, J., Giannella, C., Bhargava, R., Kargupta, H., Klusch, M.: Distributed Data Mining and Agents. Engineering Applications of Artificial Intelligence Journal 18, 791–807 (2005)
179. Skalak, D.B.: Prototype and Feature Selection by Sampling and Random Mutation Hill Climbing Algorithm. In: Proceedings of the International Conference on Machine Learning, pp. 293–301 (1994)
180. Skillicorn, D.: Strategies for Parallel Data Mining. IEEE Concurrency 7(4), 26–35 (1999)
181. Skowron, A., Stepniuk, J.: Tolerance Approximation Spaces. Fundamenta Informaticea 27, 245–253 (1996)
182. Skowron, A., Stepniuk, J., Swiniarski, R.: Approximation Spaces in Machine Learning and Pattern Recognition. In: Pal, S.K., Bandyopadhyay, S., Biswas, S. (eds.) PReMI 2005. LNCS, vol. 3776, pp. 750–755. Springer, Heidelberg (2005)
183. Sian, S.: Extending Learning to Multiple Agents: Issues and a Model for Multi-Agent Machine Learning (Ma-Ml). In: Kodratoff, Y. (ed.) EWSL 1991. LNCS, vol. 482, pp. 440–456. Springer, Heidelberg (1991)

184. Smyth, B., McKenna, E.: Footprint-based Retrieval. In: Third International Conference on Case-Based Reasoning, Munich, Germany, pp. 343–357 (1999)

185. Song, H.H., Lee, S.W.: LVQ Combined with Simulated Annealing for Optimal Design of Large-set Reference Models. Neural Networks 9(2), 329–336 (1996)

186. Stolfo, S., Prodromidis, A.L., Tselepis, S., Lee, W., Fan, D.W.: JAM: Java Agents for Meta-learning over Distributed Databases. In: 3rd International Conference on Knowledge Discovery and Data Mining, pp. 74–81. AAAI Press, Newport Beach (1997)

187. Stefanowski, J.: Multiple and Hybrid Classifiers. In: Polkowski, L. (ed.) Formal Methods and Intelligent Techniques in Control, Decision Making, Warszawa. Multimedia and Robotics, pp. 174–188 (2001)

188. Stefanowski, J.: Algorytmy ndukcji reguł decyzyjnych w odkrywaniu wiedzy. Habilitation Thesis 361. Poznań University of Technology, Poznań (2001) (in Polish)

189. Struyf, A., Hubert, M., Rousseeuw, P.J.: Clustering in Object-oriented Environment. Journal of Statistical Software 1(4), 1–30 (1996)

190. Symeonidis, A.L., Chatzidimtriou, K.C., Athanasiadis, I.N., Mitkas, P.A.: Data Mining for Agent Reasoning: A Synergy for Training Intelligent Agents. Engineering Applications of Artificial Intelligence 20, 1097–1111 (2007)

191. Talukdar, S.N., Pyo, S.S., Giras, T.: Asynchronous Procedures for Parallel Processing. IEEE Trans. on PAS PAS-102(11), 3652–3659 (1983)

192. Talukdar, S.N., de Souza, P.: Scale Efficient Organizations. In: IEEE International Conference on Systems, Man, and Cybernetics, Chicago, pp. 1458–1463 (1992)

193. Talukdar, S.N., Ramesh, V.C.: A Multi-agent Technique for Contingency Constrained Optimal Power Flows. IEEE Transactions on Power Systems 9(2), 855–861 (1994)

194. Talukdar, S., Baerentzen, L., Gove, A., de Souza, P.: Asynchronous Teams: Co-operation Schemes for Autonomous, Computer-based Agents. Technical Report EDRC 18-59-96, Carnegie Mellon University, Pittsburgh (1996)

195. Talukdar, S., Baerentzen, L., Gove, A., de Souza, P.: Asynchronous Teams: Cooperation Schemes for Autonomous Agents. Journal of Heuristics 4(4), 295–332 (1998)

196. Talukdar, S.N.: Collaboration Rules for Autonomous Software Agents. Decision Support Systems 24, 269–278 (1999)

197. The European Network of Excellence on Intelligence Technologies for Smart Adaptive Systems (EUNITE) - EUNITE World Competition in domain of Intelligent Technologies (2002), http://neuron.tuke.sk/competition2 (accessed April 30, 2002)

198. Ting, K.M., Low, B.T.: Model Combination in the Multiple-data-base Scenario. In: van Someren, M., Widmer, G. (eds.) ECML 1997. LNCS (LNAI), vol. 1224, pp. 250–265. Springer, Heidelberg (1997)

199. Tomek, I.: An Experiment with the Edited Nearest-Neighbour Rule. IEEE Trans. on Systems, Man, and Cybernetics 6(6), 448–452 (1976)

200. Tozicka, J., Rovatsos, M., Pechoucek, M., Urban, U.: MALEF: Framework for Distributed Machine Learning and Data Mining. International Journal of Intelligent Information and Database Systems 2(1), 6–24 (2008)

201. Tsoumakas, G., Angelis, L., Vlahavas, I.: Clustering Classifiers for Knowledge Discovery from Physically Distributed Databases. Data & Knowledge Engineering 49, 223–242 (2004)

202. Tsoumakas, G., Vlahavas, I.: Effective Stacking of Distributed Classifiers. In: 15th European Conference on Artificial Intelligence, pp. 340–344 (2002)

203. Turinsky, A.L., Grossman, R.L.: A Framework for Finding Distributed data Mining Strategies that are Intermediate between Centralized and In-place Strategies. In: KDD Workshop on Distributed Data Mining (2000)

204. Tveit, A., Engum, H.: Parallelization of the Incremental Proximal Support Vector Machine Classifier Using a Heap-based Tree Topology. In: Parallel and Distributed Computing for Machine Learning. The Proceedings of the 14th European Conference on Machine Learning and the 7th European Conference on Principles and Practice of Knowledge Discovery in Databases (ECML/PKDD 2003), Cavtat-Dubrovnik, Cratia (2003)

205. Tweedale, J., Ichalkaranje, N., Sioutis, C., Jarvis, B., Consoli, A., Phillips-Wren, G.E.: Innovations in Multi-agent Systems. Journal of Network and Computer Applications 30(3), 1089–1115 (2007)

206. Uno, T.: Multi-sorting Algorithm for Finding Pairs of Similar Short Substrings from Large-scale String Data. Knowledge and Information Systems (2009), doi:10.1007/s10115-009-0271-6

207. Verleysen, M., Francois, D.: The Curse of Dimensionality in Data Mining and Time Series Prediction. In: Cabestany, J., Prieto, A.G., Sandoval, F. (eds.) IWANN 2005. LNCS, vol. 3512, pp. 758–770. Springer, Heidelberg (2005)

208. Wang, X., Yang, J., Teng, X., Xia, W., Jensen, R.: Feature Selection Based on Rough Sets and Particle Swarm Optimization. Pattern Recognition Letters 28(4), 459–471 (2007)

209. Wang, B.X., Japkowicz, N.: Boosting Support Vector Machines for Imbalanced Data Sets. Knowledge and Information Systems 25, 1–20 (2009), doi:0.1007/s10115-009-0198-y

210. Warmounth, M.K., Kivinen, J., Auer, P.: The Perceptron Algorithm Varsus Winnow: Linear Versus Logarithmic Mistake Bounds when New Input Variables are Relevant. Artificial Intelligence 97, 325–343 (1997)

211. Wei, Y., Li, T., Ge, Z.: Combining Distributed Classifies by Stacking. In: Proceedings of the Third International Conference on Genetic and Evolutionary Computing, pp. 418–421 (2009)

212. Weiss, S.M., Kulikowski, C.A.: Computer Systems That Learn: Classification and Prediction Methods from Statistics, Neural Nets. In: Machine Learning and Expert Systems. Morgan Kaufmann, San Francisco (1991)

213. Weiss, G.M., Provost, F.: The Effect of Class Distribution on Classifier Learning: An Empirical Study. Technical Report ML-TR-44, Department of Computer Science, Rutgers University (2001)

214. Wilson, D.R., Martinez, T.R.: Improved Heterogeneous Distance Functions. Journal of Artificial Intelligence Research 6, 1–34 (1997)

215. Wilson, D.R., Martinez, T.R.: An Integrated Instance-based Learning Algorithm. Computational Intelligence 16, 1–28 (2000)

216. Wilson, D.R., Martinez, T.R.: Reduction Techniques for Instance-based Learning Algorithm. Machine Learning 33(3), 257–286 (2000)

217. Widmer, G., Kubat, M.: Learning in the Presence of Concept Drift and Hidden Contexts. Machine Learning 23(1), 69–101 (1996)

218. Winton, D., Pete, E.: Using Instance Selection to Combine Multiple Models Learned from Disjoint Subsets. In: Liu, H., Motoda, H. (eds.) Instance Selection and Construction for Data Mining. Kluwer Scientific Publisher, Dordrecht (2001)

219. Witten, I.H., Frank, E.: Data Mining: Practical Machine Learning Tools and Techniques, 2nd edn. Morgan Kaufman, San Francisco (2005)

220. Wolpert, D.H.: The Supervised Learning No Free Lunch Theorem. Technical Report, NASA Ames Research Center, Moffett Field, California, USA (2001)
221. Wu, X.: Synthesizing High-Frequency Rules from Different Data Sources. IEEE Transactions on Knowledge and Data Engineering 15(2), 353–367 (2003)
222. Wu, Y., Ianakiev, K.G., Govindaraju, V.: Improvements in K-Nearest Neighbor Classification. In: Singh, S., Murshed, N., Kropatsch, W.G. (eds.) ICAPR 2001. LNCS, vol. 2013, pp. 222–229. Springer, Heidelberg (2001)
223. Xu, L., Krzyzak, A., Suen, C.Y.: Methods of Combining Multiple Classifiers and their Application to Handwriting Recognition. IEEE Transaction on Systems, Man and Cybernetics 22, 418–435 (1992)
224. Yu, K., Xu, X., Ester, M., Kriegel, H.P.: Feature Weighting and Instance Selection for Collaborative Filtering: An Information-Theoretic Approach. Knowledge and Information Systems 5(2), 201–224 (2003)
225. Yu, L., Liu, H.: Efficient Feature Selection via Analysis of Relevance and Redundancy. Journal of Machine Learning Research 5, 1205–1224 (2004)
226. Yu, T., Jan, T., Simoff, S., Debenham, J.: Incorporating Prior Domain Knowledge Into Inductive Machine Learning: A Review. In: International Conference on Advances in intelligence Systems - Theory and Applications, Luxemburg (2004)
227. Yang, P., Tao, L., Xu, L., Zhang, Z.: Multiagent Framework for Bio-data Mining. In: Wen, P., Li, Y., Polkowski, L., Yao, Y., Tsumoto, S., Wang, G. (eds.) RSKT 2009. LNCS, vol. 5589, pp. 200–207. Springer, Heidelberg (2009)
228. Yang, Q., Wu, X.: 10 Challenging Problems in Data Mining Research. International Journal of Information Technology & Decision Making 5(4), 597–604 (2006)
229. Yen, S., Lee, Y.S.: Cluster-based Under-sampling Approaches for Imbalanced Data Distributions. Expert Systems with Applications 36, 5718–5727 (2009)
230. Zaki, M.J.: Parallel and Distributed Data Mining: An Introduction. In: Zaki, M.J., Ho, C.-T. (eds.) KDD 1999. LNCS (LNAI), vol. 1759, pp. 1–23. Springer, Heidelberg (2000)
231. Zhang, S., Wu, X., Zhang, C.: Multi-Database Mining. IEEE Computational Intelligence Bulletin 2(1) (2003)
232. Zhang, Z., Zhang, C., Zhang, S.: An Agent-based Hybrid Framework for Database Mining. Applied Artificial Intelligence 17, 383–398 (2003)
233. Zhang, S., Zhang, C., Yang, Q.: Data Preparation for Data Mining. Applied Artificial Intelligence 17, 375–381 (2003)
234. Zhang, G., Rong, H., Hu, L., Jin, W.: Application of Radial Basis Probability Neural Network to Signal Recognition. In: Proceedings of the Fifth World Congress on Intelligent Control and Automation, vol. 3, pp. 1950–1953 (2004)
235. Zhang, X.F., Lam, C.M., Cheung, W.K.: Mining Local Data Sources For Learning Global Cluster Model Via Local Model Exchange. IEEE Intelligence Informatics Bulletine 4(2), 748–751 (2004)
236. Zhu, X., Wu, X.: Scalable Representative Instance Selection and Ranking. In: Proceedings of the 18th IEEE International Conference on Pattern Recognition, pp. 352–355 (2006)
237. Zhu, X., Zhang, P., Lin, X., Shi, Y.: Active Learning from Data Streams. In: Proceedings of the Seventh IEEE International Conference on Data Mining, pp. 757–762 (2007)
238. Zhang, D., Zhou, Z.H., Chen, S.: Semi-Supervised Dimensionality Reduction. In: Proceedings of the International Conference Data Mining, pp. 629–634 (2007)
239. Zongker, D., Jain, A.: Algorithm for Feature Selection: An Evaluation. In: Proceedings of the International Conference on Pattern Recognition, ICPR 1996, pp. 18–22 (1996)

Regular Papers

Data Clustering Based on an Efficient Hybrid of K-Harmonic Means, PSO and GA

Malihe Danesh[1], Mahmoud Naghibzadeh[1], Mohammad Reza Akbarzadeh Totonchi[1], Mohaddeseh Danesh[2], Behrouz Minaei[2], and Hossein Shirgahi[3]

[1] Department of Computer Engineering
Ferdowsi University of Mashhad, Mashhad, Iran
[2] Department of Computer Engineering
Iran University of Science and Technology, Tehran, Iran
[3] Islamic Azad University, Jouybar Branch, Jouybar, Iran
Ma.danesh@stu-mail.um.ac.ir, Naghibzadeh@um.ac.ir,
Akbarzadeh@ieee.org, MdDanesh@comp.iust.ac.ir,
minaeibi@cse.msu.edu, hossein.shirgahi@gmail.com

Abstract. Clustering is one of the most commonly techniques in Data Mining. Kmeans is one of the most popular clustering techniques due to its simplicity and efficiency. However, it is sensitive to initialization and easily trapped in local optima. K-harmonic means clustering solves the problem of initialization using a built-in boosting function, but it is suffering from running into local optima. Particle Swarm Optimization is a stochastic global optimization technique that is the proper solution to solve this problem. In this paper, PSOKHM not only helps KHM clustering escape from local optima but also overcomes the shortcoming of slow convergence speed of PSO. In this paper, a hybrid data clustering algorithm based on PSO and Genetic algorithm, GSOKHM, is proposed. We investigate local optima method in addition to the global optima in PSO, called LSOKHM. The experimental results on five real datasets indicate that LSOKHM is superior to the GSOKHM algorithm.

Keywords: Data clustering; PSO; KHM; Genetic algorithm.

1 Introduction

One of the critical methods for data management is data clustering with similar properties in the sets of groups. A *cluster* is a collection of objects which are "similar" between them and are "dissimilar" to the objects belonging to other clusters. Clustering techniques are applied in many application areas such as machine learning, spatial database analysis, pattern recognition, bioinformatics, information retrieval and web mining [1, 2, 3, 4]. The existing clustering algorithms can be simply classified into the following two categories: hierarchical clustering and partitional clustering [5].

K-means (KM) algorithm is one of the most popular and widespread partitioning clustering algorithms. The most common clustering objective in KM is to minimize the sum of dissimilarities between all objects and their corresponding cluster centers. The main drawback of the KM algorithm is that the cluster result is sensitive to the selection of the initial cluster centers and may converge to the local optima [6].

N.T. Nguyen (Ed.): Transactions on CCI IV, LNCS 6660, pp. 125–140, 2011.
© Springer-Verlag Berlin Heidelberg 2011

The K-harmonic means (KHM) algorithm [7, 8] is a more recent algorithm proposed in 1999 that its objective in this algorithm is to minimize the harmonic average from all points in the dataset to all cluster centers. The KHM algorithm solves the problem of initialization of the KM algorithm, but it also easily runs into local optima. So must find the solution to escape from local optima to reach the better clustering algorithm. Recently much work was done to overcome this problem.

Simulated annealing (SA) algorithm is a generic probabilistic metaheuristic that was proposed to find the equilibrium configuration of a collection of atoms at a given temperature and it is always used to solve the combinatorial problems. SA heuristic was used with K-harmonic means (SAKHMC) to overcome local optimal problem [9].

Tabu search (TS) is a search method for combinatorial optimization problems that use a local or neighborhood search procedure to solve the problems. TabuKHM (Tabu K-harmonic means) algorithm was proposed to solve local minima in K-harmonic means algorithm [10].

Particle Swarm Optimization (PSO) algorithm is a stochastic global optimization technique inspired by social behavior of bird flocking or fish schooling. A hybrid data clustering algorithm based on PSO and KHM (PSOKHM) was proposed in [11], which makes full use of the merits of both algorithms.

The Ant clustering algorithm (ACA) that it closely mimics the ant behavior, can avoid trapping in local optimal solution. a new clustering algorithm using the Ant clustering algorithm with K-harmonic means clustering (ACAKHM) was proposed [12].

Furthermore, some hybrid heuristic methods were used with clustering algorithm to solve local optimal problem [13, 14].

In this paper, we purpose two algorithms to escape from local optima. First, by new hybrid of PSO and Genetic algorithm, called GSOKHM, to clustering data vectors and second, by using local optima behavior against global optima behavior (LSOKHM) to improve clustering result. We also use four real datasets to evaluate our algorithm.

The rest of the paper is organized as follows. Section 2 describes data clustering problem that consist of partitional clustering and k-harmonic means algorithm. Section 3 introduces Particle Swarm Optimization algorithm and section 4 describes our proposed methods, GSOKHM and LSOKHM algorithms. Section 5 illustrates experimental results and compares it with previous methods. Finally, Section 6 makes conclusions.

2   Data Clustering Problem

Data clustering is a common technique for data analysis, which is used in many fields, including machine learning, data mining, pattern recognition, image analysis and bioinformatics. Clustering consists of partitioning a data set into subsets (clusters), so that the data in each subset (ideally) share some common trait - often similarity or proximity for some defined distance measure.

Data clustering algorithms can be hierarchical or partitional. Hierarchical clustering builds a hierarchy of clusters from individual elements. The traditional representation of this hierarchy is a tree, with individual elements at one end and a single cluster with every element at the other. Since it is not the subject of this study we will not mention it in detail.

2.1 The Partitional Clustering

Partitional clustering in [15] is defined as a division data objects into non-overlapping subsets (clusters) such that each data object is in exactly one subset. Giving $X = \{x_1, x_2, ..., x_n\}$, the goal of a partitional clustering algorithm is to determine a partition $C = \{C_1, C_2, ..., C_k\}$ where ($C_k \neq \phi, \forall k \in K; C_h \cap C_l = \phi, \forall h, l \in K, h \neq l$; $\bigcup_{k=1}^{K} C_k = X$) such that objects which belong to the same cluster are as similar to each other as possible, while objects which belong to different clusters are as dissimilar as possible. The clustering problem is to find the partition C^* that has an optimal adequacy with respect to all other feasible solution. Let $f(C) = f(C_1, C_2, ..., C_k)$ be the objective function of the clustering problem and the objective is to optimize $f(C)$.

K-means and K-harmonic means are both center-based clustering algorithms. K-means algorithm minimizes the total mean squared distance from each point of the data set to the point of closest center that is called hard partitional clustering. In contrast to it, the K-harmonic means is a kind of fuzzy clustering which characteristic is that a pattern belongs to all clusters with a degree of membership instead of belonging to one cluster only. It minimizes the harmonic average from all points in the data set to each center. It will be explained in detail in the following section.

2.2 K-harmonic Means Clustering

KHM [7, 8] is a class of center-based iterative clustering algorithms which is essentially insensitive to the initialization of the centers. The insensitivity to initialization is attributed to a dynamic weighting function, which increases the importance of the data points that are far from any centers in the next iteration.

The KHM clustering replace the minimum distance from a data point to the centers, used in KM, by harmonic mean of the distance from each data point to all centers. The harmonic means gives a good (low) score for each data point when that data point is close to a center. It is similar to the minimum function used by KM, but it is a smooth differentiable function. The following notations are used to formulate the KHM algorithm:

$X = \{x_1, x_2, ..., x_n\}$, the data to be clustered.
$C = \{c_1, c_2, ..., c_n\}$, the set of cluster centers.

$M(c_j | x_i)$ = the membership function defining the proportion of data point x_i that belongs to center c_j.
$W(x_i)$ = the weight function defining how much influence data point x_i has in recomputing the center parameters in the next iteration.
Basic algorithm for KHM clustering is shown as follows:

1. Initialize the algorithm with guessed centers C, i.e., randomly choose the initial centers.
2. Calculate objective function value according to

$$KHM(X,C) = \sum_{i=1}^{n} \frac{k}{\sum_{j=1}^{K} \frac{1}{\| x_i - c_j \|^p}} . \qquad (1)$$

where p is an input parameter and typically $p \geq 2$.

3. For each data point x_i, compute its membership $m(c_j | x_i)$ in each center c_j according to

$$m(c_j | x_i) = \frac{\| x_i - c_j \|^{-p-2}}{\sum_{j=1}^{k} \| x_i - c_j \|^{-p-2}} . \qquad (2)$$

4. For each data point x_i, compute its weight $w(x_i)$ according to

$$w(x_i) = \frac{\sum_{j=1}^{k} \| x_i - c_j \|^{-p-2}}{\left(\sum_{j=1}^{k} \| x_i - c_j \|^{-p} \right)^2} . \qquad (3)$$

5. For each center c_j, re-compute its location from all data points x_i according to their memberships and weights:

$$c_j = \frac{\sum_{i=1}^{n} m(c_j | x_i) w(x_i) x_i}{\sum_{i=1}^{n} m(c_j | x_i) w(x_i)} . \qquad (4)$$

6. Repeat steps 2–5 predefined number of iterations or until KHM(X,C) does not change significantly.

7. Assign data point xi to cluster j with the biggest $m(c_j | x_i)$.

It is demonstrated that KHM is essentially insensitive to the initialization of the centers. However, it tends to converge to local optima [10].

3   Particle Swarm Optimization

PSO is a sociologically inspired population based optimization algorithm [16]. Nowadays, PSO has gained much attention and wide applications in a variety of fields. Each particle is an individual, and the swarm is composed of particles. In PSO, the solution space of the problem is formulated as a search space. Each position in the search space is a correlated solution of the problem. Particles cooperate to find the best position (best solution) in the search space (solution space). Each particle moves according to its velocity. At each iteration, the particle movement is computed as follows:

$$x_i(t+1) \leftarrow x_i(t) + v_i(t) . \qquad (5)$$

$$v_i(t+1) \leftarrow \omega v_i(t) + c_1 rand_1(pbest_i(t) -$$
$$x_i(t)) + c_2 rand_2(gbest(t) - x_i(t)) \quad . \tag{6}$$

In Eqs. (5) and (6), $x_i(t)$ is the position of particle i at time t, $v_i(t)$ is the velocity of particle i at time t, $pbest_i(t)$ is the best position found by particle i itself so far, gbest(t) is the best position found by the whole swarm so far, x is an inertia weight scaling the previous time step velocity, c_1 and c_2 are two acceleration coefficients that scale the influence of the best personal position of the particle ($pbest_i(t)$) and the best global position (gbest(t)), $rand_1$ and $rand_2$ are random variables between 0 and 1. The process of PSO is shown as Fig. 1.

Initialize a population of particles with random positions and velocities in the search space.
While (termination conditions are not met)
{
For each particle i do
Update the position of particle i according to equation (5).
Update the velocity of particle i according to equation (6).
Map the position of particle i in the solution space and evaluate its fitness value according to the fitness function.
Update $pbest_i(t)$ and gbest (t) if necessary.
End for
}

Fig. 1. The process of the PSO algorithm

4   Recommended Method

We proposed two new algorithms based on KHM, PSO and GA to get advantages of faster convergence in KHM and global optima of PSO and GA algorithms. In both of them, we used a same model of particle is shown in Fig. 2. A particle is a vector of real numbers of dimension k × d, where k is the number of clusters and d is the dimension of data to be clustered. The fitness function of these algorithms is the objective function of the KHM algorithm. They will be explained in detail in the following sections.

X_{11}	X_{12}	......	X_{k1}	X_{k2}	......	x_{kd}

Fig. 2. The representation of a particle

4.1   GSOKHM Method

In this method, we try to join PSO with another evolutionary algorithm like genetic algorithm to increase PSO's performance in PSOKHM to make better data clustering.

Genetic algorithm is a kind of stochastic algorithms that uses selection, crossover and mutation operations. It is one of the most popular evolutionary algorithms and is

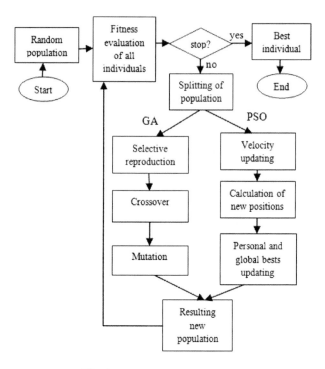

Fig. 3. The hybrid GSO algorithm

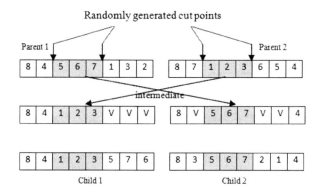

Fig. 4. The crossover operation of GSOKHM

effective to converge the local optima in KHM algorithm and also increases PSO's performance. We use GSO algorithm by hybrid of PSO and GA that its operation is shown in Fig. 3.

As it is shown in Fig.3, in each iteration the population is divided into two equal parts, then PSO and GA algorithms are applied on each part independently, finally they join with each other again to evaluate changes. This procedure is followed to gain the desired situation.

Algorithm: GSOKHM clustering

Input: uniform N datasets, with d dimensions for each dataset and k value as the number of clusters

Output: partitioning N dataset

Procedure:

1. Initialize the parameters including MAXIter, GSO_Iter, KHM_Iter, Pop_size, ω, C1, C2, Pmutation, Pcrossover

2. Initialize a population of size Pop_size

3. Set iterative count num=0

4. (GSO Hybrid Method)

    4.1. splitting the population of particles for parallel computations of PSO and GA algorithms

    4.2. apply PSO and GA operators according to fig()

    4.3. repeat step 4 as much as GSO_iter

5. (KHM Method)

    5.1. For each particle i do

        5.1.1. Take the position of particle i as the initial cluster centers of the KHM algorithm

        5.1.2. Recalculate each cluster center using the KHM algorithm

    5.2. repeat step 5 as much as KHM_iter

6. num=num+1. If num<MaxIter, go to Step 3

7. Assign data point xi to cluster j with the biggest $m(c_j|x_i)$

Fig. 5. The GSOKHM algorithm

In genetic algorithm, we use Roulette-Wheels choosing in selection operation. Crossover operation is done as Fig.4.

Finally, GSOKHM algorithm is summarized in Fig. 5.

4.2 LSOKHM Algorithm

In this method, we investigate the local optima method in addition to the global optima in PSO algorithm, called LSOKHM and try to show its performance than basic situation. Local Swarm Optimization operation is shown in Fig. 6.

Begin : Gen=0

Generate a swarm of random solutions (xi)

i=1,2,...,Swarm_Size

Divide the Swarm in n neighborhoods.

Assign equal number of particles to each neighborhood.

Initialize for each particle, xpbesti= xi, and vi(t)=0.

Do

Evaluate the fitness of the particle in each neighborhood.

Select the leader (xlBesti) of each neighborhood.

For each particle, update its velocity with (6).

by using the corresponding leader of each neighborhood xlBesti, For each particle, update its position with (5).

Evaluate the fitness of the new position for each particle.

Update the xpbesti(memory) value for each particle.

Gen=Gen+1

Until Gen=Gmax

End

Fig. 6. LSO algorithm pseudocode

As it is obvious, we understand from this psoudocode that the best local optima ($lbest_i$) of each particle i, in that the neighborhood is selected instead of calculating general best (gbest) of each generation. We use $lbest_i$ to update formulas of speed and particles' locations in that local population.

5   Experimental Results

Four datasets are employed to validate our method. These datasets, named Wine, Glass, Iris, Contraceptive Method Choice (denoted as CMC) and Image Segmentation, cover examples of data of low, medium and high dimensions. All datasets are available at ftp://ftp.ics.uci.edu./pub/machine-learning-databases/. Table 1 summarizes the characteristics of these datasets. Table 2 shows the parameters set in our algorithm that we achieved them with experimental results.

Table 1. Characteristics of datasets considered

Name of dataset	No. Of classes	No. Of features	Size of dataset (size of classes in parentheses)
Iris	3	4	150 (50, 50, 50)
Glass	6	9	214 (70, 17, 76, 13, 9, 29)
CMC	3	9	1473 (629, 334, 510)
Wine	3	13	178 (59, 71, 48)
Image Segmentation	7	19	210 (30, 30, 30, 30, 30, 30, 30)

5.1 Datasets

Fisher's iris dataset (n = 150, d = 4, k=3), which consists of three different species of iris flower: Iris Setosa, Iris Versicolour and Iris Virginica. For each species, 50 samples with four features (sepal length, sepal width, petal length, and petal width) were collected.

Glass (n = 214, d = 9, k = 6), which consists of six different types of glass: building windows float processed (70 objects), building windows non-float processed (76 objects), vehicle windows float processed (17 objects), containers (13 objects), tableware (9 objects), and headlamps (29 objects). Each type has nine features, which are refractive index, sodium, magnesium, aluminum, silicon, potassium, calcium, barium, and iron.

Contraceptive Method Choice (n=1473, d = 9, k = 3): This dataset is a subset of the 1987 National Indonesia Contraceptive Prevalence Survey. The samples are married women who either were not pregnant or did not know if they were at the time of interview. The problem is to predict the choice of current contraceptive method (no use has 629 objects, long-term methods have 334 objects, and short-term methods have 510 objects) of a woman based on her demographic and socioeconomic characteristics.

Wine (n = 178, d = 13, k = 3): These data, consisting of 178 objects characterized by 13 such features as alcohol, malic acid, ash, alkalinity of ash, magnesium, total phenols, flavanoids, nonflavanoid phenols, proanthocyanins, color intensity, hue, OD280/OD315 of diluted wines, and praline, are the results of a chemical analysis of wines brewed in the same region in Italy but derived from three different *cultivars*. There are three categories in the data: class 1 (59 objects), class 2 (71 objects), and class 3 (48 objects).

Image Segmentation (n = 210, d = 19, k = 7): The instances were drawn randomly from a database of 7 outdoor images. The images were hand segmented to create a classification for every pixel.

5.2 Experimental Results

In this section, we evaluate and compare the performances of the following methods: KHM, PSOKHM and LSOKHM algorithms as means of solution for the objective

Table 2. Initialization of the parameters in proposed methods

Parameter	Value
Pop_size	18
ω	0.73
C1	1.5
C2	1.5
Pmutation	0.02
Pcrossover	0.5
MaxIter	5
GSO_Iter	8
KHM_Iter	4

Table 3. Results of KHM, GSO, PSOKHM, and GSOKHM clustering when p = 2

	KHM	GSO	PSOKHM	GSOKHM	LSOKHM
IRIS					
F-Measure	0.8923	0.9025	0.8990	**0.9129**	**0.9151**
KHM (X,C)	74.95	87.31	58.14	**11.72**	**18.02**
Runtime(sec)	0.1811	2.567	2.19	2.73	2.13
Glass					
F-Measure	**0.4831**	0.4348	0.4245	**0.4354**	0.4326
KHM (X,C)	376.33	256.99	118.80	**105.25**	**118.57**
Runtime(sec)	0.3244	6.9471	5.43	6.89	5.42
Wine					
F-Measure	0.6900	0.6635	0.7023	**0.7090**	**0.7082**
KHM (X,C)	7,479,216	326,400	71,092	**64,490**	**59,278**
Runtime(sec)	0.2406	3.548	2.55	3.48	2.57
CMC					
F-Measure	0.4491	0.4438	0.4436	**0.4510**	**0.4511**
KHM (X,C)	150,950	40,271	49,163	**9,424**	**9,509**
Runtime(sec)	0.7720	20.467	18.68	20.45	19.09
Image					
F-Measure	0.6031	0.5812	0.6169	**0.6373**	**0.6394**
KHM (X,C)	1,316,910	881,410	435,860	**259,120**	**238,950**
Runtime(sec)	0.2258	9.1421	6.6787	9.0539	6.6981

Table 4. Results of KHM, GSO, PSOKHM, and GSOKHM clustering when p = 2.5

	KHM	GSO	PSOKHM	GSOKHM	LSOKHM
IRIS					
F-Measure	0.8853	0.8919	0.8951	**0.9017**	**0.9005**
KHM (X,C)	44.07	26.54	23.159	**3.687**	**3.878**
Runtime(sec)	0.1331	2.668	2.19	2.93	2.13
Glass					
F-Measure	0.4130	0.4063	**0.4180**	0.4100	**0.4286**
KHM (X,C)	633.40	321.44	89.98	**70.89**	**86.10**
Runtime(sec)	0.2898	7.304	5.88	7.27	5.82
Wine					
F-Measure	0.6694	0.6598	0.6835	**0.6902**	**0.6940**
KHM (X,C)	194,607,300	10,812,000	8,442,950	**3,572,228**	**5,618,170**
Runtime(sec)	0.1554	3.8087	2.78	3.71	2.76
CMC					
F-Measure	**0.4496**	0.4460	0.4447	0.4445	**0.4474**
KHM (X,C)	687,737.3	14,807	82,307.2	**12,921**	**13,128.3**
Runtime(sec)	1.5656	21.50	19.45	21.45	19.43
Image					
F-Measure	0.5840	0.5173	0.5919	**0.6086**	**0.6113**
KHM (X,C)	4,156,800	2,364,400	2,451,900	**2,034,000**	**2,083,900**
Runtime(sec)	0.2905	9.2204	6.6980	9.1244	6.7156

function of the KHM algorithm. The quality of the respective clustering will also be compared, where the quality is measured by the following two criteria:

The sum over all data points of the harmonic average of the distance from a data point to all the centers, as defined in Eq (10-2). Clearly, the smaller the sum is, the higher the quality of clustering is.

The F-Measure uses the ideas of precision and recall from information retrieval [17]. Each class i (as given by the class labels of the used benchmark dataset) is regarded as the set of n_i items desired for a query; each cluster j (generated by the algorithm) is regarded as the set of n_j items retrieved for a query; n_{ij} gives the number of elements of class i within cluster j. For each class i and cluster j precision and recall are then defined as:

$$r(i, j) = \frac{n_{ij}}{n_i} \tag{7}$$

$$p(i, j) = \frac{n_{ij}}{n_j} \tag{8}$$

Table 5. Results of KHM, GSO, PSOKHM, and GSOKHM clustering when p = 3

	KHM	GSO	PSOKHM	GSOKHM	LSOKHM
IRIS					
F-Measure	0.8853	0.8851	0.8934	**0.8950**	0.9035
KHM (X,C)	51.22	46.537	10.32	**7.49**	1.0087
Runtime(sec)	0.1499	2.6813	2.22	2.19	2.88
Glass					
F-Measure	0.3874	0.3724	0.3873	**0.4259**	0.4067
KHM (X,C)	418.32	347.92	87.43	**66.65**	74.66
Runtime(sec)	0.3276	7.430	5.81	7.32	5.76
Wine					
F-Measure	0.6421	0.6704	0.6533	**0.6733**	0.6851
KHM (X,C)	3,177,367,000	50,257,800	361,404,860	**97,070,697**	12,331,994
Runtime(sec)	0.2074	3.7810	2.97	3.68	2.87
CMC					
F-Measure	**0.4515**	0.4462	0.4435	0.4462	**0.4480**
KHM (X,C)	1,499,943	12,616	135,074	**17,557**	20,255
Runtime(sec)	0.8635	21.276	20.02	21.19	20.14
Image					
F-Measure	0.5259	0.5098	0.5375	**0.5523**	0.5564
KHM (X,C)	11,460,000	6,685,000	5,568,600	**3,872,300**	4,139,600
Runtime(sec)	0.2728	9.3302	6.5887	9.1303	6.6677

And the corresponding value under the F-Measure is:

$$F(i, j) = \frac{(b^2 + 1).p(i, j).r(i, j)}{b^2.p(i, j) + r(i, j)} \tag{9}$$

Where we chose b = 1 to obtain equal weighting for p(i, j) and r(i, j). The overall fmeasure for the dataset of size n is given by:

$$F = \sum_i \frac{n_i}{n} \max_j \{F(i, j)\} \tag{10}$$

Obviously, the bigger F-Measure is, the higher the quality of clustering is.

The experimental results are averages of 10 runs of simulation. The algorithms are implemented using MATLAB 7.6.0(r2008a) on Vista Home Premium OS with CPU 2.4 GHz and 6 GB RAM. It is known that p is a key parameter to get good objective function values. For this reason we conduct our experiments with different p values. Tables 3, 4, 5 give the means and standard deviations (over 10 runs) obtained for each

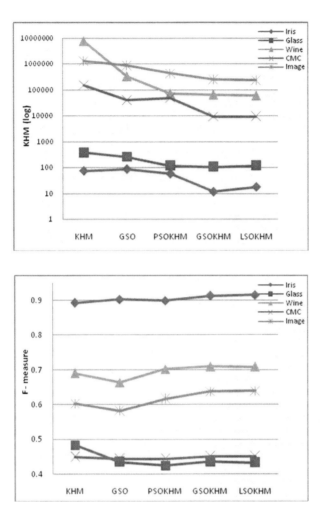

Fig. 7. Graph of F-measure and KHM values when p=2

of these measures when p is 2.5, 3 and 3.5, respectively. Additionally, they show the runtimes of the algorithms.

We typed bold two best methods in result tables. Experimental results show that in both proposed algorithms GSOKHM, LSOKHM the means of KHM(X,C) algorithm obtained in each value of p is less than KHM and PSOKHM algorithms, so we obtain better results in our algorithms. Besides, having checked F-Measure mean value and comparing it with other results, we find that for all datasets except CMC, this value in GSOKHM and LSOKHM is more than previous results, so higher performance is achieved.

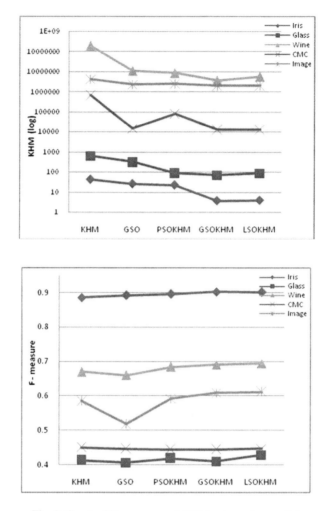

Fig. 8. Graph of F-measure and KHM values when p=2.5

From runtime view, these two algorithms require more time rather than KHM but as performance view these are comparable with hybrid PSOKHM algorithm. Also with comparing the performance of these two algorithms, we conclude that their effect is equal in optimizing clustering algorithm but in GSOKHM the need time is more because it should call genetic function.

Finally, we conclude that the GSOKHM and LSOKHM algorithms improve quality of clustering because of surprisingly decrease of KHM value and increase of F-Measure value. LSOKHM needs less run time than GSOKHM in all testing datasets. This ratio is different in various datasets. Therefore LSOKHM is more suitable as time view.

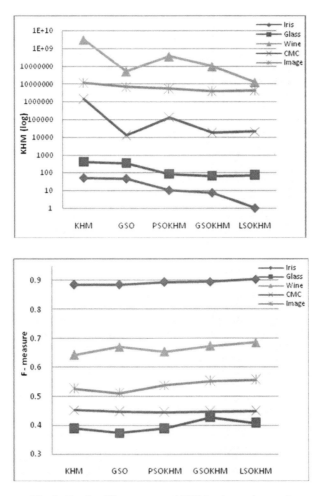

Fig. 9. Graph of F-measure and KHM values when p=3

6 Conclusions

This paper investigates a hybrid clustering algorithm called PSOKHM based on the advantages of KHM and PSO algorithms. This hybrid algorithm improves the convergence speed of PSO and also inhibits KHM from local optima. The proposed algorithms in this paper called GSOKHM and LSOKHM which GSOKHM is investigated by the help of local optima and global optima of PSO and LSOKHM is done by the hybrid of genetic evolutionary and PSO on hybrid PSOKHM algorithm. The experiment is done on five real datasets. These algorithms calculate the data clusters' centers by using overall sum of all data points based on the harmonic average of the distance between one point to all centers. So this method has better results than KHM and PSOKHM. Also as F-Measure metric, it has better results too. Moreover it is understood from the experiments that LSOKHM is almost equal with PSOKHM as run time. Therefore LSOKHM algorithm as a better substitution in data clustering.

This algorithm is so efficient in clustering but its run time is more than KHM. Therefore it can't be used when the time has a vital effect in the system. In the future, we intend to use more efficient combinatorial optimization techniques so as to reduce the runtime of our clustering algorithm.

References

[1] Hu, G., Zhou, S., Guan, J., Hu, X.: Towards effective document clustering: A constrained K-means based approach. Information Processing & Management 44, 1397–1409 (2008)

[2] Tan, P.N., Steinbach, M., Kumar, V.: Introduction to data mining, pp. 487–559. Addison-Wesley, Boston (2005)

[3] Tjhi, W.C., Chen, L.H.: A heuristic-based fuzzy co-clustering algorithm for categorization of high-dimensional data. Fuzzy Sets and Systems 159, 371–389 (2008)

[4] Zhou, H., Liu, Y.H.: Accurate integration of multi-view range images using k-means clustering. Pattern Recognition 41, 152–175 (2008)

[5] Jain, A.K., Murty, M.N., Flynn, P.j.: Data clustering: A review. ACM Computational Survey 31, 264–323 (1999)

[6] Cui, X., Potok, T.E., Palathingal, P.: Document clustering using Particle Swarm Optimization. In: Proceedings 2005 IEEE Swarm Intelligence Symposium, pp. 185–191 (2005)

[7] Zhang, B., Hsu, M., Dayal, U.: K-harmonic means – a data clustering algorithm. Technical Report HPL-1999-124, Hewlett-Packard Laboratories (1999)

[8] Hammerly, G., Elkan, C.: Alternatives to the k-means algorithm that find better clusterings. In: Proceedings of the 11th International Conference on Information and Knowledge Management, Virginia, USA, pp. 600–607 (2002)

[9] Güngör, Z., Ünler, A.: K-harmonic means data clustering with simulated annealing heuristic. Applied Mathematics and Computation, 199–209 (2007)

[10] Güngör, Z., Ünler, A.: K-harmonic means data clustering with tabu-search method. Applied Mathematical Modelling 32, 1115–1125 (2008)

[11] Yang, F., Sun, T., Zhang, C.: An efficient hybrid data clustering method based on K-harmonic means and Particle Swarm Optimization. Expert Systems with Applications: An International Journal 36, 9847–9852 (2009)

[12] Jiang, H., Yi, S., Li, J., Yang, F., Hu, X.: Ant clustering algorithm with k-harmonic means clustering. Expert Systems with Applications 37, 8679–8684 (2010)

[13] Chu, S., Roddick, J.: A clustering algorithm using Tabu search approach with simulated annealing for vector quantization. Chinese Journal of Electronics 12, 349–353 (2003)

[14] Huang, C.H., Pan, J.S., Lu, Z.H., Sun, S.H., Hang, H.M.: Vector quantization based on genetic simulated annealing. Signal Processing 81, 1513–1523 (2001)

[15] Xu, R.: Survey of clustering algorithms. IEEE Transactions on Neural Networks 16, 645–678 (2005)

[16] Kennedy, J., Eberhart, R.C.: Particle swarm optimization. In: Proceedings of the 1995 IEEE International Conference on Neural Networks, pp. 1942–1948. IEEE Press, New Jersey (1985)

[17] Dalli, A.: Adaptation of the F-measure to cluster-based Lexicon quality evaluation. In: EACL (2003)

A Study of Probability Collectives Multi-agent Systems on Optimization and Robustness

Chien-Feng Huang and Bao Rong Chang[*]

Department of Computer Science and Information Engineering,
National University of Kaohsiung, Taiwan, R.O.C.
{cfhuang15,brchang}@nuk.edu.tw

Abstract. We present a study on optimization and robustness of Probability Collectives Multi-agent Systems (PCMAS). This framework for distributed optimization is deeply connected with both game theory and statistical physics. In contrast to traditional biologically-inspired algorithms, Probability-Collectives (PC) based methods do not update populations of solutions. Instead, they update an explicitly parameterized probability distribution p over the space of solutions by a collective of agents. That updating of p arises as the optimization of a functional of p. The functional is chosen so that any p that optimizes it should be p peaked about good solutions. By comparing with genetic algorithms, we show that the PCMAS method appeared superior to the GA method in initial rate of decent, long term performance as well as the robustness of the search on complex optimization problems.

Keywords: Probability collectives; multi-agent systems; genetic algorithms; optimization; search robustness.

1 Introduction

Biologically-inspired algorithms, such as Genetic algorithms(GA) [1], Ant Colony Optimization (ACO) [2], Particle Swarm Optimization (PSO) [3], have been used as computational models to mimic evolutionary and social learning systems and as adaptive algorithms to solve complex problems. The core component of this class of optimization algorithms is a population of solutions that are employed to search for optimal solutions to the problem at hand. In the past decade, the research on Multi-agent Systems (MAS) has advanced the population-based algorithms with theoretical principles that shed light on the mechanism of system's decomposition and interacting agents' coordinating behavior in complex systems. As the complexity of a system grow, a generally more effective way to handle the system is through decomposition of the system into distributed and decentralized sub-systems and a given optimization task can be accomplished collectively by the sub-systems. In this scenario, the smaller subsystems can be regarded as a group of learning agents. These agents are self-interested and are

---

[*] Corresponding author.

N.T. Nguyen (Ed.): Transactions on CCI IV, LNCS 6660, pp. 141–159, 2011.

dedicated to optimizing their individual rewards or payoffs that in turn collectively optimize the global goal on the systems level.

Probability Collectives (PC) theory [4] refers to the systems-level objective as the world utility, which measures the performance of the whole system. PC is a broad framework for modeling and controlling distributed systems, and has deep connections to game theory, statistical physics, distributed control and optimization. Typically the search of adaptive, distributed agent-based algorithms is conducted by having each agent run its own reinforcement learning algorithm [5]. In this methodology the global utility function $G(x)$ in the system maps a joint move of the agents, $x \in X$, to the performance of the overall system. Moreover, in practice the agents in a MAS are bounded rational. The equilibrium they reach typically involves mixed strategies rather than pure strategies; i.e., they don't settle on a single point x that optimizes $G(x)$. This suggests formulating a framework to explicitly account for the bounded rational, mixed strategy characteristics of the agents. PC adopts this perspective to show that the equilibrium of a MAS is the minimizer of a Lagrangian $L(P)$ (derived using information theory) that quantifies the expected value of G for the joint distribution $P(x_1, x_2, \ldots, x_n)$ [4].

PC considers a bounded rational game in which each agent i chooses its move x_i independently at any instant by sampling its probability distribution (mixed strategy), $q_i(x_i)$. Accordingly, the probability distribution of the joint-moves is a product distribution; i.e.

$$P(x) = P(x_1, x_2, \ldots, x_n) = \prod_{i=1}^{N} q_i(x_i), \tag{1}$$

if there are N agents participate in the game. In this representation, all coupling between the agents occurs indirectly; it is the separate distributions of the agents q_i that are statistically coupled, yet the actual moves of the agents are independent. The core of the PCMAS[1] methodology is thus to approximate the joint distribution by the product distribution, and to concentrate on how the agents update the probability distributions across their possible actions instead of specifically on the joint action generated by sampling those distributions. This embodies a notion of a region where the optimum is likely to be located as well as an uncertainty due to both imperfect sampling, and the stochastic independence of the agents' actions.

The PC approach differs from traditional optimization methods such as gradient descent, GA and PSO that concentrate on a specific choice for the design variables (i.e., pure strategies) and on how to update that choice. Since the PC approach operates directly on probability distributions that optimize an associated Lagrangian, it offers a direct treatment for incorporating uncertainty, which is also represented through probabilities [6]. This is the most salient feature that this class of algorithms possesses – the search course is guided by a probability

---

[1] PCMAS is used here to reflect the nature of PC in the context of multi-agent systems. In this paper, PC and PCMAS are two exchangeable terms.

distribution over x, rather than a single value of x. By building such a probabilistic model of promising solutions and sampling the built model to generate new candidate solutions, PC allows the agents to significantly expand the range of exploration of the search space, and simultaneously focus on promising areas of solutions. As a result, this class of algorithms may provide a more robust and scalable solution to many important classes of optimization problems.

In [7] several benchmark testbeds were first studied to compare PCMAS with GA, which bear important characteristics of search space such as multimodality, nonlinearity and non-separability. Using these problems Huang et al. [7] showed that PCMAS can outperform GA in the rate of descent, trapping in false minima and long term optimization. More recently, Huang and Chang [8] presented a preliminary study on PCMAS that showed the search by the PCMAS is more robust than that of the GA.

Also recently, Kulkarni and Tai [9] compared PC with other optimization algorithms, including Chaos Genetic Algorithm (CGA) [10], Punctuated Anytime Learning (PAL) system [11] and Loosely Coupled GA (LCGA) [12]. They stated several advantages of PC that make it a competitive choice over other algorithms. In a nutshell, PC has the following advantages that can facilitate optimization tasks:

1. PC is a distributed solution approach in which each agent independently updates its probability distribution at any instant. In PC the probability of the strategy set is always a vector of real numbers, thereby allowing the techniques of the straightforward optimization for Euclidean vectors, such as gradient descent, to be applicable.
2. PC is robust in the sense that the cost function can be irregular or noisy. PC also provides the sensitivity information about the problem in the sense that a variable with a peaky distribution plays a more important role in the optimization task than a variable with a broad distribution. In essence, peaky distribution provides the best choice of action that contributes most to the optimization of the global utility.
3. The computational and communication load is marginally less and equally distributed among all the agents. Thus the framework of PC enables an efficient way to handle large-scale problems with many variables.

In this paper we report a further comparison on the search performance and robustness on function optimization between the PCMAS and GA. The goal is to investigate how agents in the PCMAS search for solutions in complex optimization problems. The organization of this paper is as follows. In Section 2, a review of PC is provided. Section 3 presents the experimental results. We then conclude this paper in Section 4.

2   Review of Probability Collectives

2.1   Non-cooperative Game Theory

Assume that a set of N agents participate in a noncooperative game in which a mixed strategy that agent i adopts is a distribution $q_i(x_i)$ over its allowed pure strategies [13]. Each agent i also has a private utility function $g_i(x)$ that maps a joint move of all the N agents, x (i.e., pure strategies adopted by all the agents) into the real numbers. Given mixed strategies of all the agents, the expected utility of agent i is

$$
E(g_i) = \int dx P(x) g_i(x)
$$
$$
= \int dx \prod_j q_j(x_j) g_i(x). \tag{2}
$$

Given the mixed strategies of the other agents, a Nash equilibrium indicates that every agent adopts a mixed strategy to maximize its own expected utility. In theory, Nash equilibria require the assumption of full rationality, that is, every agent i can calculate the strategies of the other agents and its own associated optimal distribution.

However, in the absence of full rationality the equilibrium is determined using the knowledge available to the agents. As a means to quantify this knowledge, the Shannon entropy,

$$
S(P) = -\int dy P(x) \ln(P(x)),
$$

describes a unique real-valued amount of syntactic information in a distribution $P(x)$. Given incomplete prior knowledge about $P(x)$, the maximum entropy (maxent) principle states that the best estimate of $P(x)$ is the distribution with the largest entropy, constrained by the prior knowledge. This approach has proven useful in domains ranging from signal processing to supervised learning [14].

In the case of maximal prior knowledge available to agent i, the actual joint-strategy of the agents and thus all of their expected utilities are known. For this situation, trivially, the maxent principle states that the estimated q is that joint-strategy (it being the q with maximal entropy that is consistent with the prior knowledge).

Removing agent i's strategy from this maximal prior knowledge leaves the mixed strategies of all agents other than i, together with agent i's expected utility. For prior knowledge concerning agent i's expected utility ε_i, the maxent estimate of the associated q_i is obtained by the minimizer of the Lagrangian:

$$
L_i(q_i) \equiv \beta_i[\varepsilon_i - E(g_i)] - S_i(q_i) \tag{3}
$$
$$
= \beta_i[\varepsilon_i - \int dx \prod_j q_j(x_j) g_i(x)] - S_i(q_i),
$$

where β_i denotes the inverse temperatures (i.e., $\beta_i = 1/T_i$) implicitly set by the constraint on the expected utility.

The solution is a set of coupled Boltzmann distributions:

$$q_i(x_i) \; \alpha \; e^{-\beta_i E_{q(i)}[g_i|x_i]}, \tag{4}$$

where the subscript $q(i)$ on the expectation value indicates that it is evaluated according to the distribution $\prod_{j\neq i} q_j$; and the expectation is conditioned on agent i making move x_i.

The first term in L_i of Eq. (3) is minimized by a perfectly rational agent, whereas the second term is minimized by a perfectly irrational agent, i.e., by a perfectly uniform mixed strategy q_i. Thus β_i in the maxent Lagrangian explicitly specifies the balance between the rational and irrational behavior of the agent. When $\beta \rightarrow \infty$, the set of q that simultaneously minimize the Lagrangians will recover the Nash equilibria of the game, which is the set of delta functions about the Nash equilibria.

In team games, the individual private utilities g_i's are the same and can be replaced with a single world utility G. In this case, the mixed strategies minimizing the Lagrangian are related to each other via

$$q_i(x_i) \; \alpha \; e^{-E_{q(i)}[G|x_i]}, \tag{5}$$

where the overall proportionality constant for each i is set by normalization, and

$$G(x) \equiv \sum_i \beta_i g_i(x). \tag{6}$$

Eq. (5) and (6) show that the probability of agent i choosing pure strategy x_i depends on the effect of that choice on the utilities of the other agents. Therefore, in the PC framework, even though the actual moves of the agents are independent, the probability distributions are coupled through expectation. Once all $q_i(x_i)$'s are determined, the probability distribution of the joint-moves by all the agents is a production distribution and can be obtained through Eq. (1).

2.2   Formulation of Optimization Problems

Given that the agents in PC are bounded rational, if they play a team game with world utility G, their equilibrium will be the optimizer of G. Furthermore, if constraints are included, the equilibrium will be the optimizer of G subject to the constraints. The equilibrium can be found by minimizing the Lagrangian:

$$L_q \equiv \sum_i \beta_i[E_q(g_i) - \varepsilon_i] - S(q), \tag{7}$$

with the prior information set being empty, i.e. for all i, $\varepsilon_i = 0$ [4].

Specifically for the unconstrained optimization problem,

$$\min_{x} G(\boldsymbol{x})$$

assumes each agent sets one component of x as that agent's action. The Lagrangian $L_i(q_i)$ for each agent as a function of the probability distribution across its actions (replacing β_i with $1 / T_i$) is,

$$L_i(q_i) = E[G(x_i, x_{(i)})] - T_i S(q_i)$$
$$= \sum_{x_i} q_i(x_i) E[G(x_i, x_{(i)})|X_i] + T_i \sum_{x_j} q_i(x_j) \ln(q_i(x_j)),$$

where G is the world utility (system objective), which depends upon the action of agent i, x_i, and the actions of the other agents, $x(i)$, simultaneously. During the minimization of the Lagrangian, the temperature T_i offers a means to adjust the degree of the exploitation of existing promising solutions (low temperature) and that of the exploration of the search space (high temperature).

The expectation $E[G(x_i, x_{(i)})]$ is evaluated according to the distributions of the agents other than i:

$$p(x_{(i)}) = \prod_{j \neq i} q_j(x_j).$$

Each agent then addresses the following local optimization problem:

$$\min_{q_i} L_i(q_i)$$

$$s.t. \sum_{x_i} q_i(x_i) = 1, q_i(x_i) \geq 0, \forall x_i.$$

One can employ gradient descent or Newton updating to minimize the Lagrangian since both the gradient and the Hessian are obtained in closed forms. Using Newton updating and enforcing the constraint on total probability, the following update rule at each iteration is obtained [15]:

$$q_i(x_i) \rightarrow q_i(x_i) - \alpha q_i(x_i) \times$$

$$\{(E[G|x_i] - E[G])/T_i + S(q_i) + \ln q_i(x_i)\}, \tag{8}$$

where α plays the role of a step size. The step size is required since the expectations result from the current probability distributions of all the agents. The update rule ensures that the total probability sums to unity but does not prevent negative probabilities. To ensure this, all negative components are set to a small positive value, typically 1×10^{-6}, and then the probability distribution is re-normalized.

2.3   Implementation of Probability Collectives

To perform the gradient descent in probability space each agent must estimate the expected value of any of its actions, $E[G|x_i]$, from Monte-Carlo samples. Briefly, optimization proceeds in alternating rounds of Monte-Carlo sampling blocks, and updates to the agent's probability distribution over the parameter

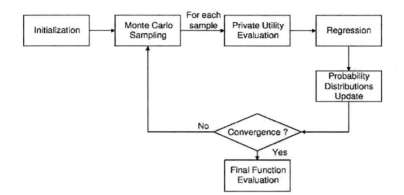

Fig. 1. PCMAS Flow Chart

value. To draw a Monte-Carlo sample each agent chooses the value for its parameter x_i from its current probability distribution, and the world cost function $G(x)$ is evaluated.

The number of samples in each Monte-Carlo block determines accuracy of the expected cost estimate. If sampling the objective function is costly, one may wish to gain the most information from the least number of samples. The kernel density estimation implies and exploits weak prior knowledge about smooth interpolation between the sample points. Additionally, as long as each iteration update does not dramatically change the PD, samples from the previous iterations may be re-used by geometrically weighting them according to their "age" in iterations. The imperfections that these augmentations introduce can be considered as another contribution to the bounded rationality term that broadens the probability distribution. The primary free parameters in the optimization are the Gaussian kernel width (τ), the rate of cooling ($\delta T/T$), the number of Monte-Carlo samples per iteration, the proportional step size in the gradient descent (α), and data-aging rate (γ).

The procedure for updating temperature T in PCMAS, referred to as the annealing schedule, plays an important role in the efficiency and reliability of the approach [16]. If the temperature is reduced too rapidly, the PCMAS is more likely to find a local minimum; however, if too slowly, then a large number of iterations and Monte-Carlo samples are required. Typically, a geometric schedule is applied, which involves multiplying the temperature by some fixed factor every several iterations.

The flow chart of the PCMAS is displayed in Figure 1 and its detailed steps are described in the following [16].

1. Initialize
   (a) Set the initial parameters, including temperature T and assign the annealing schedule for T as a function of iteration number.

    (b) Specify the number of Monte-Carlo samples N for each iteration.

    (c) Assign agents to the variables in the problem, with their actions representing choices for values. Set the starting probabilities for each agent to uniform over its possible actions.

    (d) Set the termination criteria.

2. Minimize the lagrangian

    (a) Monte-Carlo sample the agent probabilities to obtain N joint actions.

    (b) For each sample, evaluate the objective function and compute the private utility for each agent.

    (c) Compute the expected utilities for the agents for each of their possible moves using a regression.

    (d) Update the probability distributions according to Eq. (8).

    (e) Update the parameters. Use the assigned annealing schedule for T.

    (f) Evaluate the termination criteria. If not satisfied, return to step 2(a), otherwise proceed to 3.

3. Evaluation

    (a) Determine the highest probability action for each agent.

    (b) Evaluate the objective function with this set of actions.

3   Experimental Results

In this section, we report a comparison of the PCMAS with genetic algorithms in searching for the minima of several complex functions of various complexity and difficulty. Many of the characteristics in these testbeds are considered important by evolutionary algorithm practitioners, such as multimodality, nonlinearity and non-separability, etc. The study of search efficiency usually involves defining a performance measure that embodies the idea of rate of improvement, so that its change over time can be monitored for investigation. In many practical problems, a traditional performance metric is the "best-so-far" curve that plots the fitness of the best individual that has been seen thus far by generation n for the GA, i.e., a point in the search space that optimizes the objective function thus far. Due to the stochastic nature of the search processes, statistical measures using averaged best-so-far curves (over 50 runs at each generation) are presented for each testbed. The 95% confidence intervals about the means are then provided in order to illustrate the robustness of the search – narrower confidence intervals imply the search is more robust and reproducible over many runs.

    In contrast, in the PCMAS, the result returned is a probability distribution across the variable space that optimizes an associated Lagrangian. It embodies a notion of a region where the minimum is likely to be located as well as an uncertainty due to both imperfect sampling, and the stochastic independence of the agents' actions. To compare this on even ground to the GA, we focus solely on the samples themselves. We note however, this is an imperfect summary: for example, generally the maximum of the PD will not actually be one of the samples, though it is one's best single guess of the minimum.

Table 1. Mechanism of a simple GA

1. Randomly generate an initial population of l n-bit genotypes (individuals).
2. Evaluate each individual's fitness.
3. Repeat until l offspring have been created.
a. select a pair of parents for mating;
b. apply crossover operator;
c. apply mutation operator.
4. Replace the current population with the new population.
5. Re-interate from Step 2 until terminating condition.

In a basic genetic algorithm the population consists of genotypes that encode solutions (phenotypes) to some problems. Evolution occurs by iterated stochastic variation of genotypes, and selection of the best phenotypes is according to how well they optimize the function of interest. Table 1 depicts the process of a simple genetic algorithm by which we use to compare with the PCMAS algorithm.

For the GA to be compared, we examined a range of population sizes (50 and 100) to bracket a range of initial descent rates, long term performance and robustness tests. The 50 member populations generally descended quickly but converged to less satisfactory sub-optimal solutions than the 100 member GA did. Parameter values were finely discretized to approximate a continuous range, and encoded as bit strings. The GA experiments employ a binary tournament selection [17], one-point crossover and mutation rates of 0.7/pair and 0.005/bit, respectively.

In the following examples the optimization free parameters for the PCMAS were set as follows: step size $\alpha = 0.2$, data-ageing rate $\gamma = 0.5$, cooling rate $\delta_T/T = 0.01$, Gaussian kernel width τ is set to 1% of the range of the search parameter, and $T = 0.1$ was a sufficiently high starting temperature. Monte-calro block sizes of 25 and 50 were examined.

3.1   The Schaffer Function F_7

Schaffer's test function F_7 [18] is defined as:

$$f(\overline{x}) = (x_1^2 + x_2^2)^{0.25}[sin^2(50(x_1^2 + x_2^2)^{0.1}) + 1],$$

where $-1 \leq x_i \leq 1$ for $1 \leq i \leq 2$. Figure 2 displays the surface which is plotted upside down for easier viewing of the inverted minimum as a peak. Since there are many local optima in the search space, the population in the GA can easily converge on any of them. The barriers would also present considerable difficulty to search approaches that evolve a single point x using local gradient information.

For this simple 2-dimensional case one could feasibly model the probability distribution in the full joint PC space rather than approximating it as a product distribution. However since we are, in fact, exploring multi-agent systems, instead two agents will carry out the search in the two parameters independently. For the GA, each variable is encoded by 50 bits; thus each agent in the GA consists of a bit string of length 100 (two blocks of 50 bits are concatenated to form a string).

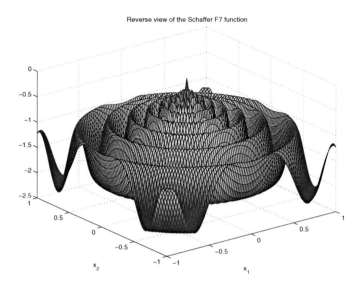

Fig. 2. Reverse view of the Schaffer F_7 function

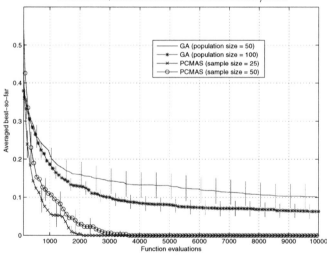

Fig. 3. Best-so-far performance on Schaffer F_7

Figure 3 displays the best-so-far values attained by the PCMAS and the GA as a function of the number of sample evaluations of the objective function. The curves are the mean values over 50 repetitions and the vertical bars are the 95% confidence intervals on the means. Curves for different population sizes of the GA are shown. The methods distinguish themselves with different rates of initial descent of the objective function (on left) and the long-term performance

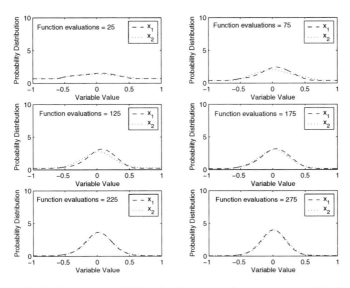

Fig. 4. Evolution of probability distributions of x_1 and x_2 on Schaffer F_7

(on right). Notably, the run-to-run variation of the performance trajectory is much lower on the PCMAS than for the GA (see vertical bars). As a result, the PCMAS best-so-far trajectory was far more reproducible than that of the GA, thereby implying the robustness of the search process in PCMAS.

Figure 4 displays the evolution of the probability distributions of the two variables for a typical PCMAS run. As can be seen, the probability density quickly centers about the optimum. This explains why the PCMAS is able to locate the optimum in a rather short period of time. Furthermore, since the agents in the PCMAS search the solution space by parameterizing the probability distributions of solutions, this algorithm actually explores a broader range of the search space than the point-based search by the GA does (i.e., searching for single points optimizing the objective function). This is the main reason that the search in the PCMAS is more robust than in the GA.

3.2   The Rosenbrock Function

The second testbed is the generalized Rosenbrock function in ten dimensions. The definition of this function is [19]:

$$f(\overline{x}) = \sum_{i=1}^{N-1} [100(x_i^2 - x_{i+1})^2 + (1 - x_i)^2], \tag{9}$$

where $\overline{x} = [x_1, x_2, \dots, x_N]^T$, $-5.12 \leq x_i \leq 5.12$.

Although the problem studied here is 10 dimensional ($N{=}10$) with ten agents, in Figure 5 we provide a visual gist of the reversed surface by showing the Rosenbrock function in two-dimensions. For easy viewing of the minimum as a peak, a logarithmic vertical axis is displayed in this figure to illustrate the sharp spike.

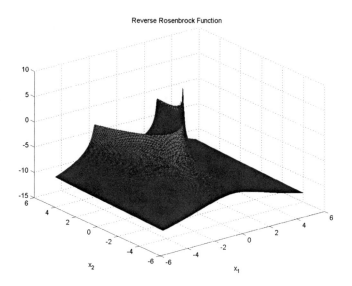

Fig. 5. Reverse view of the logarithm of the Rosenbrock function

Rosenbrock's saddle is a classic optimization problem with a narrow global optimum hidden inside a long, narrow, curved flat valley. Monte-carlo methods will have difficulty landing a point in the narrow spike and thus will not efficiently locate it. The U-shape will also tend to make decomposition of the PCMAS into a product distribution challenging. Since it has no barriers the surface would be ripe for gradient descent; however while the valley will be found quickly the curvature and flatness of the valley floor will frustrate sampled gradient estimation.

Here we examine the case for 10 dimensions. Each individual in the GA is a 200 bit-string concatenated by ten blocks of 20 bits each encoding a variable. The empirical results are displayed in Figure 6. The top of this figure shows the best-so-far values attained by the algorithms. The bottom plot displays a detailed view from the range of the objective's value on the interval [0, 70]. One can clearly see that the PCMAS technique can locate the global optimum more quickly than the GA, along with the narrower 95% confidence intervals that again imply the search process in PCMAS is more robust than in the GA.

3.3   De Jong Function F_3

The third testbed studied is De Jong's function F_3 [20]:

$$f(\overline{x}) = \sum_{i=1}^{N} \text{integer}(x_i), \tag{10}$$

where $\overline{x} = [x_1, x_2, \ldots, x_N]^T$, $-5.12 \leq x_i \leq 5.12$ for $1 \leq i \leq N$. A two-dimensional sketch of this function is illustrated in Figure 7, which displays

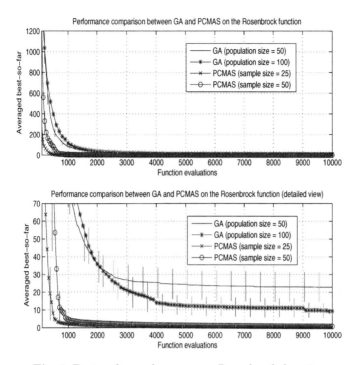

Fig. 6. Best-so-far performance on Rosenbrock function

the characteristics of a simple, unimodal step function. One thus expects that the global minimum is easy to locate by the GA or PCMAS.

For this testbed, each individual of the population of the GA is a 100 bit-string concatenated by two blocks of 50 bits each encoding a variable. The empirical results are displayed in Figure 8. Notably, the PCMAS is able to identify the optimum almost immediately after the the algorithm starts, yet it takes many functions for the GA to accomplish the same goal. One can also see that the 95% confidence intervals of the PCMAS are virtually invisible, especially when being compared with those of the GA. The results here again show that the search process in PCMAS is more robust than that in the GA.

3.4   The Ackley Path Function

Ackley's Path [21] is a widely used multimodal test function. The function's definition is:

$$f(\overline{x}) = -ae^{-b(\frac{\sum_i x_i^2}{N})^{\frac{1}{2}}} - e^{\frac{\sum_i cos(cx_i)}{N}} + a + e^1,$$

where $a=20$, $b=0.2$, $c = 2\pi$, and $-32.768 \leq x_i \leq 32.768$ for $1 \leq i \leq n$.

The problem we use here is again 10 dimensional (N=10); thus the PCMAS will use ten agents to search for the optimum. For the GA, each individual of the population is a 200 bit-string concatenated by ten blocks of 20 bits each

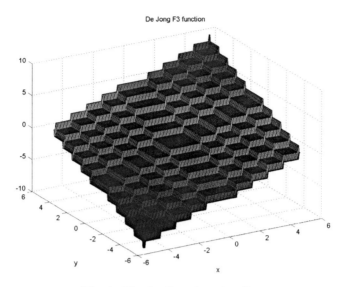

Fig. 7. The De Jong function F_3

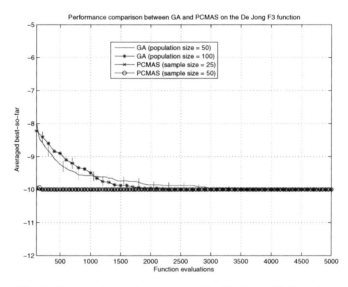

Fig. 8. Best-so-far performance on the De Jong F3 Function

encoding a variable. Figure 9 gives a visual gist of the function in a lower 2-dimensional form. The surface is overall a single deep well with a locally rough surface. For easy viewing of the details the figure is enlarged, showing the region in the neighborhood of the minimum.

The empirical results of the search algorithms on this surface are displayed in Figure 10. The PCMAS again outperforms the GA in early decent towards the minimum and the search is more reproducible than that of the GA.

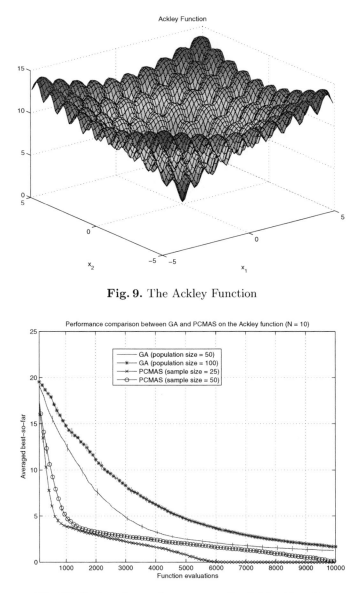

Fig. 9. The Ackley Function

Fig. 10. Best-so-far performance on the Ackley Function

3.5   The Michalewicz Function

The final testbed employed in this section is Michalewicz's epistatic function
[22]:

$$f(\overline{x}) = - \sum_{i=1}^{N} sin(y_i) sin^{2m}(\frac{iy_i^2}{\pi}),$$

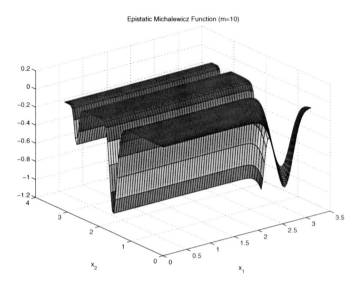

Fig. 11. The Michalewicz Function ($m{=}10$)

where

$$y_i = x_i cos\frac{\pi}{6} - x_{i+1} sin\frac{\pi}{6}, \quad \text{if } i \mod 2 = 1 \text{ and } i \neq N;$$

$$y_i = x_{i-1} sin\frac{\pi}{6} + x_i cos\frac{\pi}{6}, \quad \text{if } i \mod 2 = 0 \text{ and } i \neq N;$$

$$y_N = x_N,$$

$0 \leq x_i \leq \pi$ for $1 \leq i \leq N$.

A system is highly epistatic if the optimal allele for any locus depends on a large number of alleles at other loci. The concept of epistasis in nature corresponds to nonlinearity in the context of GA [23]. This function is a highly multimodal, nonlinear and nonseparable testbed ($n!$ local optima). A sketch of a two-dimensional version of this function is displayed in Figure 11 for the steepness parameter $m = 10$. Larger m leads to more difficult search. For very large m the function behaves like a needle in the haystack since the function values for points in the space outside the narrow peaks give very little information on the location of the global optimum.

The periodic, self-similar valleys can be expected to create more local minima in the product space PD than in the true fully coupled representation. Thus this surface will be hard for PCMAS. Another difficulty comes from the simple rotation of the valleys that couple all the axes in pairs. This explicit coupling is well designed to frustrate the explicitly decoupled multi-agent probability system. Conversely, because only consecutive alleles are coupled by the rotation, cross-over is well prepared to conserve this coupling in evolution.

We searched a ten dimensional ($N{=}10$) space for the cases of $m = 10$ and $m = 200$. As before the GA used 20 bits per variable. The empirical results are displayed in Figure 12 and Figure 13 for $m = 10$ and $m = 200$, respectively.

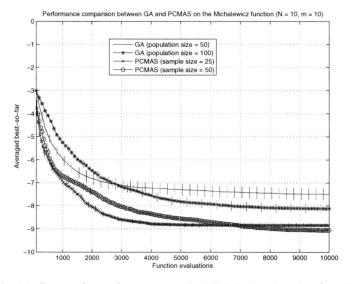

Fig. 12. Best-so-far performance on the Michalewicz function (m=10)

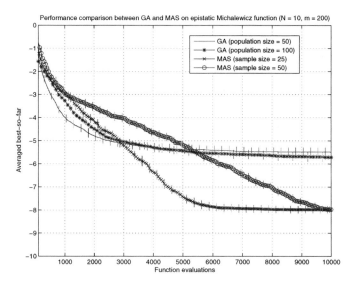

Fig. 13. Best-so-far performance on the Michalewicz function (m=200)

It is clear that the PCMAS technique again outperforms the GA. In particular, in case of $m = 200$, the PCMAS still demonstrates a surprisingly effective and robust search power even though the function behaves like a needle in the haystack and is very difficult to search.

4   Conclusions

We presented a comparative study of two agent-based adaptive algorithms – the PCMAS and the GA approaches. The PCMAS approach introduces a methodology by which the search course in this system is guided by probability distribution over variables, rather than using single values derived from those variables. We have shown that the PCMAS method appeared superior to the GA method both in initial rate of decent and long term performance. In addition, since the best-so-far trajectories of the PCMAS were far more reproducible than those of the GA, the search of the PCMAS is thus shown to be more robust than the GA on these complex optimization problems.

References

[1] Holland, J.H.: Adaptation in Natural and Artificial Systems. University of Michigan Press, Ann Arbor (1975)

[2] Dorigo, M.: Optimization, learning and natural algorithms. Ph.D. thesis, Politecnico di Milano (1992)

[3] Kennedy, J., Eberhart, R.C.: Particle swarm optimization. In: Proc. of IEEE International Conference on Neural Networks, pp. 1942–1948 (1995)

[4] Wolpert, D.H.: Theory of collectives. The Design and Analysis of Collectives. Springer, New York (2003), http://ic.arc.nasa.gov/dhw

[5] Wolpert, D.H.: Information theory – the bridge connecting bounded rational game theory and statistical physicsy. In: Braha, D., Bar-Yam, Y. (eds.) Complex Engineering Systems. Perseus Books, Cambridge (2004)

[6] Bieniawski, S., Wolpert, D. H., Kroo, I.: Discrete, continuous, and constrained optimization using collectives. In: Proc. of the 10th AIAA/ISSMO Multidisciplinary Analysis and Optimization Conference, AIAA Paper 2004–4580 (2004)

[7] Huang, C.F., Bieniawski, S., Wolpert, D.H., Strauss, C.: Comparative study of probability collectives based multi–agent systems and genetic algorithms. In: Proc. of the 2005 Genetic and Evolutionary Computation Conference (GECCO 2005), pp. 751–752 (2005)

[8] Huang, C.-F., Chang, B.R.: Probability collectives multi-agent systems: A study of robustness in search. In: Pan, J.-S., Chen, S.-M., Nguyen, N.T. (eds.) ICCCI 2010. LNCS (LNAI), vol. 6422, pp. 334–343. Springer, Heidelberg (2010)

[9] Kulkarni, A., Tai, K.: Probability collectives: a multi-agent approach for solving combinatorial optimization problems. Applied Soft Computing 10(3), 759–771 (2010)

[10] Cheng, C., Wang, W., Xu, D., Chau, K.: Optimizing hydropower reservoir operation using hybrid genetic algorithm and chaos. Water Resource Management 22, 895–909 (2008)

[11] Blumenthal, H., Parker, G.: Benchmarking punctuated anytime learning for evolving a multi-agent team's binary controllers. In: World Automation Congress (2006)

[12] Bouvry, P., Arbab, F., Seredynski, F.: Distributed evolutionary optimization, in Manifold: Rosenbrock's function case study. Information Sciences 122, 141–159 (2000)

[13] Fudenberg, D., Tirole, J.: Game Theory. MIT Press, Cambridge (1991)

[14] Mackay, D.: Information Theory, Inference, and Learning Algorithms. Cambridge University Press, Cambridge (2003)

[15] Wolpert, D., Bieniawski, S.: Distributed control by lagrangian steepest descent. In: Proc. of the 43rd IEEE Conference on Decision and Control, pp. 1562–1567 (2004)

[16] Bieniawski, S.: Distributed optimization and flight control using collectives. Ph.D. thesis, Stanford University, CA (2005)

[17] Goldberg, D. E., Deb, K.: A comparative analysis of selection schemes used in genetic algorithms. Foundation of Genetic Algorithms, 69–93 (1991)

[18] Schaffer, J.D., Caruana, R.A., Eshelman, L.J., Das, R.: A study of control parameters affecting online performance of genetic algorithms for function optimization. In: Proc. 3rd International Conference on Genetic Algorithms, pp. 51–60. Morgan Kaufmann, San Francisco (1989)

[19] Second International Contest on Evolutionary Optimization, held in the IEEE-ICEC 1997 Conference (1997)

[20] De Jong, K.: Analysis of the Behavior of a Class of Genetic Adaptive Systems. PhD thesis, University of Michigan, Ann Arbor (1975)

[21] Ackley, D.H.: A connectionist machine for genetic hillclimbing. Kluwer Academic Publishers, Boston (1987)

[22] Michalewicz, Z.: Genetic Algorithms + Data Structures = Evolution Programs. Springer, Heidelberg (1992)

[23] Goldberg, D.E.: Genetic Algorithms in search, Optimization, and Machine Learning. Addison Wesley, Reading (1989)

Inference Rules in Multi-agents' Temporal Logics

Vladimir Rybakov

School of Computing, Mathematics & Digital Technology,
Manchester Metropolitan University, Manchester, U.K. and, part time,
Siberian Federal University, Krasnoyarsk, Russia
V.Rybakov@mmu.ac.uk

Abstract. Aim of this paper[1] is to work out a framework for computation inference rules valid in agents' temporal logics. Coordinated, rational actions of agents use logical reasoning, derivations (in order to predict results). As a tool, describing human reasoning procedure, we suggest valid inference rules (valid semantically - in Kripke-like frames generating logic). Our paper studies inference rules valid in temporal agents' logics admitting various representations of time, in particular, we consider logics with linear and branching intransitive time. We suggest algorithms which allow to compute valid inference rules in agents' liner time logics $\mathcal{LTL}_K$ and $\mathcal{LTL}_K(Z)$, agents' logic with branching intransitive time $\mathcal{L}_{TA_i}$, and the logic with branching transitive time $\mathcal{L}_{TA_t}$.

Keywords: multi-agents' logics, temporal logics, linear temporal logic, inference rules, valid inference rules.

1   Introduction, Research Background

We can view a multi-agent system as a system composed of multiple interacting intelligent agents. Such systems as usual are applied to solve problems which are difficult or impossible for an individual agent or monolithic system to solve (take as trivial examples high school teaching, online trading etc). From theoretical viewpoint, these systems are classified and studied in a special branches of AI. In particular, a special field in AL is properties of logical reasoning in multi-agent environment modeled by various multi-agent logical systems. In general, prime objective of AI is: to describe the property of humans, intelligence - the sapience of Homo sapiens - so precisely that it can be simulated by a machine. This grandiose task been standing a set of issues about the nature of the mind and limits of scientific hubris, and one of most intriguing questions was what is human reasoning procedure.

In turn, this generated research based on mathematical symbolic logic which describes reasoning and true statements. Today, it has become an essential part

---

[1] This research is supported by Engineering and Physical Sciences Research Council (EPSRC), U.K., grant EP/F014406/1.

N.T. Nguyen (Ed.): Transactions on CCI IV, LNCS 6660, pp. 160–176, 2011.

of AI, providing the heavy lifting for many difficult problems in computer science. Usage of symbolic mathematical logic, and especially various systems of non-classical logic in AI is very popular (cf. van Benthem [1,2], - temporal and modal logic, Gabbay (et.al) [3,4,5] - modal, multi-modal, temporal logics, inference, Hodkinson (at. al) [6,7,8,9] - temporal, temporal linear and real time logic, first-order branching time logic, time and automata). A corner part of representation for human reasoning is inference: the process of drawing a conclusion by applying rules to observations or hypotheses.

Human inference (i.e. how humans draw conclusions) is traditionally studied within the field of cognitive psychology. Mathematical logic studies the laws of valid inference, and we would like work out a logical framework for computation valid inference in multi-agents' logics, which are combinations (or hybrids) of multi-modal and temporal logics.

Various applications of multi-modal logic to AI and CS is a popular area. In particular, they are based on usage of multi-agent logic, as a part (or implementation) of epistemic logic. Among epistemic logics to model knowledge a range from $S4$ over the intermediate systems $S4.2 - S4.4$ to $S5$ has been investigated (Hintikka – S4 (1962), Kutschera argued for S4.4 (1976), Lenzen suggested S4.2 (1978), van der Hoek has proposed to strengthen knowledge according to system S4.3 (1996), van Ditmarsch, van der Hoek and Kooi together with Fagin, Halpern, Moses and Vardi (Fagin et al. 1995 [10], cf. also [11]) and others assume knowledge to be S5 valid). The developed approach to model multi-agent environment in AI often combines, not only modal operations for agents' knowledge and Boolean logical operations, but also other ones - e.g. operations for time - temporal operations, dynamic logic operations (cf. R.Schmidt et.al [12]). Through multi-agent approach we may view the logic of discovery, which has a solid prehistory, maybe, starting from the monograph Logic of Discovery and Logic of Discourse by Jaakko Hintikka and Fernand Vandamme [13]. The mentioned above logical systems are, as a rule, some hybrids of individual ones.

They are usually introduced by combination (fusion) of several non-classical logics. Among these logics, the linear temporal logic LTL was very popular. Temporal logics and, in particular, LTL, is currently the most widely used specification formalism for reactive systems. They were first suggested to be used for specifying properties of programs in late 1970's (cf. Pnueli [14]). The most used temporal framework is the linear-time propositional temporal logic LTL, which has been studied from various viewpoints (cf. e.g. Manna and Pnueli [15,16], Clark E. et al. [17]). Temporal logics have numerous applications to safety, liveness and fairness, to various problems arising in computing. Model checking for LTL formed a noticeable trend in applications of logic in Computer Science, which uses, in particular, applications of automata theory (cf. Vardi [18,19]). Temporal logics themselves can be considered as special cases of hybrid logics, e.g. as a bimodal logic with some additional laws imposed on interaction of modalities to emulate the flow of time.

The mathematical theory dedicated to study of various aspects concerning interaction of temporal operations (e.g. axiomatizations of temporal logics) and to construction of effective semantic theory based on Kripke/Hintikka-like models and temporal Boolean algebras, formed a highly technical branch in non-classical logics (cf. e.g. van Benthem [20,21], Goldblatt [22], Gabbay and Hodkinson [23], Hodkinson [24]). Admissible inference rules is some temporal logics where investigated in Rybakov [25,26,27].

Multi-agents' knowledge logics may be referred to hybrid logics as well, they form active area in AI and Knowledge Representation (cf. Bordini et al. [28], Dix et al. [29], Hoek et al. [30], Fisher [31], Hendler [32], Kacprzak [33], Wooldridge [34]). In a sense, multi-agent logics came from a particular application of multi-modal logics to reasoning about knowledge (cf. Fagin et al. [10,35], Halpern and Shore [11]), where modal-like operations K_i (responsible for knowledge of individual agents) were embedded in the language of propositional logic. These operations are intended to model effects and properties of agents' knowledge in changing environment. When we going to make combination of a multi-agent logic and a background logic (say for time), a reasonable question appears: which logic should be used as the basic logic. For instance, if the logic used as the basis is too expressive — the undecidability phenomenon can occur (cf. Kacprzak [33] with reduction of the decidability to the domino problem). If the basic logic is just the boolean logic, and the agents are autonomous, decidability for the standard systems usually can be obtained by techniques from modal logic, e.g. filtration, (cf. [10,35]).

In this our paper (it is an extended version of conference paper [36]) we would like to consider more complicated case: linear temporal logic and other temporal logics as a background logics. The main aim is to work out a framework for computation inference rules valid in agents' temporal logics, in particular, to find algorithms for computation valid inference rules. We will consider some extensions of the linear temporal logic LTL (which is simplest case) and branching temporal logic with potentially intransitive time accessibility relation (though the technique work for transitive time as well). For this, we adopt and extend our approach applied previously in Rybakov et al. [37,38,39]. Proposed algorithms reduce verification of validity for inference rules in considered logics to the computation of truth of special inference rules in finite (effectively finite) models. In the final part of the paper we briefly discuss extension our research to verification of admissible rules. Some necessary conditions for admissibility immediately follow from obtained results.

2   Definitions, Notation Preliminaries

We proceed by necessary definitions and notation to follow the paper (though some preliminary acquaintance with non-classical propositional logics (mathematical approach) and their algebraic and Kripke-Hintikka semantics is advisable). Our main aim is to work out a framework, which would allow correctly compute valid inference rules, valid logical inference. Let us consider any propositional logic (modal, temporal, intuitionistic etc.) Λ, whose set of all formulas is denoted by Fm_Λ. A (an inference) rule is an expression

$$\frac{\alpha_1, \ldots, \alpha_n}{\beta}$$

(often, for short, we write $\alpha_1, \ldots, \alpha_n / \beta$), where $\alpha_i, \beta \in Fm_\Lambda$. An informal meaning of this inference rule is: (i) β follows from premisses (assumptions, hypothesis) $\alpha_1, \ldots, \alpha_n$, or (ii) this rule infers β from $\alpha_1, \ldots, \alpha_n$. As an informal example, consider: "When it rains, the grass gets wet. It rains. Therefore, the grass is wet." For the formalization the notions of intelligence and argumentation in all forms, logical inference is of fundamental importance. Which inference rules may be taken as correct formalism is non-trivial question. In this paper we will study so called valid inference rules.

Given a logic Λ defined by a class K of Kripke models M, based on a class F of Kripke frames. A rule $r = \alpha_1 \ldots \alpha_m / \beta$ is *valid in a model* $\mathcal{M} = \langle \mathcal{F}, Val \rangle \in M$, where $\mathcal{F} \in F$, (symbolically $\mathcal{M} \Vdash r$), if

$$[\forall_i (\mathcal{M} \Vdash_{Val} \alpha_i)] \Longrightarrow \mathcal{M} \Vdash_{Val} \beta.$$

So, the meaning of the rule r to be valid in $\mathcal{M}$ is as follows: if all premisses of r are valid in the model then the conclusion is valid as well.

A rule r is *valid in a frame* $\mathcal{F} \in F$, if, for every valuation Val of variables from r, $\mathcal{F} \Vdash_{Val} r$. Finally, r is valid in logic Λ generated by a class of frames F, if for any frame $\mathcal{F} \in F$, r is valid in $\mathcal{F}$. This definition looks quite correct from general viewpoint: the rule is valid if it is valid everywhere - in all models generating Λ. Basic question which we are dealing with is how to compute valid inference (how verify if a given rule is valid). Below we start from illustration on how to compute valid inference in agents' logics based on linear time background.

The logic $\mathcal{LTL}_K$ introduced in [40] is the agents' logic based on linear time. We recall basis definition and facts concerning this logic. The generating this logic frames

$$\mathcal{N}_C := \langle \bigcup_{i \in N} C(i), R, R_1, \ldots R_m, Next \rangle$$

are tuples, where N is the set of natural numbers, $C(i), i \in N$ are some pairwise disjoint nonempty sets, $R, R_1, \ldots, R_m$ are binary relations, emulating agents' accessibility. For all elements a and b from $\bigcup_{i \in N} C(i)$

$$aRb \iff [a \in C(i) \text{ and } b \in C(j) \text{ and } i < j] \text{ or } [a, b \in C(i) \text{ for some } i];$$

any R_j is a reflexive, transitive and symmetric relation (i.e an equivalence relation), and

$$\forall a, b \in \bigcup_{i \in N} C(i), \ aR_j b \Longrightarrow [a, b \in C(i) \text{ for some } i];$$

$$a \ Next \ b \iff \exists i [a \in C(i) \ \& \ b \in C(i+1)].$$

These frames are intended to model the reasoning (or computation) in discrete time, so each $i \in N$ (any natural number i) is the time index for a cluster of states arising at a step in current computation. Any $C(i)$ is a set of all possible states in the time point i, and the relation R models discrete current of time. Relations R_j are intended to model knowledge-accessibility relations of agents in any cluster of states $C(i)$ at the time point i. Thus any R_j is supposed to be $S5$-like relation, i.e an equivalence relation. The *Next* relation is the standard one – it describes all states available in the next time point cluster.

The language of $\mathcal{LTL}_K$ uses the language of Boolean logic, operations $\mathbf{N}$ (next), $\mathbf{U}$ (until)), $\mathbf{U}_w$ (weak until), $\mathbf{U}_s$ (strong until), agents' knowledge (unary) operations K_j, $1 \leq j \leq m$ and *knowledge via interaction operation* $\mathbf{IntK}$. Formation rules for formulas are as usual. For any collection of propositional letters *Prop* and any frame $\mathcal{N}_C$, a valuation in $\mathcal{N}_C$ is a mapping which assigns truth values to elements of *Prop* in $\mathcal{N}_C$. So, for any $p \in Prop$, $V(p) \subseteq \mathcal{N}_C$. We will call $\langle \mathcal{N}_C, V \rangle$ a model (a Kripke/Hintikka model). For any model $\mathcal{M}$, the truth values are extended from propositions (in *Prop*) to arbitrary formulas (built over *Prop*) as follows (for $a \in \mathcal{N}_C$, notation $(\mathcal{N}_C, a) \Vdash_V \varphi$ says that the formula φ is true at a in $\mathcal{N}_C$ w.r.t. V).

The rules are as follows:

$\forall p \in Prop, \quad (\mathcal{M}, a) \Vdash_V p \Leftrightarrow a \in V(p)$;

$(\mathcal{M}, a) \Vdash_V \varphi \wedge \psi \Leftrightarrow (\mathcal{M}, a) \Vdash_V \varphi \ \& \ (\mathcal{M}, a) \Vdash_V \psi$;

$(\mathcal{M}, a) \Vdash_V \neg \varphi \Leftrightarrow \mathrm{not}[(\mathcal{M}, a) \Vdash_V \varphi]$;

$(\mathcal{M}, a) \Vdash_V \mathbf{N}\varphi \Leftrightarrow \forall b[(a \text{ Next } b) \Rightarrow (\mathcal{M}, b) \Vdash_V \varphi]$;

$(\mathcal{M}, a) \Vdash_V \varphi \mathbf{U}\psi \Leftrightarrow \exists b[(aRb) \& ((\mathcal{M}, b) \Vdash_V \psi) \& \forall c[(aRcRb) \& \neg(bRc) \Rightarrow (\mathcal{M}, c) \Vdash_V \varphi]]$.

Similar rules work for $\mathbf{U}_w$ and $\mathbf{U}_s$.

$(\mathcal{M}, a) \Vdash_V \varphi \mathbf{U}_w\psi \Leftrightarrow \exists b[(aRb) \& ((\mathcal{M}, b) \Vdash_V \psi) \wedge \forall c[(aRcRb) \& \neg(bRc) \& (c \in C(i)) \Rightarrow$

$\exists d \in C(i)(\mathcal{M}, d) \Vdash_V \varphi]]$;

$(\mathcal{M}, a) \Vdash_V \varphi \mathbf{U}_s\psi \Leftrightarrow \exists b[(aRb) \& b \in C(i) \& \forall c \in C(i)((\mathcal{M}, c) \Vdash_V \psi) \&$

$\forall c[(aRcRb) \& \neg(bRc) \Rightarrow (\mathcal{M}, c) \Vdash_V \varphi]]$;

Further, for operations K_j and $\mathbf{IntK}$ we use rules:

$(\mathcal{M}, a) \Vdash_V K_j\varphi \Leftrightarrow \forall b[(a \ R_j \ b) \Rightarrow (\mathcal{M}, b) \Vdash_V \varphi]$;

$(\mathcal{M}, a) \Vdash_V \mathbf{IntK}\varphi \Leftrightarrow \exists a_{i_1}, \ldots, a_{i_s} \in \mathcal{M}[aR_{i_1}a_{i_1}R_{i_2}a_{i_2} \ldots R_{i_s}a_{i_s} \ \&$

$(\mathcal{M}, a_{i_s}) \Vdash_V \varphi]$.

$\mathbf{N}\varphi$ has meaning: φ holds in the next time cluster of states
(at all states of that cluster);
$\varphi\mathbf{U}\psi$ can be read: φ holds until ψ will hold;
$\varphi\mathbf{U}_w\psi$ has meaning: φ weakly holds until ψ will hold;
$\varphi\mathbf{U}_s\psi$ says: φ strongly holds until ψ will hold;
$K_j\varphi$ means: the agent j *knows* φ at the current state of a time cluster.
$\mathbf{IntK}\varphi$ means: φ is known by interaction between agents.

$(\mathcal{M}, a) \Vdash_V \mathbf{IntK}\varphi$ says that there is a finite path (of unbounded length) of interchanging agents' accessibility relations which leads to a state where φ is true. Intuitively it looks as agents interact and pass each other the information that φ is true at some state. So, φ is known in a via an *interaction* of agents. It looks as an interesting application of the common knowledge operation introduced in e.g. [10].

Notice also that, in the rules above, the treatment of $\mathbf{U}$ is slightly different from standard one – it is sufficient for ψ to be true at least at one state of the achievable current time cluster. The operation $\mathbf{U}_w$ more drastically differs from the standard $\mathbf{U}$, – it is sufficient for φ to be true only in a certain state of all time clusters before ψ will become true at a state. And the strong until – $\varphi\mathbf{U}_s\psi$ – means that there is a time point i, where the formula ψ is true at all states in the time cluster $C(i)$, and φ holds in all states of all time points j preceding i.

3   Possible Applications of Suggested Logical Operations

The operations $\mathbf{U}_w$ and $\mathbf{U}_s$ may be implemented for reasoning about network computations and their supervision. Assume that any $C(i)$ in the model

$$\mathcal{N}_C := \langle \bigcup_{i \in N} C(i), R, R_1, \ldots, R_m, Next, V \rangle$$

consists of CPUs available at the time moment i. Any p from *Prop* is a computational task, and $(\mathcal{N}_C, a) \Vdash_V p$ means that the CPU a performs a computation for p.

(i) *Persistence.* The truth relation:

$$(\mathcal{N}_C, a) \Vdash_V p \, \mathbf{U}_w q$$

means that, in the future, some CPU will start computation for q and before this, in any time point there is a CPU which performs computation for p. Thus $\mathbf{U}_w$ allows us to check *persistence* in computations for p. (Here and below we can interpret latter q in operation $\mathbf{U}_w$ and other $\mathbf{U}$-like operations as a termination condition).

(ii) *Idleness.* The statement

$$(\mathcal{N}_C, a) \Vdash_V p \, \mathbf{U}_s q$$

means that in some future time point all CPUs will compute q and before this all CPUs make computations for p. So, $\mathbf{U}_s$ can check that there no *idle* CPUs w.r.t. p.

(iii) *Distributed computation.* The fact

$$(\mathcal{N}_C, a) \Vdash_V \neg(p \wedge q)\mathbf{U}_s r$$

means that before a computation for r will start no CPUs are performing computations for p and q simultaneously. So, this way we can check a kind of *distribution* of computations for p and q: no CPUs computing both p and q (so to say computations for p and q must be *disjunctive*).

(iv) *Parallel computation.* The relation

$$(\mathcal{N}_C, a) \Vdash_V (\neg(p \wedge q)\mathbf{U}_s r) \wedge (p \ \mathbf{U}_w r) \wedge (q \ \mathbf{U}_w r)$$

represents parallel computation of tasks p and q. The formula above says that the computation for p and q are distributed (before the termination signal r) and *parallel:* in any time (before termination by r) there are two distinct CPUs one of which perform computation for p and another one – for q. These examples illustrate some of motives for introduction new operations $\mathbf{U}_w$ and $\mathbf{U}_s$.

The major distinction of our logic from the standard propositional temporal logic LTL is embedding of a *structure* into the states. We replace a single state i (which (usually) is a world in a linear Kripke model) with a structure $C(i)$ (which is a Kripke model for multi-agents' logic $\mathbf{KD45_m}$, the latter is the multi-modal logic $S5_m$). Every $C(i)$ is a set with a collection of agents' binary accessibility relations R_j. In terms of implementation, we can present any $C(i)$ as a collection of all possible web sites in a network at a time moment i, and any R_j is all web links available for the agent j.

Therefore the introduction of the operation $\mathbf{IntK}$, *to be known via interaction between agents* (cf. definition of the rule for the computation of its truth value above), is very relevant to this approach. Indeed, $\mathbf{IntK}$ means that the information about the truth of a proposition may be transferred via agents' interaction: an agent passes the information to another one, etc. until it will reach the state (web site) where it has been requested.

To briefly compare the suggested logical operations with standard ones, note that using operations $\mathbf{U}$ and $\mathbf{N}$ we can define all standard temporal and modal operations. For instance, $\mathbf{F}\varphi$ (φ *holds eventually*, which, in terms of modal logic, means φ is possible (denotation $\Diamond\varphi$)), can be described as $true\mathbf{U}\varphi$. Therefore, we can also define the modal operation $\Box$ (as $\Box\varphi := \neg\Diamond\neg\varphi$) in this language. The temporal operation $\mathbf{G}$, where $\mathbf{G}\varphi$ means φ *holds henceforth*, can be defined as $\neg\mathbf{F}\neg\varphi$. We can describe within this language various properties of transition systems and Kripke structures. For instance, the formula $\mathbf{G}(\neg request \vee (request \ \mathbf{U} \ grant))$ says that whenever a request is made it holds continuously until it is eventually granted.

The standard temporal operations together with knowledge operations add more expressive power to the language.

(v) *Discoverability.* The formula $\Box\neg K_1\neg\varphi$ says that, for any future time cluster and for any state a of this cluster the knowledge φ is *discoverable* for agent 1, it has access to a state b where φ holds. So φ is always discoverable for the agent 1.

(vi) *Weak necessity.* The formula

$$\Box_w\varphi := \neg(\top\mathbf{U}_s\neg\varphi)$$

expresses the *weak necessity*, it says that in any time cluster $C(i)$ there is a state where φ is true.

To give more examples, the formula

$$(\neg\varphi\mathbf{U}_w\Box\varphi) \wedge \Diamond\Box\varphi$$

signifies that there is a minimal time point i since which φ holds in all states of all future time clusters, but before the time point i the formula φ is false in a state of any time cluster. Such properties are difficult to express in terms of standard modal or temporal operations.

The operations $\mathbf{U}_s$ and $\mathbf{U}_w$ may be presented using standard operation $\mathbf{U}$ and the *belief* operation (universal modality on whole $C(i)$ for each i). Vice versa, the *belief* operation *locally* may be expressed by $\mathbf{U}_s$. Also the operation *belief* is too strong: it covers all agents' knowledge operations and **IntK**, and its introduction into the language would collapse the approach. Introduction the operation *believe* in $C(i)$ (in the context of the paper) would not much intended interpretations (as network computation, web surfing), e.g. it does not look realistic to assume that there is a omniscient supervisor: agent who can use any web link and can open any web site. The expressions for standard modal and temporal operations presented above are only for illustration of expressive power of our language, below we use only postulated language and notation.

4   Temporal Logics: Linear Case – $\mathcal{LTL}_K$ and Close Logics

Definition 1. For a Kripke structure $\mathcal{M} := \langle \mathcal{N}_C, \leq, V \rangle$ and a formula φ, we say that

(i) φ is satisfiable in $\mathcal{M}$ (denotation – $\mathcal{M} \Vdash_{Sat}\varphi$) if there is a state b of $\mathcal{M}$ ($b \in \mathcal{N}_C$) where φ is true: $(\mathcal{M}, b) \Vdash_V \varphi$.

(ii) φ is valid in $\mathcal{M}$ (denotation – $\mathcal{M} \Vdash \varphi$) if, for any b of $\mathcal{M}$ ($b \in \mathcal{N}_C$), the formula φ is true at b $((\mathcal{M}, b) \Vdash_V \varphi)$.

Definition 2. For a Kripke frame $\mathcal{N}_C$ and a formula φ, we say that

(i) φ is satisfiable in $\mathcal{N}_C$ (denotation $\mathcal{N}_C \Vdash_{Sat}\varphi$) if there is a valuation V in the frame $\mathcal{N}_C$ such that $\langle \mathcal{N}_C, V \rangle \Vdash_{Sat}\varphi$.

(ii) φ is valid in $\mathcal{N}_C$ (denotation $\mathcal{N}_C \Vdash \varphi$) if $not(\mathcal{N}_C \Vdash_{Sat}\neg\varphi)$.

Definition 3. The logic $\mathcal{LTL}_K$ is the set of all formulas which are valid in all frames $\mathcal{N}_C$.

A formula φ is a theorem of $\mathcal{LTL}_K$ if $\varphi \in \mathcal{LTL}_K$. To connect satisfiability and theorems of $\mathcal{LTL}_K$, it is sufficient to recall that a formula φ in the language of $\mathcal{LTL}_K$ is said to be *satisfiable* in $\mathcal{LTL}_K$ iff there is a valuation V in a Kripke frame $\mathcal{N}_C$ which makes φ satisfiable: $\langle \mathcal{N}_C, V \rangle \Vdash_{Sat} \varphi$. It is clear that a formula φ is satisfiable iff $\neg\varphi$ is not a theorem of $\mathcal{LTL}_K$: $\neg\varphi \notin \mathcal{LTL}_K$. And vise versa, φ is a theorem of $\mathcal{LTL}_K$ ($\varphi \in \mathcal{LTL}_K$) if $\neg\varphi$ is not satisfiable.

In fact, $\mathcal{LTL}_K$ is a fusion of a special temporal-like logic and the agent knowledge logic, thus $\mathcal{LTL}_K$ is a logic with modal and time operations. Therefore to approach decidability issue we can borrow some techniques from these areas. We will apply a technique using elements of previous research concerning truth and admissibility of inference rules (cf. [25,26,41,42]) in non-classical logics. This approach uses a representation of formulas by rules, and transformation of rules into their normal reduced forms. Such translation of formulas into these rules is essential for (i) implicit representation of not-nested universal modality, and (ii) simplification of proofs (using the specific structure of these rules), in particular, by avoiding proofs of inductive steps on nested logical operations.

All necessary notation, known facts and results are given below. By definition, a (sequential) rule is an expression

$$\mathbf{r} := \frac{\varphi_1(x_1,\ldots,x_n),\ldots,\varphi_m(x_1,\ldots,x_n)}{\psi(x_1,\ldots,x_n)},$$

where $\varphi_1(x_1,\ldots,x_n),\ldots,\varphi_m(x_1,\ldots,x_n)$ and $\psi(x_1,\ldots,x_n)$ are some formulas constructed out of letters $x_1,\ldots,x_n$. Letters $x_1,\ldots,x_n$ are variables of $\mathbf{r}$, we use notation $x_i \in Var(\mathbf{r})$ to say x_i is a variable of $\mathbf{r}$.

Definition 4. *A rule $\mathbf{r}$ is said to be* valid *in a Kripke model $\langle \mathcal{N}_C, V \rangle$ with the valuation V (we will use notation $\mathcal{N}_C \Vdash_V \mathbf{r}$) if*

$$[\forall a\ ((\mathcal{N}_C, a) \Vdash_V \bigwedge_{1 \le i \le m} \varphi_i)] \Rightarrow [\forall a\ ((\mathcal{N}_C, a) \Vdash_V \psi)].$$

Otherwise we say $\mathbf{r}$ is refuted in $\mathcal{N}_C$, or refuted in $\mathcal{N}_C$ by V, and write $\mathcal{N}_C \not\Vdash_V \mathbf{r}$.

A rule $\mathbf{r}$ is *valid* in a frame $\mathcal{N}_C$ (notation $\mathcal{N}_C \Vdash \mathbf{r}$) if, for any valuation V of letters from $Var(\mathbf{r})$, $\mathcal{N}_C \Vdash_V \mathbf{r}$ (again, otherwise we say $\mathcal{N}_C$ *refutes* $\mathbf{r}$, notation $\mathcal{N}_C \not\Vdash \mathbf{r}$). Material implication has standard meaning: $x \to y := \neg x \lor y$. For any formula φ we can consider the rule $x \to x/\varphi$ (with the premise $x \to x$ and the conclusion φ) and employ the technique of reduced normal forms for inference rules as follows.

Lemma 1. *A formula φ is a theorem of $\mathcal{LTL}_K$ iff the rule $(x \to x/\varphi)$ is valid in any frame $\mathcal{N}_C$.*

The proof is evident. □

In the sequel, for simplicity of notation and utilization of intuition, concerning the action of modal logical operations, we will use symbols $\Diamond_i$ for $\neg K_i \neg$ and $\Box_i := K_i$ respectively. This will also help to maintain a well balanced notation. A rule $\mathbf{r}$ is (said to be) in a *reduced normal form* if $\mathbf{r} = \varepsilon_r / x_1$, where

$$\varepsilon_r := \bigvee_{1 \leq j \leq s} \theta_j; \quad \theta_j := (\bigwedge_{1 \leq i \leq n} [\quad x_i^{t(j,i,0)} \wedge (\mathbf{N} x_i)^{t(j,i,1)} \wedge$$

$$\bigwedge_{k \in [1,n], k \neq i} (x_i \mathbf{U} x_k)^{t(j,i,k,0)} \wedge \bigwedge_{k \in [1,n], k \neq i} (x_i \mathbf{U}_w x_k)^{t(j,i,k,1)} \wedge$$

$$\bigwedge_{k \in [1,n], k \neq i} (x_i \mathbf{U}_s x_k)^{t(j,i,k,2)} \wedge \mathbf{IntK} x_i^{t(j,i,2)} \wedge \bigwedge_{1 \leq l \leq m} (\Diamond_l x_i)^{t(j,i,l,3)}]),$$

and all x_t are certain letters (variables), $t(j,i,z), t(j,i,k,z) \in \{0,1\}$ and, for any formula α above, $\alpha^0 := \alpha, \alpha^1 := \neg\alpha$.

Definition 5. *Given a rule* $\mathbf{r_{nf}}$ *in the reduced normal form,* $\mathbf{r_{nf}}$ *is said to be a normal reduced form for a rule* $\mathbf{r}$ *iff, for any frame* $\mathcal{N}_C$, $\mathcal{N}_C \Vdash \mathbf{r} \Leftrightarrow \mathcal{N}_C \Vdash \mathbf{r_{nf}}$.

Based on proofs of Lemma 3.1.3 and Theorem 3.1.11 from [42], by similar technique, following closely to the proof in [42], we obtain

Theorem 1. *There exists an algorithm running in (single) exponential time, which, for any given rule* $\mathbf{r}$, *constructs its normal reduced form* $\mathbf{r_{nf}}$.

Lemma 2. *If a rule* $\mathbf{r_{nf}}$ *is refuted in a frame* $\mathcal{N}_C$, *then* $\mathbf{r_{nf}}$ *may be refuted by a valuation* V *in such frame with (i) clusters* $C(i)$ *at most square polynomial in size of* $\mathbf{r_{nf}}$, *where (ii) the number of non-isomorphic models with the valuation* V *on the time clusters* $C(i)$ *is at most exponential in size of* $\mathbf{r_{nf}}$.

Based on this lemma we may derive

Theorem 2. *The logic* $\mathcal{LTL}_K$ *is decidable. The algorithm for checking a formula to be a theorem of* $\mathcal{LTL}_K$ *consists in validity verification for rules in the reduced normal form in some special finite Kripke/Hintikka frames* $\mathcal{N}_C(k_1, m_1)$ *of size effectively bounded on the size of the rules (single-exponential from a square polynomial on size of the rules).*

Recall, that a logic $\mathcal{L}$ has finite model property (fmp) iff, for any formula φ, where $\varphi \notin \mathcal{L}$, there is a finite Kripke frame $\mathcal{F}$ such that $\mathcal{F} \not\Vdash \varphi$, but for any formula $\psi \in \mathcal{L}$, $\mathcal{F} \Vdash \psi$ (in this case $\mathcal{F}$ is said to be an $\mathcal{L}$-frame). Using Lemma 1 and Theorem 3 we proved

Corollary 1. *The logic* $\mathcal{LTL}_K$ *has the finite model property.*

There are some variations of the logic $\mathcal{LTL}_K$ that use other logical operations to model $\mathbf{U}_s$ and $\mathbf{U}_w$. Consider the following new relation R_s on frames $\mathcal{N}_C$:

$$\forall i \in N, \forall a, b \in C(i)(aR_sb).$$

The relation R_s plays a special role in modeling the knowledge of a supervisor (omniscient agent) who knows the information in all states of the current time point. Let $\square_s := K_s$, $\lozenge_s := \neg K_s\neg$. We use notation $\equiv_{sem}$ to say that the truth values of formulas in frames $\mathcal{N}_C$ coincide. It is easy to see that

Proposition 1. *The following holds*

$$(i)\ \varphi\mathbf{U}_w\psi \equiv_{sem} \lozenge_s\varphi\mathbf{U}\lozenge_s\psi; \quad (ii)\ \varphi\mathbf{U}_s\psi \equiv_{sem} \square_s\varphi\mathbf{U}\square_s\psi.$$

So, having at our disposal a supervisor agent, we can obtain weak and strong *until*. The logic LTL_{KS} in the language with K_s and without $\mathbf{U}_s$ and $\mathbf{U}_w$ obeys the technique for $\mathcal{LTL}_K$ presented in this paper, and we can get the decidability with the same bound of complexity. Another way to vary or extend the language is to add variants of the operation $\mathbf{N}$. For instance, we could consider an operation $\mathbf{N}_w$ – *weak next* with interpretation

$$(\mathcal{M}, a) \Vdash_V \mathbf{N}_w\varphi \Leftrightarrow \exists b[(a\ \text{Next}\ b)\&(\mathcal{M}, b) \Vdash_V \varphi],$$

and the logic with this new operation again will be decidable. Moving in this direction further, we can consider a new operation $Next_w$ on frames $\mathcal{N}_C$ being a restriction of $Next$, for instance, satisfying the conditions:

$$\forall a, b \in \bigcup_{i \in N} C(i), a\ Next_w\ b \Rightarrow [a \in C(i)\ \text{for some}\ i\ \text{and}\ b \in C(i+1)];$$

$$\forall a \in \bigcup_{i \in N} C(i)[a \in C(i) \Rightarrow [\exists b \in C(i+1)(a\ Next_wb)]\ \&$$

$$\forall c \in C(i)\forall d \in C(i+1)[(cNext_wd) \Leftrightarrow (a\ Next_w\ d)]].$$

Again, the method of the Theorem 2 will works for this case and we get decision algorithm. The logic $\mathcal{LTL}_K$ is the set of all formulas valid in all models. The paper [40] proves that this logic is decidable: there is an algorithm which for any formula α computes if $\alpha \in \mathcal{LTL}_K$.

Therefore in order to compute valid for $\mathcal{LTL}_K$ inference rules, it is very easy to observe that, for any rule $r = \alpha_1 \ldots \alpha_m/\beta$, r is valid in $\mathcal{LTL}_K$ iff

$$[\bigwedge_{1 \leq i \leq m} (\square\alpha_i) \to \beta] \in \mathcal{LTL}_K.$$

Therefore, from decidability of $\mathcal{LTL}_K$ we immediately obtain

Proposition 2. *There is an algorithm computing inference rules valid in $\mathcal{LTL}_K$.*

Similar statement holds for linear temporal logic with past. To be precise we give definition of this logic and the detailed statement. First we introduce (cf. [40]) the logic $\mathcal{LTL}_K(Z)$. The logic $\mathcal{LTL}_K$ is based on a flow of time modeled by natural numbers, which matches well with human intuition. If we intend to model past, first candidate for time indexes is the set Z of all integer numbers with standard ordering. Semantic definition of the logic is as follows. The frame

$$\mathcal{Z}_C := \langle \bigcup_{i \in Z} C(i), R, R_1, \ldots R_m, Next, Prev \rangle$$

is a tuple, where Z is the set of all integer numbers, $C(i)$ are some nonempty (pairwise disjoint) sets, R is a binary linear relation for time, $R_1, \ldots, R_m$ are binary accessibility relations imitating possible agents' transitions.

$$\forall a, b \in \bigcup_{i \in Z} C(i)(aRb) \Leftrightarrow [a \in C(i) \& b \in C(j) \& i \leq j].$$

As before, R_j are reflexive, transitive and symmetric relations, and

$$\forall a, b \in \bigcup_{i \in Z} C(i), aR_j b \Rightarrow \exists i \in Z[a, b \in C(i)].$$

Any R_j is an equivalence relation, at clusters $C(i)$. Further,

$$a \; Next \; b \Leftrightarrow [\exists i((a \in C(i)) \& (b \in C(i+1)))];$$

$$a \; Prev \; b \Leftrightarrow [\exists i((a \in C(i)) \& (b \in C(i-1)))].$$

The language of $\mathcal{LTL}_K(Z)$ extends the language of $\mathcal{LTL}_K$ by four more logical operations: $\mathbf{S}$ (since), $\mathbf{S}_w$ (weak since), $\mathbf{S}_s$ (strong since), $\mathbf{N}^{-1}$ (previous). For a frame $\mathcal{Z}_C$ with a valuation V, the rules of computation for truth values of formulas in the model $\mathcal{M} := \langle \mathcal{Z}_C, V \rangle$ are similar to given above ones for the case of logic $\mathcal{LTL}_K$, only we compute operations $\mathbf{S}, \mathbf{S}_w, \mathbf{S}_s$ and $\mathbf{N}^{-1}$ towards past.

Again, in the paper [40] it was proved that $\mathcal{LTL}_K(Z)$ is decidable, and an algorithm for computation of true and satisfiable formulas was found. And if we wont to compute valid in $\mathcal{LTL}_K(Z)$ inferences, we may use the following simple observation: for any rule $r = \alpha_1 \ldots \alpha_m / \beta$, r is valid in $\mathcal{LTL}_K(Z)$ iff

$$[\bigwedge_{1 \leq i \leq m} (\Box^+ \alpha_i \wedge \Box^- \alpha_i) \rightarrow \beta] \in \mathcal{LTL}_K(Z).$$

Hence, using decidability of $\mathcal{LTL}_K(Z)$ we derive

Proposition 3. *The logic $\mathcal{LTL}_K(Z)$ is decidable w.r.t. valid inference rules. There is an algorithm computing inference rules valid in $\mathcal{LTL}_K(Z)$.*

If we will take to consideration agents' logics with non-linear, or not transitive time then the question is already does not follow from all known and future possible results about decidability of logics themselves. We describe a suitable technique to handle this case in next section.

5 Temporal Logics with Non-linear and Intransitive Time

We will consider in this section logics with non-linear and intransitive time. Be begin with a semantical definition of such logics. The models for these logics are based on the Kripke/Hintikka frames

$$C_Y := \langle \bigcup_{i \in Y} C(i), R, R_1, \ldots, R_m \rangle,$$

where $Y = \langle Y, R_t \rangle$ can be any set with a binary relation R_t, each $i \in Y$ is the time index for a set $C(i)$ of possible states (so, any $C(i)$ is just a non-empty set of worlds – states).

$Y := \langle Y, R_t \rangle$ is the time frame (viewed as steps in a computation or stages of evolving a system).

In own turn, any $i \in Y$ is a time point, and $C(i)$ is a set of states/elements (*worlds* or *states of affairs* in terms of Kripke/Hintikka semantics) in the current time point i.

The branching-time flow is modeled by the binary accessibility relation R in $C_Y := \langle \bigcup_{i \in Y} C(i), R, R_1, \ldots, R_m \rangle$ where for all elements a and b from $\bigcup_{i \in Y} C(i)$,

$$aRb \iff \exists i, j \in Y : iR_t j \ \& \ a \in C(i) \ \& \ b \in C(j).$$

Less formally, R imitates the flow of time connecting the states, so, aRb means that the state b is situated in a time point, which is accessible from the time point where a is situated.

We do not assume now that R is transitive, because it would not correspond to all possible interpretations. For instance, if R is imitated by possible links within WEB, it could be not transitive (if we see a web page wp_a and yet some else web page wp_b is visible from the intermediate wp_a, this does not mean that we can see wp_b from the starting web page). Relations $R_1, \ldots, R_m$ are binary relations on $\bigcup_{i \in Y} C(i)$ imitating agents' accessibility within time clusters $C(i)$. So, any R_j is a reflexive, transitive and symmetric relation, and

$$\forall a, b \in \bigcup_{i \in Y} C(i), \ aR_j b \Rightarrow [a, b \in C(i) \ for \ some \ i].$$

The language of the corresponding logic includes propositional letters, Boolean logical operations, operations K_i, $1 \le i \le m$ for agents' knowledge, and temporal operations: $\diamond^+$ (will be in future), $\diamond^-$ (was in past). (Since relations R is not obligatory linear, no very natural way to input operations *until* and *next*, as well as similar ones for past)). Formation rules for formulas are as usual.

A model M on a frame C_Y is this frame together with a valuation V of propositional letters, i.e. V maps letters in subsets of the base set of C_Y. As in previous section this valuation may be extended from propositional letters to arbitrary formulas. The rules are as follows,

$$\forall a \in \bigcup_{i \in Y} C(i), \forall p \in Prop, \ (\mathcal{M}, a) \Vdash_V p \ \Leftrightarrow \ a \in V(p),$$

then the similar, as earlier, steps for Boolean operations and agents' knowledge operations; for temporal operations the rules are

$$\forall a \in \bigcup_{i \in Y} C(i), \forall p \in Prop(C_Y, a) \Vdash_V \Diamond^+ \varphi \iff$$

$$\exists b \in C_Y[(aRb) \text{ and } (C_Y, b) \Vdash_V \varphi;]$$

$$\forall a \in \bigcup_{i \in Y} C(i), \forall p \in Prop(C_Y, a) \Vdash_V \Diamond^- \varphi \iff$$

$$\exists b \in C_Y[(bRa) \text{ and } (C_Y, b) \Vdash_V \varphi.]$$

Definition 6. *The logic $\mathcal{L}_{TA_i}$ is the set of all formulas valid in all worlds of all models based on all possible frames C_Y.*

If we wish to describe inference rules valid in $\mathcal{L}_{TA_i}$, approach from previous section do not work because we cannot say that a rule $r = \alpha_1 \ldots \alpha_m/\beta$, r is valid in $\mathcal{L}_{TA_i}$ iff $[\bigwedge_{1 \leq i < m}(\Box^+\alpha_i \wedge \Box^-\alpha_i) \to \beta] \in \mathcal{L}_{TA_i}$ (because both possible intransitivity of accessibility relations and full temporal language for future and past - possible time zigzags). So, even decidability of $\mathcal{L}_{TA_i}$ itself cannot be used directly.

But using some translation inference rules to reduced forms and some technique based on advanced filtration may help. First we define reduced forms for inference rules. A rule $\mathbf{r}$ is said to have the *reduced normal form* if $\mathbf{r} = \varepsilon/x_1$ where

$$\varepsilon := \bigvee_{1 \leq j \leq n} (\bigwedge_{1 \leq i \leq n} [x_i^{t(j,i,0)} \wedge (\Diamond^+ x_i)^{t(j,i,1)} \wedge (\Diamond^- x_i)^{t(j,i,2)} \wedge$$

$$\bigwedge_{1 \leq s \leq m} (\neg \mathbf{K}_s \neg x_i)^{t(j,i,s,3)}),$$

and all x_s are certain letters (variables), $t(j, i, z), t(j, i, k, z) \in \{0, 1\}$ and, for any formula α above, $\alpha^0 := \alpha$, $\alpha^1 := \neg\alpha$.

Similar to Lemma 3.1.3 and Theorem 3.1.11 from [42], it follows

Theorem 3. *There exists an algorithm running in (single) exponential time, which, for any given rule $\mathbf{r}$, constructs its equivalent normal reduced form $\mathbf{r}_{nf}$.*

Most important for us is

Theorem 4. *If a rule in reduced form $\mathbf{r}_{nf}$ is invalid in a model based at some C_Y then $\mathbf{r}_{nf}$ is invalid in some such finite model of size computable from $\mathbf{r}_{nf}$.*

And combining these two theorems we obtain

Theorem 5. *The logic $\mathcal{L}_{TA_i}$ is decidable w.r.t. valid inference rules. There is an algorithm which by any rule $\mathbf{r}$ checks if $\mathbf{r}$ is valid in $\mathcal{L}_{TA_i}$.*

It is relevant to say that this theorem just reduce validity problem for inference rules to model checking which itself is a difficult computational task.

Approach applied in this section is rather flexible, in particular, we may to impose some restrictions on possible time admissibility relations, and yet the approach can work. For instance if possible time accessibility relations R at frames C_Y may be only transitive, we obtain the logic $\mathcal{L}_{TA_r}$. Using exactly the same approach and scheme of proofs we obtain

Theorem 6. *The logic $\mathcal{L}_{TA_r}$ is decidable w.r.t. valid inference rules. There is an algorithm which by any rule $\mathbf{r}$ checks if $\mathbf{r}$ is valid in $\mathcal{L}_{TA_r}$.*

Valid rules are a subclass of more general class of admissible rules, which were introduced to consideration by P.Lorentzen (1955). A rule r is admissible in a propositional logic $\mathcal{L}$ if $\mathcal{L}$, as the set of formulas, is closed w.r.t. applications of r. That is, for any substitution σ, if σ turns all premisses of r to theorems of $\mathcal{L}$, then the conclusion ψ turns in a theorem after application of σ. It is very interesting and challenging to develop a technique to determine inference rules admissible in described logics, but up to day we see no closure solution. Only a point is: it is immediate to see that if a rule r is not admissible then r is not valid. Therefore theorems of this paper concerning decidability w.r.t. valid rules give a necessary condition for rules to be admissible.

6   Concluding Comments

In this our paper we develop methods for verification inference rules to be valid for several agents' temporal logics. Some methods, if applicable, merely reduce the problem to model checking via decidability of logics (for linear time), others (for more complex cases) are using more intelligent technique involving construction of reduced forms for inference rules and an advanced filtration technique. In sum, in mathematical terms, we show that considered agents' temporal logics are decidable w.r.t. valid inference rules.

There are many open venues for the future research, including (i) extensions of results to other logics from AI area, in particular with another structures of time frames (non-discrete, various non-linear, etc.), (ii) construction of more efficient algorithms checking validity of inference rules in considered logics.

The mentioned above area of questions concerning admissibility of inference rues in agents' temporal logics is very interesting and actual as well. The results of our paper might be useful for researchers from AI community interested in logical inference in agents' logics, knowledge representation, and human(automated) reasoning.

References

1. van Benthem, J.: The Logic of Time.- A Model-Theoretic Investigation into the Varieties Temporal Ontology and Temporal Discourse. Kluwer, Dordrecht (1991)
2. van Benthem, J.: Modality, bisimulation and interpolation in infinitary logic. Ann. Pure Appl. Logic 96 (1999)

3. Gabbay, D.M., Schlechta, K.: A theory of hierarchical consequence and conditionals. Journal of Logic, Language and Information 19(1), 3–32 (2010)
4. Gabbay, D.M., Rodrigues, O., Pigozzi, G.: Connections between belief revision, belief merging and social choice. J. Log. Comput. 19(3), 445–446 (2009)
5. Gabbay, D., Kurucz, A., Wolter, F., Zakharyaschev, M.: Stud. Logic Found. Math. Elsevier Sci. Publ, Noth-Holland (2003)
6. Hodkinson, I., Montanari, A., Sciavicco, G.: Non-finite axiomatizability and undecidability of interval temporal logics with C, D, and T. In: Kaminski, M., Martini, S. (eds.) CSL 2008. LNCS, vol. 5213, pp. 308–322. Springer, Heidelberg (2008)
7. Hodkinson, I.M.: Complexity of monodic guarded fragments over linear and real time. Ann. Pure Appl. Logic 138(1-3), 94–125 (2006)
8. Hodkinson, I., Woter, F., Zakharyaschev, M.: Undecidable fragments of first-order branching time logic. In: LICS 2002, pp. 393–402 (2002)
9. Hodkinson, I.: Temporal logic and automata. In: Templal Logic: Math. Found. and Comp. Asp., vol. 2, ch. 2, pp. 30–72. Clarendon Press, Oxford (2000)
10. Fagin, R., Halpern, J., Moses, Y., Vardi, M.: Reasoning About Knowledge. The MIT Press, Cambridge (1995)
11. Halpern, J., Shore, R.: Reasoning about common knowledge with infinitely many agents. Information and Computation 191(1), 1–40 (2004)
12. Schmidt, R., Tishkovsky, D.: Multi-agent dynamic logics with informational test. Annals of Mathematics and Artificial Intelligence 42(1-3), 5–36 (2004)
13. Hintikka, J., Vandamme, F.: Logic of Discovery and Logic of Discourse. Springer, Heidelberg (1986)
14. Pnueli, A.: The temporal logic of programs. In: Proc. of the 18th Annual Symp. on Foundations of Computer Science, pp. 46–57. IEEE, Los Alamitos (1977)
15. Manna, Z., Pnueli, A.: Temporal Verification of Reactive Systems: Safety. Springer, Heidelberg (1995)
16. Manna, Z., Pnueli, A.: The Temporal Logic of Reactive and Concurrent Systems: Specification. Springer, Heidelberg (1992)
17. Clarke, E., Grumberg, O., Hamaguchi, K.P.: Another look at ltl model checking. In: Dill, D.L. (ed.) CAV 1994. LNCS, vol. 818. Springer, Heidelberg (1994)
18. Daniele, M., Giunchiglia, F., Vardi, M.Y.: Improved automata generation for linear temporal logic. In: Halbwachs, N., Peled, D.A. (eds.) CAV 1999. LNCS, vol. 1633, pp. 249–260. Springer, Heidelberg (1999)
19. Vardi, M.: An automata-theoretic approach to linear temporal logic. In: Proceedings of the Banff Workshop on Knowledge Acquisition, Banff 1994 (1994)
20. van Benthem, J.: The Logic of Time. Kluwer, Dordrecht (1991)
21. van Benthem, J., Bergstra, J.: Logic of transition systems. Journal of Logic, Language and Information 3(4), 247–283 (1994)
22. Goldblatt, R.: Logics of Time and Computation. CSLI Lecture Notes, vol. 7 (1992)
23. Gabbay, D., Hodkinson, I.: An axiomatisation of the temporal logic with until and since over the real numbers. Journal of Logic and Computation 1(2), 229–260 (1990)
24. Hodkinson, I.: Temporal Logic. In: Gabbay, D.M., Reynolds, M.A., Finger, M. (eds.) Temporal Logic and Automata, vol. 2, ch. II, pp. 30–72. Clarendon Press, Oxford (2000)
25. Rybakov, V.: Logical consecutions in discrete linear temporal logic. Journal of Symbolic Logic 70(4), 1137–1149 (2005)
26. Rybakov, V.: Logical consecutions in intransitive temporal linear logic of finite intervals. Journal of Logic Computation 15(5), 633–657 (2005)

27. Rybakov, V.: Until-Since Temporal Logic Based on Parallel Time with Common Past. Deciding Algorithms. In: Artemov, S., Nerode, A. (eds.) LFCS 2007. LNCS, vol. 4514, pp. 486–497. Springer, Heidelberg (2007)

28. Bordini, R.H., Fisher, M., Visser, W., Wooldridge, M.: Model checking rational agents. IEEE Intelligent Systems 19, 46–52 (2004)

29. Dix, J., Fisher, M., Levesque, H., Sterling, L.: Editorial. Annals of Mathematics and Artificial Intelligence 41(2-4), 131–133 (2004)

30. van der Hoek, W., Wooldridge, M.: Towards a logic of rational agency. Logic Journal of the IGPL 11(2), 133–157 (2003)

31. Fisher, M.: Temporal development methods for agent-based systems. Journal of Autonomous Agents and Multi-Agent Systems 10(1), 41–66 (2005)

32. Hendler, J.: Agents and the semantic web. IEEE Intelligent Systems 16(2), 30–37 (2001)

33. Kacprzak, M.: Undecidability of a multi-agent logic. Fundamenta Informaticae 45(2-3), 213–220 (2003)

34. Wooldridge, M.J., Weiß, G., Ciancarini, P. (eds.): AOSE 2001. LNCS, vol. 2222. Springer, Heidelberg (2002)

35. Fagin, R., Geanakoplos, J., Halpern, J., Vardi, M.J.: The hierarchical approach to modeling knowledge and common knowledge. International Journal of Game Theory 28(3), 331–365 (1999)

36. Babenyshev, S., Rybakov, V.: A framework to compute inference rules valid in agents' temporal logics. In: Setchi, R., Jordanov, I., Howlett, R.J., Jain, L.C. (eds.) KES 2010. LNCS (LNAI), vol. 6276, pp. 230–239. Springer, Heidelberg (2010)

37. Rybakov, V.: Logic of discovery in uncertain situations– deciding algorithms. In: Apolloni, B., Howlett, R.J., Jain, L. (eds.) KES 2007, Part II. LNCS (LNAI), vol. 4693, pp. 950–958. Springer, Heidelberg (2007)

38. Babenyshev, S., Rybakov, V.: Decidability of hybrid logic with local common knowledge based on linear temporal logic LTL. In: Beckmann, A., Dimitracopoulos, C., Löwe, B. (eds.) CiE 2008. LNCS, vol. 5028, pp. 32–41. Springer, Heidelberg (2008)

39. Babenyshev, S., Rybakov, V.: Describing evolutions of multi-agent systems. In: Velásquez, J.D., Ríos, S.A., Howlett, R.J., Jain, L.C. (eds.) KES 2009. LNCS (LNAI), vol. 5711, pp. 38–45. Springer, Heidelberg (2009)

40. Rybakov, V.: Linear temporal logic K extended by multi-agent logic K_n with interacting agents. J. of Logic Computation 19, 989–1017 (2009)

41. Rybakov, V.: Rules of inference with parameters for intuitionistic logic. Journal of Symbolic Logic 57(3), 912–923 (1992)

42. Rybakov, V.: Admissible Logical Inference Rules. Studies in Logic and the Foundations of Mathematics, vol. 136. Elsevier Sci. Publ., North-Holland (1997)

Selecting ISPs

Siemiński Andrzej

Institute for Informatics
Technical University of Wrocław
Wybrzeże Wyspiańskiego 27
53-370 Wrocław, Poland
andrzej.sieminski@pwr.wroc.pl

Abstract. The users have now many ISPs (Internet Service Providers) to choose from. Selecting an offer with best price/performance ratio is not an easy task. The key factor is the user perceived latency while displaying the Internet pages. Up to now there is no comprehensive theoretical model of the relationship that links the offered network throughput to the browser latency. Therefore an experiment was necessary to measure the actual browser latency for different ISPs. In the paper several properties of the network connection that is offered by ISPs were recorded and analyzed. The results clearly indicate that some of the popular assumptions do not hold. The network throughput and the browser latency are not tightly bound. The use of Content Delivery Networks does not always result in the shortening of the browser response time. On the other hand the internal (within one IPS) trace routs to a WWW server exhibit substantial stability while they are dissimilar for different ISPs. The analysis of the trace routs suggests that the presence of particular hosts in a trace routes indicates slower than usual download time. This property could be used to select an ISP.

Keywords: browser latency, network throughput, ISP, trace route.

1 Introduction

The browser latency is the key factor in the satisfaction of WEB users. The studies on human cognition [2,9] revealed that on the average a man easily accepts a latency lower than 10 seconds. Too long download time means not only user dissatisfaction but causes more measurable losses. Zona Research in its heavily cited study [15] estimated that each year Web sites lose several billions of dollars due to what they call "unacceptable download speed and resulting user bailout behavior."

The browser latency could be reduced in many ways. Loading some of the objects from a local cache or a proxy cache can considerably speed up the browsing. The effects of caching on browser latency and on the so called page cacheability were discussed in depth in [12] and [13]. Another option is the technique of incremental loading of items. A good programmer of web pages can fool the person into thinking a page is loading faster than what actually is by loading first the text and then including secondary menu graphics or high resolution graphics etc. This gives the

N.T. Nguyen (Ed.): Transactions on CCI IV, LNCS 6660, pp. 177–191, 2011.

user something to start scanning and changes the perception of how fast a page loads. This technique does not decrease the latency but merely the its perception [1]. One can use also page compression and decompression to speed up browsing as described in [3].

All the above techniques are useful but an individual user has hardly any influence upon them. On the other hand he/she has a number of ISPs (Internet Service Providers) to choose from. Usually the decision which ISP to select depends on three factors: the reliability of the service, its cost, and the offered bandwidth. The general belief is that the higher the bandwidth is the shorter is the latency. The precise nature if the relationship is difficult to model. The paper tries to identify the properties of Internet connections that have influence upon the browsing speed. During the study the Internet connections provided by four ISPs operating in Poland were tested.

The paper is organized as follows. The next section describes the basic properties of Internet traffic and the adverse effects of the Internet protocols on the browsing speed. The protocol introduced deficiencies could be mitigated but not eliminated. They are responsible for the fact that increasing the ISP bandwidth does not necessary result in a corresponding increase in browsing speed. The relationship is described by a formula discussed at the end of the section. The Section 3 presents the results of the conducted experiment. During the study several pages from different severs were periodically loaded and the download time and other transmission properties were recorded. The measurements were done for four ISPs. The servers were located in many parts of the world. Some of the servers were supported by Content Delivery Networks (CDNs). The 4th Section studies the correlation between the browser latency and low level connection properties. The Section 5 introduces the concept of black spots – host in trace routes that indicate lower than average transfer rate. The obtained results should help the user to select an ISP. The future research work areas are discussed in the last 6th Section.

2   Basics of Internet Traffic

The TCP (Transmission Control Protocol) is used by the Web to deliver requests for objects from users to servers and then the Web objects in the opposite direction. The following TCP features have a profound effect on the performance of the Web:

- TCP ensures that lost packets of data are retransmitted.
- TCP is as a connection-oriented protocol.
- TCP regulates the rate with which the sending host transmits data so that the receiver can absorb it.

It is well known that the protocol was designed to maximize the reliability of data delivery not the speed of data transmission. The protocol a notorious slow-starter. All objects with sizes not exceeding a few kilobytes are transmitted in the same time [8]. The reasons of the phenomena are twofold: firstly the overhead of the transmission initialization does not depend on the size of an object and secondly the protocol adopts the size of transmitted packets of data to the current network load. As a result the average bit rate transfer for large objects is considerably higher than for small

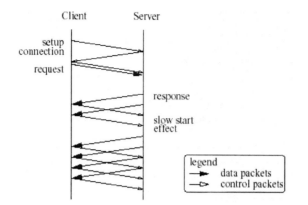

Fig. 1. Establishing a HTTP connection between a client and a server [8]

objects. This is rather unfortunate as the Web traffic is characterized by the burst-outs of numerous requests for small objects.

The need to open and maintain a connection also slows down the transmission. The message exchange to start a transaction (a three way handshake, see Fig. 1) is necessary because the TCP uses the unreliable IP protocol to transfer segments. The obvious inefficiency of the solution prompted the introduction of the persistent connections in the new HTTP/1.1 version of the protocol. The idea is to use the same TCP connection to send and receive multiple HTTP requests/responses thus reducing both network congestion (fewer TCP connections are made) and the latency in subsequent requests (no handshaking). Modifying the infrastructure of a network that spans the whole world is not an easy task – even now many servers still use the previous versions of the protocol. Another problem is the extent to which different browsers are capable of exploiting the persistent connection [14].

The physical limitations are another, often overlooked, reason for the slow transfer rate. They could not be overcome at all. The minimal RTT (round time trip) between two servers is limited by the speed of light and usually does not exceed 2/3 of its value. This is a serious constraint particularly for cross continent transmissions. Let us suppose that 1 KB of data is to be transmitted over a connection with a raw throughput of 2,48 Gbits. The average RTT between New York and Los Angeles is 85 ms. This translates into maximum data throughput of 4 Kbytes per second. The Figure 2 shows the relationship between the maximum throughput and the RTT.

That phenomenon is extremely worrisome because it means that even large improvements in the throughput in the backbone network have only marginal effect on transmission time of small objects.

Up to now there is no reliable model that could be used to predict the latency of downloading a page from a server. A preliminary formula for estimating the download time of a single WWW object was proposed in [10]. Below is its revised version, published in [11]. The response time (Rtime) is the sum of the discovery (Rd), transfer (Rt) and computer/render (Rc) time. The Rc is just the sum of client application render time and server applications compute time. The formulas for estimating the Rd and Rt are more complex.

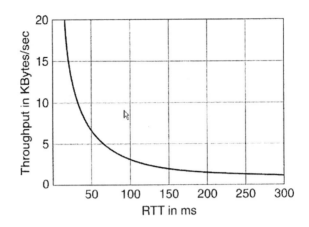

Fig. 2. Theoretical TCP throughput for different RTTs for 1KB over a 2,48 Gps link [8]

$$Rtime = Rd + Rt + Rc$$

$$Rd = (D+TPc+TPs) \left(\frac{T-1}{M} + \ln\left(\left(\frac{T-1}{M} +1 \right) +1 \right) \right) KT \frac{L}{L-1}$$

$$Rt = \max\left(\frac{8P(1+OHD)}{B} , \frac{DP(1-sqrt(L))}{W} \right)$$

Where:
P – payload (120000 bytes)
T – application turns (40)
TPc – client turn processing time (0.005 sec)
TPs – server turn processing time (0.005 sec)
M – multiplexing factor, thread number (3)
OHD – protocol header overhead (10%)
W – effective window size (3000 bytes)
K – retransmission timeout K (1,25 sec)
B – line speed (1500000 bps)
D – round trip delay (0,1 sec)
L – packet loss (2%)

The values in brackets are typical for transmission across the USA. As you can see the Rd does not depend on the size of an object. As could be expected the factor most contributing to its value is usually D – the round trip delay. The formula for Rt states that the increasing of line speed shortens the transfer time only to a certain point. If it passes it then the second parameter of the max function determines the value of Rt. The maximal values of B that have influence on Rt are surprisingly small. The fig. 3 depicts the boarder values of B for different round trip delays.

As you can see with round trip delay of 1 second the ancient dialup modems are as good as the up to date broad band access Internet links. For more common delays of 0,1 second increasing the line speeds over 300 Kbps does not effect the download time, no matter what the size of the object is. This is valid only for transactional applications such as Internet browsing and does not apply to streaming, progressive download video or file download. For such applications increasing the line speed is shortens transmission.

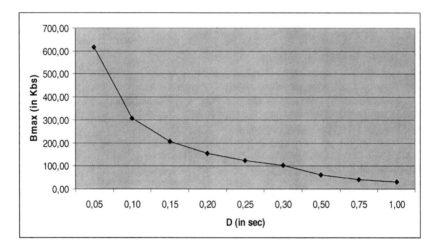

Fig. 3. The delay – transfer rate relationship

This rather astonishing conclusion is confirmed by empirical data. The surf speed recorded by the SurfSpeed service [4] does not show any significant improvement in the recent years despite the dramatic improvement in the throughput of backbone links and the spreading broadband Internet access. This is true even for the most technologically advanced countries, see the Fig. 4. The yellow, blue, and green dots represent respectively the surf speed inside country, outside country, and world wide. According to the data the surf speed outside country has actually decreased in the recent years.

3 Measuring Browser Latency

The discussed above limitations effect all ISPs. The main aim of this study is to find out what is the influence of ISP selection on the browser latency. Surprisingly there are no tools that can facilitate the selection of the best ISP. The ideal tool should measure the browser latency for a user defined set of sites, gather the results and expedite them to all that have interest in them. The most widespread tools check the actual bandwidth, like the net speed test [6]. There is no guarantee that the result will have direct impact on user perceived latency. Another type of tests attempts to mimic the user behavior by downloading a predefined set of objects from popular servers. The Numion [4] tool follows this way of operation. This is a more accurate measure. However, if sites that are particularly interesting to a user are not included in the predefined set then the usefulness of the results is lower. In both cases the tools gather and make available statistical data obtained from their users. They are invaluable source of data that covers the whole world and in many cases spans over the period of several years.

An individual user wants to check an arbitrary set of sites. Unfortunately tools that are capable of that are not popular. The Charlotte package is to our knowledge the only such a tool that belongs to the freeware domain and sufficiently well developed. Unfortunately it works only with outdated and no longer supported browsers [7]. Therefore the data for the presented below experiment were collected by a Java program developed specially for that purpose.

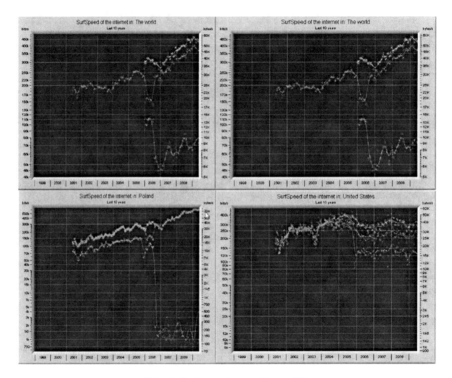

Fig. 4. Surf speed according to [4]

During the study 4 ISP's were tested. For each ISP the download durance of the same set of front pages of 16 websites were recorded. The websites were located on servers that were spread all over the world. The download was performed periodically. The observation was conducted for about a week and for each site at least 2 thousand measurements were made. The aim of the paper is to study the performance of various Internet connections and therefore the caching was carefully eliminated. Only the dynamically generated main HTML object was downloaded and as an additional precaution measure the local cache was cleared after each download.

All tested websites ware of newspaper or news services. They were divided into 4 groups:

- Local (located in Poland),
- Close (located in Germany),
- Distant (located on some other continent)
- CDN (supported by a CDN service).

The Table 1 shows the tested websites. The experiment was conducted on 4 ISPs. In what follows they are referred to as test beds or environments:

- HM1: local residential IPS, the throughput of 1155 Kbps;
- HM2: nationwide ISP, the throughput of 1076 Kbps;
- UNI: main university network, the throughput of 2838 Kbps;
- SUB: subsidiary university network, the throughput of 530 Kbps.

The throughput was measured by the net tool available on the Test Speed Webpage [6]. The throughput was similar but the measured download times were strikingly different. The mean of the recorded transfer rates are presented in the next table, the uMax and uMin columns specify the confidence interval of 95 percent for the Uni ISP environment.

Table 1. The Internet sites used in the experiment

Type	Code	Url	Type	Code	Url
CDN	COR	corel.com	Local	GAZ	gazeta.pl
CDN	NEW	news.com.au	Local	ONET	onet.pl
CDN	NYP	nypost.com	Local	WP	wp.pl
DIST	DAIL	168.com.au	Distant	SUN	suntoday.com.au
Close	FAZ	faz.net	Distant	LIFE	lifescript.com
Close	LOGI	logitech.pl	Distant	MOLY	mollyrocket.com
Close	SUED	sueddeutsche.de	Distant	OHIO	citynewsohio.com
Close	WELT	welt.de	Distant	PAR	parable.com

Table 2. The mean transfer rates in Kbps

Type	Site	UNI	uMin	uMax	HM1	HM2	SUB
CDN	COR	14.66	14.44	14.88	21.70	24.38	19.43
CDN	LIFE	159.78	156.92	162.64	354.39	104.36	97.98
CDN	NEWS	78.26	76.57	79.95	136.00	71.11	70.48
CDN	NYP	3.79	3.76	3.82	4.57	4.30	4.03
CLOSE	FAZ	65.22	64.25	66.19	247.38	116.54	102.81
CLOSE	LOGI	77.75	76.56	78.93	68.72	59.88	43.45
CLOSE	SUED	110.91	109.30	112.53	98.79	96.40	68.91
CLOSE	WELT	61.15	60.45	61.84	180.24	92.90	79.56
DIST	DAIL	28.27	28.01	28.52	74.32	79.02	73.29
DIST	MOLY	5.97	5.92	6.02	5.30	5.36	4.59
DIST	OHIO	3.50	3.46	3.53	3.60	3.73	3.51
DIST	PAR	15.40	15.16	15.64	21.51	19.64	17.40
DIST	SUN	13.67	13.61	13.74	10.44	10.87	9.03
LOCAL	GAZETA	125.16	118.71	131.61	292.08	104.32	85.61
LOCAL	ONET	376.27	361.67	390.88	263.93	109.07	89.82
LOCAL	WP	307.34	299.84	314.84	301.86	111.41	91.44

At first glance each ISP follows the same predictable pattern: the transfer rate for local sites is the fastest and it is the slowest for the distant sites, the CDN sites being the most erratic case. The situation changes however when we compare the performance of individual ISP. The UNI test-bed has the highest throughput but it is not a clear winner. Its has the highest transfer rate for only 6 sites (LOGI, SUED, MOLY, SUN, ONET, WP) and only in one case (the ONET site) its performance is considerably better than that of other competitors. On the other hand there are sites (e.g. FAZ) for which its transfer rate is only the half of that of any other ISP. The HM1 is performs best in 7 cases and the HM2 in 3. The clear looser is the SUB ISP.

The CDN powered sites have surprisingly low values of transfer rate. What is even worse is the poor performance for popular sites such as NYP or COR. On the other hand the far less popular LIFE site, also powered by an CDN service, is at least 20 times faster than the NYP site.

The mean transfer rate is not the only one factor in the human assessment of download duration. The other is its variation. People tend to forget about frequent short downloads and tend to remember the few exceptionally long ones. The Table 3 shows the values of Vs - the normalized standard deviation data calculated using the following equation:

$$Vs = 100 \ \frac{std.dev.}{mean}$$

Table 3. Normalized Standard Deviation of Download Durations

Type	Site	UNI	HM1	HM2	SUB
CDN	COREL	38.27	46.64	33.88	38,45
CDN	LIFE	45.62	24.55	19.38	63,92
CDN	NEWS	55.14	71.19	29.08	63,14
CDN	NYP	21.37	89.28	22.09	67,74
CLOSE	FAZ	37.99	22.77	10.05	60,88
CLOSE	LOGI	38.91	14.00	14.61	52,80
CLOSE	SUED	37.10	22.95	13.42	55,17
CLOSE	WELT	28.99	22.08	14.60	59,64
DIST	DAIL	21.72	18.26	13.36	51,92
DIST	MOLY	22.28	22.64	18.66	27,23
DIST	OHIO	24.29	20.56	18.23	21,65
DIST	PAR	39.48	13.76	9.06	24,83
DIST	SUN	11.85	11.97	13.98	28,79
LOCAL	GAZETA	131.20	25.93	12.31	66,59
LOCAL	ONET	99.19	20.66	15.53	67,45
LOCAL	WP	62.20	17.60	11.35	65,69
SUM		715.60	464.84	269.59	815.89

The SUB ISP is once more again the clear looser but the other University environment is not much better. The empirical data is confirmed by the feelings of many staff members which do complain about the erratic nature of browsing and prefer the sometimes slower but more reliable service provided by other ISPs. This could be partially explained by the fact that the university network is used by drastically changing number of users, it supports e-learning servers and many others services. The CDN service does not provide neither faster nor more stable transfer rate. The data prove that the selection of an ISP could influence the user perceived browser latency.

4 Low Level Measures

The throughput alone has not direct impact on the user perceived latency. The aim of the section is to present some low level measures hoping that they will provide some clues for the ISP selection process. The low level measures are based on two basic network tools: ping and trace route. They include: ping duration, trace route duration, and trace route size (number of hops), trace route length (number of geographical locations) and trace route distance. The ping and trace route data were collected simultaneously with the download durations. Analyzing the results one should take into account that both ping and trace route tools do not use the HTTP protocol.

4.1 Ping

Ping is a computer network tool used to test whether a particular host is reachable across an IP network. It works by sending ICMP "echo request" packets to the target host and listening for ICMP "echo response" replies. Although is does not measure the download time of a page, the Ping tool is widely used to estimate the RTT round-trip time, expressed generally in milliseconds. As stated in the Section 2 the RTT time has a profound influence on the HTTP performance.

Table 4. Ping Durations in milliseconds

Type	Code	UNI	uMin	uMax	HM1	HM2	SUB
CDN	COREL	4.4	4.4	4.4	22.8	38.9	71.3
CDN	LIFE	4.5	4.4	4.5	19.1	39.9	66.7
CDN	NEWS	4.5	4.5	4.6	18.8	38.1	65.2
CDN	NYP	4.6	4.6	4.6	24.3	38.3	66.5
CLOSE	FAZ	32.0	31.9	32.1	44.5	45.2	104.8
CLOSE	LOGI	33.0	33.0	33.0	51.7	48.6	94.8
CLOSE	SUED	29.3	29.2	29.3	47.3	44.9	100.4
CLOSE	WELT	41.2	41.1	41.3	45.3	57.9	121.3
DIST	DAIL	125.2	125.1	125.2	152.2	152.4	182.6
DIST	MOLY	172.6	172.3	172.9	202.1	201.0	240.1
DIST	OHIO	125.4	125.2	125.5	140.5	133.7	205.9
DIST	PAR	182.6	182.5	182.8	203.1	214.4	257.1
DIST	SUN	151.8	151.8	151.9	198.6	176.1	216.3
LOCAL	GAZETA	9.2	9.1	9.2	17.1	25.2	88.2
LOCAL	ONET	5.9	5.9	5.9	24.7	23.2	71.5
LOCAL	WP	11.2	11.1	11.2	25.8	23.3	90.9

The Table 4 compares the ping durations of the UNI test-bed with the results of SUB and the two HM test-beds. The table contains the mean PING duration together with the usual confidence interval.

This time the UNI test-bed is the clear winner, the HM2 coming in second place. The data allow us to draw further conclusions:

- Ping transmits small packets of data so the ISP throughput does not have much influence on its duration. The remarkable differences in values in the table suggest that the packets follow different routs.
- The longer the distance to the original server the more uniform distribution of ping durations – compare the performance of the WP and AUSD servers.
- In all cases the best results have the CDN powered servers.
- The SUB environment has disproportionately long Ping durations the only. exception are the distant servers.

4.2 Traceroute

Traceroute is a computer network tool used to determine the route taken by packets across an IP network on their path to destination server. The three timestamp values returned for each host along the path are the latency values in milliseconds for each packet in the batch. The IP protocol does not guarantee that all the packets take the same route. The trace route data could be used only if:

- the routes to a destination server in a given test bed are stable, that is the packets follow usually the same route;
- the routes taken by packets in different environments differ markedly.

The experiment had shown that both of the above assumptions hold.

4.2.1 Traceroute Stability
The TCP/IP protocol does not guarantee that the packets pass the same sequence of hosts, it may be even possible that each one of them takes a different route. Using trace route based measures makes sense only if the observed routes show considerable level of stability.

Let n be the number of routes or measurements, h be the total number of visits to all hosts of in trace routes and h_i be the number of times the host i has been visited. The proposed stability measure St of the trace routes is defined as follows:

$$St = \sum_{i=1}^{h} \frac{h_i * h_i}{n * h}$$

The value of h_i/n the probability that a route would include the h_i host whereas h_i/h is a weighting factor.

If all routes are identical then each $h_i=n$ and the thus St=1, with the increasing number of hosts and diversity of paths taken the stability approaches 0. The Table 5 contains the stability St of all environments.

As could be anticipated most stable are routs to the local servers. The least stable are routs to the CDN powered sites. This is because of the rerouting that often takes place in the CDN. In general all of sites show substantial degree of similarity.

4.2.2 Trace Route Based Measures
In the study the following trace route properties were analyzed:

- the number of steps on the route,
- the number of leaps on the route,
- the total duration,
- total route length.

The number of steps was equal to the number of visited hosts. The second property is equal to the number of different geographical locations at which the hosts are located. The service provided by MaxMind [5] makes it possible to convert an IP number to the longitude and latitude of its Web host. Knowing this location it is possible to calculate the distance covered by packets on their route which is shown in the last column. From the wealth data we have selected some typical items which is presented in the Table 6.

Table 5. The stability of trace route data

Type	Site	UNI	HM1	HM2	SUB	Average
CDN	COR	0.82	0.78	0.46	0.96	0.76
CDN	LIFE	0.69	0.80	0.45	0.96	0.73
CDN	NEWS	0.68	0.80	0.46	0.95	0.72
CDN	NYP	0.82	0.80	0.46	0.95	0.76
CLOSE	FAZ	0.75	0.86	0.95	0.96	0.88
CLOSE	LOGI	0.76	0.93	0.93	0.96	0.90
CLOSE	SEUD	0.81	0.97	0.96	0.97	0.93
CLOSE	WELT	0.70	0.85	0.56	0.83	0.74
DIST	DAIL	0.76	0.99	0.87	0.93	0.89
DIST	MOLY	0.82	0.79	0.80	0.95	0.84
DIST	OHIO	0.83	0.91	0.64	0.89	0.82
DIST	PAR	0.47	0.51	0.44	0.49	0.48
DIST	SUN	0.88	0.70	0.60	0.93	0.78
LOCAL	GAZE	0.71	0.98	0.94	0.95	0.90
LOCAL	ONET	0.86	0.99	1.00	0.97	0.96
LOCAL	WP	0.89	0.98	0.98	0.94	0.95
	Average	0.77	0.85	0.72	0.91	

One of the CDN servers is located in Poland but only the for the UNI and SUB test-beds the packets usually follow the shortest trace. The difference in Dist values between the SUB and UNI reflects the fact that for HM1 and HM2 environments the stability of routes is not great and the packets are often directed to other CDN servers located in other European countries. Note that the frequent redirection has little impact on the transfer rate.

The farther is the location of tested site is, the more alike the trace routes from different environments are, see the data on OHIO. On the other hand the local sites demonstrate considerable differences in trace route properties, see the GAZETA data.

Of all the properties the number of leaps is the most uniform. Comparing the data on GAZETA and OHIO web sites we discover that the number of leaps is only two times larger in the case of the OHIO server although the distance covered is more than 30 times longer.

Table 6. The properties of trace route data

Env	Type	Site	Steps	Leaps	Dur	Dist
HM1	CDN	COREL	6.5	2.1	74.6	1196.1
HM2	CDN	COREL	6.3	2.7	206.9	1613.8
SUB	CDN	COREL	10.9	2.0	516.8	237.9
UNI	CDN	COREL	8.8	1.0	59.1	148.8
HM1	DIST	OHIO	21.7	4.0	1625.8	11144.0
HM2	DIST	OHIO	14.2	5.6	1363.6	11493.5
SUB	DIST	OHIO	22.1	6.0	2597.7	11595.4
UNI	DIST	OHIO	20.2	5.4	1220.8	11707.7
HM1	CLOSE	FAZ	15.7	4.3	417.0	2649.9
HM2	CLOSE	FAZ	9.0	4.0	310.2	2109.4
SUB	CLOSE	FAZ	14.7	5.9	993.0	1849.9
UNI	CLOSE	FAZ	12.8	5.0	211.7	1821.1
HM1	LOCAL	GAZETA	7.0	1.0	79.8	302.0
HM2	LOCAL	GAZETA	6.0	3.0	156.0	402.0
SUB	LOCAL	GAZETA	12.7	3.0	758.9	390.8
UNI	LOCAL	GAZETA	10.6	2.0	98.8	299.6

Table 7. The values of the Spearman coefficient for different trace route properties

	Steps	Leaps	Dur	Dist	Ping	total
UNI	-0.37	-0.43	-0.46	-0.56	-0.47	-2.29
HM1	-0.36	-0.42	-0.52	-0.7	-0.58	-2.58
HM2	-0.44	-0.47	-0.63	-0.61	-0.54	-2.69
SUB	-0.31	-0.22	-0.37	-0.44	-0.34	-1.68
total	-1.48	-1.54	-1.98	-2.31	-1.93	

In what follows we try identify the measures that provide results most similar to the browser transfer rate. Collecting data on the browser transfer rate is time consuming. Replacing it with lower level measures has practical value.

In what follows we study the similarity of distribution of various low level measures to the browser transfer rate. The coefficient compares the various rankings of tested pages, separately for each test-bed. The similarity was measured by the Spearman coefficient. The raw scores are converted to ranks, and the differences d_i between the ranks for each observation are calculated. The coefficient is calculated according to the following formula:

$$\rho = 1 - \frac{6 \sum d_i^2}{n(n^2 - 1)}$$

where:

d_i: the difference between ranks in corresponding orderings.

n: number of pairs of values.

The value of the coefficient is always in the range from -1 to 1. The greater is its absolute value is the more significant is the correlation. Negative values indicate, that the increase of value of one property is correlated with the decrease of value of the corresponding second property. The values of the Spearman coefficient for all other columns are given in the Table 7.

The coefficient values are negative because usually the e.g. the longer the distance is the lower the transfer rate is. The relationship is present but it is not significant. The best measure is the geographical distance. Far more evident relationship exists if we eliminate the CDN sites from the data. The results are shown in the next Table 8.

The cumulative value of coefficients has increased by almost 60%. Once more again the geographical distance covered by the packets is most reliable measure but its predominance over other measures is not great.

Table 8. The values of the Spearman coefficient for different trace route properties without CDN supported sites

	Steps	Leaps	TDur	Dist	Ping	total
UNI	-0.80	-0.71	-0.89	-0.94	-0.92	-4.26
HM1	-0.80	-0.72	-0.84	-0.9	-0.87	-4.13
HM2	-0.67	-0.80	-0.86	-0.86	-0.8	-3.99
SUB	-0.76	-0.63	-0.78	-0.80	-0.72	-3.69
total	-3.03	-2.86	-3.37	-3.50	-3.31	

5 Black Spots

The low level measures are undoubtedly correlated to the transfer rate but even in the case of Dist measure the correlation is not impressive. Moreover, the transformation of IP to geographical location is not easy. The MaxMind service offers for free the transformation of only 25 IP's per day. The obtained results are also not 100% valid. In the study several hundred IP's were converted and a detailed analysis revealed that in two cases the obtained geographical location was false - the trace routes contained unjustified over Atlantic hops.

In another attempt to find an easy way of evaluating serviced provided by IPS the individual hosts were evaluated. It is assumed that the presence of some hosts in the

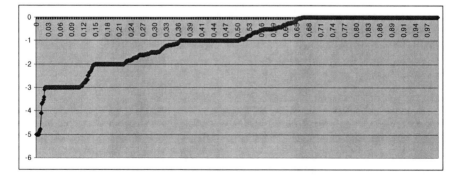

Fig. 5. The distribution of trace route host Utility Measures

trace route indicates lower transfer rates. The process starts with the assignment of Qm(env, site) - the quality measure for each environment and site according to the formula:

$$Q_m(env, site) = \frac{Tr\,(env, site) - Tr_{\max}\,(site)}{Dev(site)}$$

where:

$Tr(env, site)$ – the average transfer rate for the environment and site.

$Tr_{max}(site)$ – the maximal transfer rate for this site

$Dev(site)$ – the standard deviation of the $Tr_{max}(site)$

For each host a Utility Value is calculated. The Utility Value the average value of all the values of Qm(env, site) in which it is present. The data revealed that Utility Value for about 10% of was less or equal to -3. Having such host in the trace routes is a strong indication of a poor transfer performance. The neutral values (equal to 0) characterize 33% of all host. The distribution of the values of Utility Value for the tested host is shown on the Figure 6.

6   Conclusions and Further Area of Study

The user perceived browser response time, especially from far located servers, is often too long. Due to the limitations described in the Section 2 we can not expect, that the problem could be rectified solely by a individual user broad band access to Internet or by increasing the throughput of backbone network. The paper shows that the different IPS do differ in the actual provided transfer rate. Therefore, the selection of proper ISP is so important. Due to the complexity of Internet structure and the erratic nature of its traffic proposing a general model that could be used for evaluation of ISP is very difficult.

The aim of the reported here study was to try to identify the factors that contribute to the transfer rate. Although the raw throughput was similar for all tested ISPs the found transfer rates had differed considerably. The influence of the trace route path is far greater. As far as we know that phenomena was not reported previously. The IP protocol is the reason of the unpredictability of the routes taken by packets. That has probably discouraged research on the area. The obtained results suggest however that there is a fair amount of stability in the trace routes.

The Dist measure of ISP performance is most alike the transfer rate. The proposed "black spot" identification of the poor performance indicating hosts could be of value if data from individual users we collected and made available as a community service in a manner similar to the SurfSpeed service.

Another interesting result of the study is the actual performance of the CDN services. Their recorded transfer rate was surprisingly low. The distance to the nearest CDN server was small, the ping durations were the shortest of all those recorded but still the transfer rate was poor. The low stability of trace routes for some test-beds indicates that often the packets were rerouted to other, geographically distant servers. The CDN server processing time has much more influence on performance than in the case of regular web servers.

References and WEB Sources ·

1. Bhatti, N., Bouch, A., Kuchinsky, A.: Integrating User-Perceived Quality into Web Server Design. Computer Networks 33(1-6), 1–16 (2000)
2. Card, S.A., Moran, T.P., Newell, A.: The psychology of Human-computer Interaction. Lawrence Erlbaum Associates, NJ (1983)
3. Destounis, P., Garofalakis, J., Kappos, P.: Measuring the Mean Web Page Size and Its Compression To Limit Latency and Improve Download Time. J. Internet Research 11(1), 10–17 (2001)
4. http://numion.com
5. http://www.maxmind.com/
6. http://www.speedtest.net/index.php
7. Lamplugh, L., Porter, D.: Charlotte: An Automated Tool for Measuring Internet Response Time. Novell research (1998)
8. Rabinowich, M., Spatschech, O.: Web Caching and Replication. Addison-Wesley, USA (2002)
9. Ramsay, J., Barbesi, J., Preece, I.: Psychological Investigation of Long Retrieval Times on the World Wide Web. Interacting with Computers 10, 1 (1998)
10. Sevcik, P., Bartlett, J.: Understanding Web Performance, NetForecast, Inc. Report 5055 (2001)
11. Sevcik, P.: NetForecast Formula for Web Response Time Over a WAN, http://www.netforecast.com/
12. Siemiński, A.: Changeability of Web objects - browser perspective. In: Proceedings of 5th International Conference on Intelligent Systems Design and Applications, Wrocław, September 8-10, pp. 476–481. IEEE Computer Society [Press], Los Alamitos (2005)
13. Siemiński, A.: Browser latency impact factors. In: Apolloni, B., Howlett, R.J., Jain, L. (eds.) KES 2007, Part II. LNCS (LNAI), vol. 4693, pp. 263–270. Springer, Heidelberg (2007)
14. Wang, Z., Cao, P.: Persistent Connection Behavior of PopularBrowsers, http://pages.cs.wisc.edu/~cao/papers/persistent-connection.html
15. Zona Research: The economic impacts of unacceptable Web Site download speeds, White paper, http://www.zonaresearch.com/deliverables/while-papers/wp17/index.html

AbSM – Agent-Based Session Mobility

Günther Hölbling, Wolfgang Pfnür, and Harald Kosch

Chair of Distributed Information Systems
University of Passau,Germany
{hoelblin,pfnuer,kosch}@fim.uni-passau.de
http://www.dimis.fim.uni-passau.de

Abstract. In most cases a program, its execution state and saved files - the latter two are commonly called "session" - are confined to a physical host. We present a novel system for supporting session mobility that enables the user to break this law of locality, and instead creates a relation between the session and himself. Nowadays most people own several devices, like a notebook or a smartphone, for satisfying their mobility and flexibility needs. To support an almost automatic session handover between different devices a mobile agent system has been used. The selection of target devices has also been automated based on the usage context, the device's capabilities and a rough estimation of the actual location. To demonstrate the capabilities of our Agent-based Session Mobility platform (AbSM) a "multimedia session" use case has been realized where a video session is migrated from a notebook to a smartphone and vice versa. Please note that security issues concerning the session migration are out of scope.

Introduction

With the increasing number and use of different devices more and more users are in the unpleasant situation of having their programs and data spread over several devices. Keeping the appropriate data available on the appropriate device becomes a nuisance. To be able to continue the actual work on another system without losing much time, an automated system is needed. Session Mobility enables the user to detach a session from an actual device. The user can access his data on any physical host that is part of the AbSM platform. The system utilizes the technology of mobile agents to meet the user's need for mobility. Thus the user does not have to care about the location of the actual session of his work, instead the session takes care of the user's location. For compatibility reasons and assuring future prospects a standardized format - MPEG-21 - has been used for representing the actual session.

Usage examples. The following usage examples should illustrate the benefits of AbSM.

The introduction of session mobility makes it possible to enhance and ease the way of content selection for the system's users. A user profile and a filtering engine encapsulated within the session can be used to personalize the access

N.T. Nguyen (Ed.): Transactions on CCI IV, LNCS 6660, pp. 192–209, 2011.

to different content types and enable user preference based filtering in various situations and without worrying about the current device in use. Based on the transparent usage of the filtering component in different usage contexts (e.g. at home, in the office, etc.) and on different devices, the profile also could be enriched and adapted according to the context.

Another usage example of the system would be mobility of "browsing sessions". The simplest form of a "browsing session" could be made up by a collection of websites and their associated metadata (e.g. their access dates or cookies). For example, this would enable a user to move the active session from his PC to his smartphone. Thus the user is able to continue scouring the web on his/her way.

Consider a more concrete scenario: Someone is sitting in the living room in front of his TV-set and watching football. As nothing important seems to happen, that person decides to go to watch the game with a good friend only two blocks away. After leaving his house he hears a multitude of screams from his neighbors. When he arrives at his friend he realizes that he missed the decisive goal. By the use of AbSM that person could have continued watching or at least hearing the broadcast on his PDA or smartphone by moving the actual session, describing the multimedia content in use and its current status, from his settop-box to his mobile device. By tracking the location of the user the session migration to the mobile device could be done automatically when the user is on the move.

The rest of the paper is organized as follows. In section 1, we take a look at several similar projects and discuss the main differences compared to our proposal. Sections 2 and 3 give background information on the MPEG-21 standard and on mobile agent systems. A more detailed discussion of the Java Agent Development Framework and its benefits to our system is stated in section 4. Section 4 presents our system in detail. Besides the architecture, the selection of the target hosts based on a benchmark and the session migration will be discussed as well. Finally, section 6 concludes the paper with a short summary and future work.

1   Related Works

Several approaches have been made to satisfy the users needs for mobility and flexibility in their daily work. A recent and very simple form of session mobility can be obtained by using portable software on USB-sticks (e.g. The PortableApps Suite). All programs that should be "mobile" available have to be installed directly on the USB-stick. Although this approach is quite practical on a PC-platform it can not be used with most mobile devices, especially not with mobile phones. Moreover, many applications aren't suitable for the installation on a USB-stick.

In [11] a streaming system for ubiquitous environments has been defined. Based on MPEG-21 it provides a mechanism for session mobility. Thus users are enabled to continuously consume media through several terminals seamlessly. The system is able to transcode media or adapt it to the user's environment.

Even though this proposal seems to be very similar to AbSM several major differences can be identified. A very similar approach, the Ubiquitous Multimedia Framework for Context-Aware Session Mobility (UMOST), is presented in [10]. It provides seamless user-level handoffs for multimedia sessions and quality of service management based on MPEG-21. Adaptive streaming is supported as well. Compared to our proposal these systems focus on streaming media and are only capable of transferring "media" sessions. For parsing metadata, managing DI's and user sessions a central server is needed.

The Internet Indirection Infrastructure (i3) is used in [20] to achieve Personal Mobility. It suggests to use bluetooth-identifiers to locate persons. Every device that is within reach of the bluetooth-identifier of a specific person will try to register by setting an i3 trigger that represents that user. If multiple devices are within reach, an internal protocol will decide which one will handle the actual session. Compared to AbSM, there is no application-/ session-specific algorithm that will decide which device to use, and the user cannot choose a target device manually. Furthermore, the usage of applications not designed according to the client-server model is not possible, due to the lack of a direct session transfer between the originating and the target host.

Several Session Initiation Protocol (SIP) based systems for mobility of multimedia applications have been proposed. In [17] the main scenarios are re-routing of calls and streaming video depending on the location of the user. [2] proposed an architecture for mobility management supporting soft handoff for voice or video streams. While these proposals certainly share some functionality with AbSM they are focused on streaming media and there is no task-based algorithm that helps decide which device to use.

[18] uses agents to transfer sessions. Sessions are saved in XML format, and task-based agents allow to perform specific tasks. The agents also take care of their own sessions, saving and loading them as needed. Compared to AbSM, there is always a special agent per task, and there is no algorithm to help decide which device to use. In [6] a distributed multimedia communication framework and conferencing software where session information is managed within a LDAP directory server is presented. This work uses a central server for session management and focuses on multimedia content and video streaming in an e-learning environment.

[12] presents a way to enhance Universal Plug And Play (UPnP) in a home network by session mobility. This approach allows to transfer multimedia sessions using the UPnP Audio Video Architecture (AV) between different UPnP enabled devices. Discovery and selection of a target device is done manually by the user based on the mechanisms provided by the UPnP Framework. Although this approach seems to be very promising its still limited to UPnP AV and multimedia sessions.

A completely different approach is presented in [10]. By using thin client technologies, namely the X Window System (X11) and Virtual Network Computing (VNC), a whole virtual desktop or just mobility enabled applications can be moved from one device to another. VNC server and X11 are mandatory components of this system. In contrast to our approach a mobile application is located and executed on a server. Thus communication costs may become a severe issue.

The browser session preservation and migration (BSPM) infrastructure [8] enables the user to switch devices while browsing the web and continue the same active web session on the new device. It uses a proxy server to store a snapshot of the browser session and to provide it to other devices. In comparison to AbSM, BSPM is only applicable for browser sessions and does not take the capabilities of the target device into account.

2   MPEG-21

A huge amount of different frameworks for consumption and delivery of multimedia content is available. Most of them only cover functional and organizational parts. In contrast to these approaches MPEG-21 tries to realize a standard for the "big picture" of multimedia systems. It specifies a framework to create a common base for "seamless and universal delivery of multimedia" [5]. It tries to guarantee a transparent use of multimedia resources across different networks, devices, user preferences and communities for all players in the delivery and consumption chain. The standard consists of 18 parts centered around 7 key areas:

1. Digital Item Declaration
2. Digital Item Identification and Description
3. Content Handling and Usage
4. Intellectual Property Management and Protection
5. Terminals and Networks
6. Content Representation
7. Event Reporting

MPEG-21 introduces two key concepts: the Digital Item (DI) and the User. The DI encapsulates the content with its resources, metadata and structure (the "what"). The user is any element that interacts with the MPEG-21 framework or uses a DI (the "who"). For the session declaration and mobility focused in AbSM only the areas Digital Item Declaration and Terminals and Networks are of further relevance in this context. Nevertheless other applications providing presentation or playback functions have to cover also most other MPEG-21 key areas as shown [16]. For a comparative overview of the MPEG-21 standard, the reader can refer to [5].

2.1   Content DI and Context DI

AbSM makes use of two MPEG-21 specifications for describing the actual content and its associated session, the Content Digital Item (Content DI) and the Context Digital Item (Context DI)[9]. Both of them are XML files that use MPEG-21 schema definitions. The Content DI represents the actual content in form of resources, the metadata and their interrelationships. It may also offer several choices and selections for a content each providing a different quality, format, media type or resolution. Thus a Content DI can be processed on different devices in an adapted way. For example a Content DI may contain a movie at 3 selectable qualities and transcript of the movie for devices without video playback capabilities.

The Context DI saves the actual session information. It contains information about the playback conditions, e.g. what choices were made to play back the Content DI or the actual playback time. The session is saved within a Digital Item Adaption Description Unit of type SessionMobilityAppInfo. This description type is used to adapt the Content DI, it also stores information about the application that uses that content. As the information needed to preserve a session varies from application to application, the format of the session description is not standardized. [4]

2.2   Terminal Capabilities

For describing the capabilities of different devices AbSM adopts the mechanism of MPEG-21 for characterizing terminals. All relevant properties of the hardware are saved in an MPEG-21 conformant format. These capabilities can be classified into three categories. The device category including attributes like DeviceBenchmark where a measure for CPU performance could be saved, StorageCharacteristics where values like the size of main memory could be mentioned, the DeviceClass (PC, laptop, PDA, ...) and PowerCharacteristics like the remaining battery time. CodecCapabilities define the capabilities of device for encoding and decoding audio and video. The I/O category includes information about HID capabilities, visual output like displays resolution and color-depth and audio output specified by number of channels, bits per sample, sampling frequency etc. A fragment of a typical Terminal Capabilities description is shown in the listing below. By examine elements like PowerCharacteristics a slower device with a higher remaining battery time can be chosen. For choosing the way a DI is processed e.g. download, progressive download or streaming StorageCharacteristics have to be considered. Elements of the I/O category manly influence the decision if a device is able to process a DI and how it is presented.

```
<TerminalCapability xsi:type="PowerCharacteristicsType"
 batteryTimeRemaining="4200" />#
<TerminalCapability xsi:type="StoragesType">
 <Storage>
  <StorageCharacteristic
    xsi:type="StorageCharacteristicsType"
    size="5177344" />
 </Storage>
</TerminalCapability>
<TerminalCapability xsi:type="DeviceClassType">
 <DeviceClass
   href="urn:mpeg:mpeg21:2003:01−DIA−DeviceClassCS−NS:1">
   <mpeg7:Name xml:lang="en" />
 </DeviceClass>
```

```
</TerminalCapability>
<TerminalCapability xsi:type="DisplaysType">
 <Display>
  <DisplayCapability xsi:type="DisplayCapabilityType"
   colorCapable="true">
   <Mode>
    <Resolution horizontal="1920" vertical="1200" />
   </Mode>
   <ColorBitDepth blue="32" green="32" red="32" />
  </DisplayCapability >
 </Display>
</TerminalCapability>
<TerminalCapability xsi:type="AudioOutputsType">
 <AudioOutput>
  <AudioOutputCapability
   xsi:type="AudioOutputCapabilitiesType"
   numChannels="2">
   <Mode bitsPerSample="16" samplingFrequency="44100" />
  </AudioOutputCapability>
 </AudioOutput>
</TerminalCapability>
 <Decoding xsi:type="VideoCapabilitiesType">
  <Format href="urn:mpeg:mpeg7:cs:VisualFileFormatCS:2001:8" >
   <mpeg7:Name xml:lang="en">
   H263
   </mpeg7:Name>
  </Format>
 </Decoding>
</TerminalCapability>
```

3   Agent Systems

A Software Agent is a program that carries out tasks and makes decisions on behalf of a user or an other program. An example would be a search bot, that scours the web for useful information. It decides whether or not a website has relevant information and extracts that knowledge for the user. Agents are often defined by their characteristics - namely autonomy, proactivity, reactivity, adaptivity, persistence and social-ability. Autonomy means that the agent can act autonomously without the need for user interaction and proactivity means that it can act out of his own will. The agent may still have to ask for permission before doing anything that might be potentially harmful. The agent can react to its environment and adapts to changes in it - this is called reactivity. Therefore, it may need to gather information about its surrounding. Persistence means that agents continuously run and are not stopped after their task has been finished. The ability of agents to communicate and cooperate with other agents and components is called social ability. Besides these characteristics mobile agents have the ability to move from the current to another host. This action is called "migration". For a detailed explanation of agent systems see [14,1].

Several agent systems have been evaluated for their application in our Agent-based Session Mobility platform. Because of the need of mobility and the support of different platforms and devices e.g. handhelds and smartphones we focused on Java based platforms. These include Aglets, Beegent, Bond, JACK, MIA, Ubi-MAS, Mole, Voyager, Grasshoper, Gypsy, Cougaar, Agent Factory and JADE. Most of these agent systems were discarded for being out-dated and their lack of support for mobile environments. The most promising platforms were JADE and Agent Factory. Finally JADE was chosen for its mature status and the broad support for different Java Runtime Environments like J2ME in both configurations (CDC and CLDC), Personal Java and J2SE. For comparative discussion of several mobile agent platforms, the reader can refer to [19].

4   JADE

JADE (Java Agent Development Framework)[3] was developed and distributed by Telecom Italia, but published under the LGPL2 (Lesser General Public License Version 2). It is a Java based agent framework which fully complies to FIPA[1] standards [7].

A JADE platform is an execution environment for agents that may spread over several physical hosts. It consists of several agent containers, that can run on different machines. One of these containers is the main container, which hosts the organizational information and processes. All standard containers have to register at a main container, and there is only one active main container per Agent Platform. The organizational information and processes hosted by the main container are as follows (see figure 1):

- The container table (CT), acts as registry for all container storing the transport addresses and object references.
- The Global Agent Descriptor Table (GADT) provides information of all registered agents.
- The Agent Management System agent (AMS) features most organizational tasks like registering new agents, deregistering agents upon deletion and taking care of the whole migration process.
- The Directory Facilitator agent (DF) provides a registry for services provided by agents. This mechanism is similar to the yellow pages of the Universal Description, Discovery and Integration[2] (UDDI) service of the Web Service technology.

The main container is the central component of the platform. It hosts the most important agents, the Directory Facilitator (DF) and the Agent Management

---

[1] The Foundation for Intelligent Physical Agents provides a collection of standards to ensure interoperability between different FIPA compliant agent systems.

[2] http://www.oasis-open.org/committees/uddi-spec/doc/tcspecs.htm

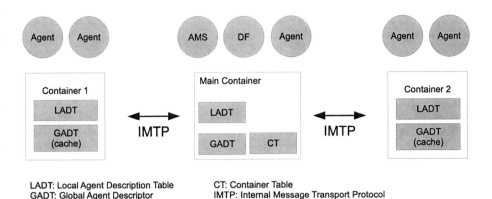

LADT: Local Agent Description Table   CT: Container Table
GADT: Global Agent Descriptor   IMTP: Internal Message Transport Protocol

Fig. 1. JADE organizational structure

System (AMS) agent which are only present on the main container. Nevertheless most operations do not include the main container at all, as every container keeps its own copy of the GADT, which is named Local Agent Descriptor Table (LADT). If the local table is out of sync, the container will refresh its cache. Typically this happens when a queried entry does not exist, or if the querying agent reports that the information was inaccurate. Due to that agent cache the main container is only involved when agents or services are created, deleted or changed (which includes agent migration). The main container is however still a single point of failure, a crash would disable the agent platform. The Main Container Replication System (MCRS) helps to overcome this situation by starting several "sleeping" main containers which simply act as a proxy to the active main container. In case of a failure, the remaining main containers are notified, and reorganize accordingly.

Message Transport is implemented in two different ways: For inter-platform communication there is a HTTP interface available at the main container. This is the FIPA-conform entry point for messages that are sent from outside into the platform. For intra-platform communication a special protocol called Internal Message Transport Protocol (IMTP) is used, which is not FIPA-conform. Besides standard message exchange between agents it is also used for system-message exchange, for example commands to shutdown a container or kill an agent.

JADE-LEAP. The limitations of the hardware of mobile devices (J2ME CLDC) made it necessary to introduce a special Lightweight Extensible Agent Platform (LEAP) for JADE. LEAP uses the so-called split-container mode: There is a lightweight front-end container on the mobile device, which keeps a constant connection to a back-end container on a J2SE host. Neither the front-end nor the back-end are a container on their own, as both only provide part of the functionality - hence the name "split-container". As serializing and deserializing of objects is not supported on J2ME CLDC, "real" migration is not possible.

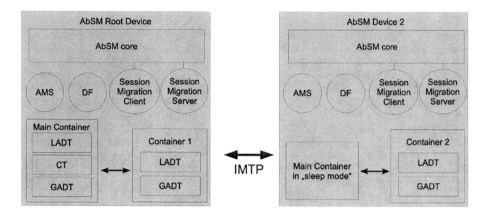

Fig. 2. Overview of AbSM's architecture

Unfortunately, this also limits the ability of Agents used in AbSM. AbSM agents can only achieve mobility by one of two distinct means: Either they are "mobile agents" as in "running on mobile devices" (using Jade-Leap and no migration), or they are "mobile agents" as per definition, able to migrate, but unable to run on mobile devices.

Benefits of Agent based Systems. Our platform strongly benefits from the employment of an agent system. The main advantages are stated in the following:

- **platform independency:** Due to the use of JADE our system can be used on all platforms with JADE support. Based on Java interoperability of routines and methods embedded in Agents is guaranteed as well.
- **management of distributed components:** Most organizational tasks for offering, finding and migrating to a target host are provided by the agent system (see CT, GADT, AMS, etc.) .
- **mobility:** The transport of the session information is fully handled by the agent system.
- **expandability:** To cope with future demands and developments the system can be easily extended by new session types and target selection mechanisms (cf. section 5.1) as they are fully embedded in the agents. Thus for extending the functionality of our system one only has to integrate new methods into the agents. JADE, as an FIPA-conform agent platform, also enables interoperability and a comfortable integration with other FIPA-conform agent platforms.
- **reliability:** In our middleware an agent migrates directly to the target device where the session is continued autonomously. Thus no connections to the originating host or a server have to be maintained and work could also be continued in situations where connection problems will often lead to communication interrupts and failures.

5   Description of the System

AbSM has been implemented in Java mainly to achieve platform independence and a broad support of mobile devices. Figure 2 shows a rough overview of a AbSM device and the relation to the services provided by the agent platform. JADE is used in the system for message delivery and migration. Every device in the AbSM platform can offer itself as a possible migration host through JADE's DF-service (cf. section 4) by registering the migration service with its MigrationServer agent.

To enhance the fault tolerance, every J2SE instance of AbSM has its own agent container as well as its own main container. Only one of the networked devices' main containers is active, the others are working as proxies. Based on the MCRS (cf. section 4) the main containers of different devices are organized in a ring, where every local main container keeps up a connection to the next main container. If the connection to the active main container is lost, the ring will re-organize and one of the other main containers changes into active state. This mechanism guarantees a maximum degree of fault tolerance. Without it, the whole System would disintegrate instantly if the JADE MainContainer crashes, due to the loss of most organizational information of the agent system.

On startup every new device has to register its MigrationServer agent at the Directory Facilitator of the agent platform. For that reason the first AbSM device creates a main container and its associated "service"-agents (DF and AMS). This device now runs the first active main container. To avoid having multiple singleton AbSM networks, every device sends a multicast request on startup. If the request is received by another instance of AbSM, it will reply, and thus give the recently started device the chance to connect to the existing network and to its MCRS. In a final step the MigrationServer Agent is started and registered. This agent manages all incoming migration requests of other devices and negotiates the session handover. The MigrationClient agent is only started if an actual session should be moved to another device. A detailed description of the migration process can be found in section 5.2. The communication between AbSM Devices is handled by JADE based on the Internal Message Transport Protocol (IMTP).

As depicted in figure 3 AbSM consists of several parts that will be described in the following.

- AbSM core: This part provides the main functionality of the system. It cares about evaluating system capabilities (see section 5.1), migration target selection (see section 5.1), the agent code (MigrationClient agent and MigrationServer agent) and the session migration process itself (see section 5.2).
- MPEG-21 Layer: All the information about content (where is the content), context (what has been done with that content) and devices (e.g. benchmark results) are saved in MPEG-21 conform XML. Thus the MPEG-21 Layer was introduced to support the creation and processing of MPEG-21 compliant XML documents. To allow random access to XML elements a Document Object Model (DOM) parser was used. Moreover, this layer adopts the Least

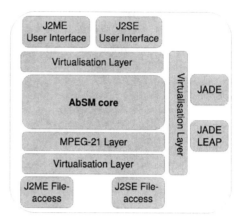

Fig. 3. AbSM's device architecture

Recently Used (LRU) strategy for buffering frequently accessed DI, making access to those items more efficient.

- Virtualisation Layer: J2SE and J2ME share many classes. However there are major differences in the way user-interfaces are realized, files are accessed or which libraries are supported. Thus several functions of AbSM, for example determine terminal capabilities (e.g. supported codecs or resolution and color-depth of the screen), or storing a digital item, have to be implemented in two editions - one for J2ME and one for J2SE. For these reasons a virtualisation layer has been created. It allows to keep as many of the classes as possible working on both editions. Basically, the classes can be compiled for both editions, while still being able to use edition-specific functions through the virtualisation layer. That way nearly all the classes except the user interface and some of the virtualisation layer's classes can be shared. The access to the agent platform is managed by this layer as well, to keep version specifics out of AbSM's core.

- J2ME/J2SE specific parts: There are several edition specific parts in AbSM like the user interfaces, file access or the agent platform (see section 4).

5.1   Benchmarking and Hardware Evaluation

To be able to decide whether or not a device is fast enough to continue a specific session, the hardware capabilities of the machine and a scale for comparison was created. Three main categories were measured on a scale between 0 and 100 points: CPU speed, resolution and color capabilities.

Additionally a session specific category, the multimedia capabilities of the devices, was evaluated. Thus for most devices a list of supported audio and video codecs is available.

CPU speed: The CPU speed was measured by calculating a total of 1 million additions, multiplications and divisions. This will take a couple of seconds on a reasonably fast mobile phone, and is very fast (split-second) on a personal computer. The time taken for this test is measured in milliseconds, with a maximum of 20 seconds for the test.

For slow devices, a good resolution can be achieved by simply using a linear function: For every 0.2 seconds that were needed to complete the test, 1 point is subtracted from a starting value of 100 points.

Unfortunately, this means that fast devices that need less than 1 second for the test (which should be most personal computers) will all receive nearly the same rating.

For fast devices a function based on indirect proportionality between points and time taken would result in a high resolution, but for slow devices, the resolution would be very bad since e.g. devices needing 10.2 to 20 seconds would all receive 1 point.

By taking the average of both functions (f1 and f2), an acceptable resolution was achieved for both fast and slow devices (f3).

The three functions can be seen at figure 4. A logarithmic scale might have been able to perform similar, but J2ME CDC 1.0 does not support logarithmic or exponential functions.

Resolution and the number of colors: As displays are 2-dimensional, the square root of the number of pixels was used as a basis for attributing points. A normalizing factor was introduced to grant 100 points to all displays

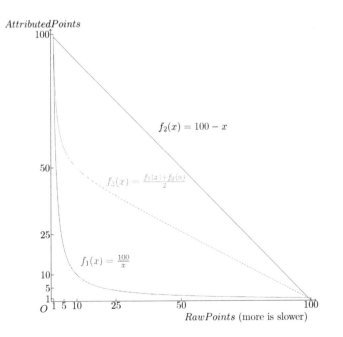

Fig. 4. CPU raw points - attributed points diagram

exceeding 2 mega pixel (2000*1000), displays with 200 pixels (20*10) would still achieve one point.

As the number of colors is usually dependent on the number of bits used to identify a specific color, this value is used for calculating the points. This allows to compare 8-bit colors with 32-bit colors. As 32-bit is the current standard for desktops, a normalizing factor was introduced so a color depth of 32-bit results in 100 points.

To prevent black-and-white displays with a high number of gray scale colors to get a better result than a simple color display, a punishing factor of 5 was used. If a display is only black-and-white, it gets only 1/5 of the points that a color display with an equal number of colors would get.

Priorities and Decision: Thanks to the pre-processing described above, there are 3 point-values each ranging from 1 to 100 points that describe the underlying hardware. Those 3 values are not enough to make a simple decision: Unless all 3 values of one benchmark are higher than those of the other, weighting factors are needed. These weighting factors should depend on the application used reflecting the importance of each benchmark category for the application e.g. for pictures, colors are important, for large data-sets like tables screen size and thus resolution is important, and for some tasks like decryption CPU power is most important. For videos, all of these are important - but only up to a certain point. If the codec is supported and the CPU is fast enough to decode the video in real-time, more CPU power will not yield further improvements. Still, if the computing power is too low, the video will stutter.

What is needed is a single value that represents the ability of the underlying hardware to perform a specific task, like playing a video, starting a game, or similar. This is done by designing special priority classes for that action, which can subsequently be used for calculating a prioritized points value.

Priorities basically assign an importance-value to every of the three main categories that were measured. The idea behind those priority-values is that they shall specify the minimum number of points needed to deliver the best service possible. If there is still an improvement from 49 to 50, but not from 50 to 51, then the priority should be 50.

To calculate a single value out of the 3 categories' values, each of them is divided by the priority value that was assigned to that category. That way, a fulfillment ratio for every of the three main aspects is created. The final value is then calculated using the bottleneck principle, as it does not matter how fast the CPU is and how brilliant the colors are if the screen is too small to recognize anything. Thus, the smallest of these three aptitude ratios determines the final points value: it is simply multiplied by 100. If a category was assigned an importance of 0 (no importance), this category is simply ignored. If all three categories are assigned an importance of 0, every system will get 100 points.

The result of these calculations is then used for automatic decisions. To be able to do this, every Content Digital Item is assigned one point value (and a corresponding priority) per component. This value is then compared with the points that were calculated for that priority during benchmark.

5.2 Session Migration

As mentioned before, the session information itself is saved and transferred as DI in MPEG-21 format. There are several agents involved in the migration process. Figure 5 shows the participants and the migration process in a simplified form. As migration is not fully supported on J2ME since it does not support serialization and reflection, there are two editions for client- and server applications. Depending on whether the actual device is the initiator or the target of a migration the corresponding application has to be started - MigrationClient for migrating to another place, or MigrationServer to accept a migration. Both components create a corresponding agent on startup. To provide a seamless migration the MigrationServer is typically started in the background, waiting for migration requests. When both the client and the server are running, the migration process can be initiated. If no benchmark and capability information is present on startup of the MigrationServer a benchmark is forced. The default means of communication within AbSM is the JADE IMTP system, which is used by all agents. The connection between different devices is established using WLAN. A typical migration consists of 7 steps (see figure 5):

Step 1. To become available on the platform for migration requests the MigrationServer has to be registered at the DF in the first place.

Step 2. For discovering all available migration targets the MigrationClient agent queries the Migration Helper agent.

Step 3 and 4. The Migration Helper Agent first queries the Directory Facilitator (DF) to get a list of all available hosts. Then a bluetooth scan, saving all bluetooth identifiers found, is performed. By comparing the bluetooth IDs of the available hosts with the list of bluetooth IDs the hosts are marked as reachable or unreachable. The bluetooth interface is only used to gain a rough estimate on the distance to a possible target.

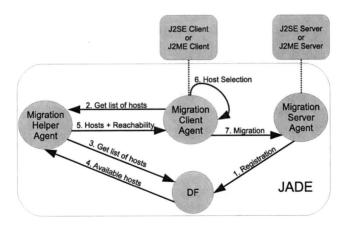

Fig. 5. Migration Process

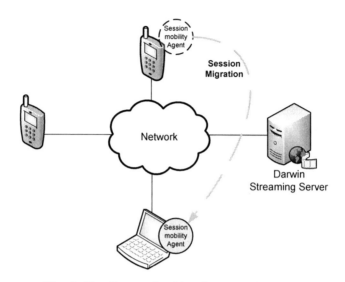

Fig. 6. Test Setup - "multimedia session" use case

Step 5. In this step the list of hosts with the additional reachability information is returned to the MigrationClient agent.

Step 6. The host selection can be done automatically or manually. In both variants the benchmark results and the capabilities of each available host are taken in account to identify the best host for the actual session. Different session types also lead to different decisions by providing different priority factors (see 5.1). For example automatic migration of a video session will simply pick the host with the highest number of Video-Points and initiates migration. In manual mode it is possible to choose from a complete list of all hosts and the number of points they achieved. It is also visible whether or not this client is within bluetooth range, so decisions can be based on locality. To be able to distinguish the hosts, their hostname is used for J2SE hosts, and their telephone number for J2ME hosts. As the telephone number is not available to a MIDlet for security reasons, it has to be manually specified in a configuration file (config.xml). In addition to the actual session other digital items of the client device can be marked for migration as well.

Step 7. Due to restrictions of JADE-LEAP "real" migration is only supported between J2SE hosts. Thus our solution to provide session migration on J2ME is to send working instructions specifying the task and the session data to a specialized agent on the server side. This agent has to provide the implementation for these instructions, otherwise the migration fails. After the migration is initiated, the digital items are sent to the new host. When all digital items are transmitted, a message is sent to indicate that the migration is complete. During a migration, all migration related messages from different hosts are discarded.